Commercial Real Estate Investing For Dummies

Cheat Sheet

P9-DGK-374

How a Deal Gets Done

This big-picture view helps you understand how a deal is closed:

1. The buyer makes an offer to purchase, and, if the seller likes the offer, the seller accepts and signs it.

2. The buyer opens escrow with an escrow/title company or attorney and sends in earnest money as a deposit to the escrow holder.

3. The buyer starts the financing process with his lender and sends necessary documents to the lender to qualify both the property and himself (and his partners).

4. The buyer does his due diligence (such as reviewing the property's financial statements and other property-related information as set forth in the contract) and does a physical inspection of the property.

5. The buyer examines the title and removes contract contingencies.

6. The buyer and the seller satisfy any remaining obligations as set forth in the contract.

7. The buyer finalizes the loan with the lender by getting an official letter of commitment from the lender.

8. The buyer reviews the closing statement and finalizes any final closing instructions with the escrow company.

9. On closing day, the buyer signs the closing paperwork with the escrow company and makes a down payment.

10. The deed is recorded, monies are disbursed, and the buyer gets the keys.

Legal Due Diligence Checklist

Due diligence is the process of "doing your homework" on the property that you're thinking about buying as an investment. Legal due diligence can be pretty extensive, and checking on the items in this list takes a team effort. Here are the items that you need to ask the seller for:

- **An environmental inspection:** The environmental inspection most often used is called a Phase I Environment Site Assessment. During this inspection the inspector explores the past use of the property and the surrounding area, looking for onsite and offsite environmental problems and liabilities.

- **A survey and title inspection:** With this inspection, a title company can verify the property size and that the title report has the same description as the survey. You can also review any easements or encroachments.

- **An inspection for building code violations:** If a violation occurs after a building is built, it's called a non-conforming use and is considered to be grandfathered in.

- **The zoning code:** You need to review the city's zoning ordinances to make sure that the property's use complies with what it's legally zoned for. If it's used illegally, the property can be shut down.

- **The insurance policy:** The property's insurance policy can be a treasure trove of information if you can get the claims history.

- **Licenses, permits, or certificates:** Oftentimes you're required to post business licenses, permits, or certificates. Make sure that you're proactive in notification of new ownership to avoid hefty fines.

- **Service and vendor contracts:** Review all service and vendor contracts to make sure that you have the right to choose or discontinue the services. These services may include maintenance and landscaping.

- **A personal property inventory:** Obtain a list of all personal items, such as equipment, tools, computers, furniture, supplies, and appliances, that are to remain with the new owner. Document all these personal items in writing or consider them gone.

- **Any police reports:** Determine past and current police reports by calling the local police department. Review the type and frequency of calls to the property. Know what's going on before you buy.

Commercial Real Estate Investing For Dummies®

Cheat Sheet

Physical Due Diligence Checklist

When investors consider physical due diligence, they need to do more than a simple walk-through of the property with an inspector. Walk-throughs are a part of physical due diligence, but only a tiny part of it. Ask the seller for the following items:

- **Site plans and specifications:** This group of documents includes all the construction documents, building plans and schematics, floor plans, and use of the land documents.
- **Photos of the property:** Photos of the exteriors, interiors, and the surrounding land and structures should be taken.
- **A structural inspection:** Inspect the walls, roofs, and foundation, and make sure there are implements in place for earthquake safety.
- **An interior systems inspection:** Inspect the interior of the property for wear and tear, including items such as doors, windows, and weatherproofing. Then inquire about the age of the roof, any building code violations, its federal compliance, and site improvements.
- **A mechanical and electrical inspection:** Make sure that every mechanical and electrical system is inspected. Such systems include heating, ventilation, air conditioning, plumbing systems, and all electrical power systems and controls.
- **A list of capital improvements performed:** Obtain receipts and documents for any capital improvements that were made. Collect these for any improvements over the past five years.
- **A pest inspection:** On some types of building, an inspection for pests, such as termites, may take place. Most apartment buildings have this inspection done as part of a lender requirement.

Financial Due Diligence Checklist

The financial aspect of due diligence focuses on why you're buying the property. It helps ensure that you make money by verifying the seller records of the property's financial performance. To perform successful financial due diligence, be sure to obtain the following from the seller:

- **Income and expense statements:** You should obtain annual income and expense statements for the past three years.
- **Rent rolls:** A rent roll is essentially an attendance sheet for all the tenants. It displays the tenant name, unit space, amount of rent paid, move-in date, lease expiration date, and security deposit.
- **Tax returns:** Obtain the property's tax returns for the past three years. Add up all of the income and expenses shown on the tax returns. These numbers should match those from the seller's °income and expense statements.
- **Lease agreements:** A lease agreement can be a complex legal document. If all of the leases are the same, such as in an apartment building, have an attorney review the first few to make sure they're valid.
- **Utility bills:** Obtain the past two years' worth of actual utility bills for the property. These bills include electricity, gas, water, sewer, trash, telephone, cable, and Internet service bills. Compare the totals of each utility category to the seller's total given on the expense statements.
- **Property tax bills:** Obtain the past two years' worth of property tax bills. Verify the amounts with those given on the seller's expense statements.

For Dummies: Bestselling Book Series for Beginners

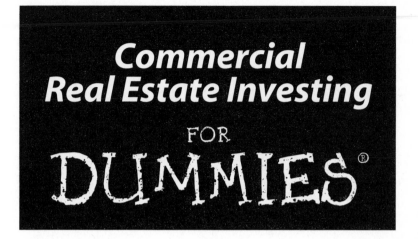

Commercial Real Estate Investing
FOR DUMMIES®

by Peter Conti and Peter Harris

Wiley Publishing, Inc.

Commercial Real Estate Investing For Dummies®

Published by
Wiley Publishing, Inc.
111 River St.
Hoboken, NJ 07030-5774
www.wiley.com

Copyright © 2008 by Wiley Publishing, Inc., Indianapolis, Indiana

Published by Wiley Publishing, Inc., Indianapolis, Indiana

Published simultaneously in Canada

For general information on our other products and services, please contact our Customer Care Department within the U.S. at 800-762-2974, outside the U.S. at 317-572-3993, or fax 317-572-4002.

For technical support, please visit www.wiley.com/techsupport.

Wiley also publishes its books in a variety of electronic formats. Some content that appears in print may not be available in electronic books.

Library of Congress Control Number: 2007941165

ISBN: 978-0-470-17491-3

Manufactured in the United States of America

10 9 8 7 6 5 4 3 2 1

WILEY

About the Authors

Peter Conti and **Peter Harris** are known as the World's #1 Greatest Commercial Real Estate Mentors. They partnered years ago by combining their existing Mentoring practices. They have both started from modest beginnings, Peter Conti was an auto mechanic, and Peter Harris was an introverted engineer. The portfolio of properties they have purchased nationwide with their Commercial Mentoring Program students continues to grow at an accelerated rate.

Peter Conti is the CEO of MentorFinancialGroup.com and lives on the Chesapeake Bay with his wife and kids in Annapolis, Maryland.

Peter Harris has purchased and put together commercial and residential real estate deals across the country for years. He has taught, mentored, and instructed many of the most successful investors across the nation. Harris and Donald Trump are coauthors of *Three Master Secrets of Real Estate Success.* He also sits on the board of advisors on several private and national real estate investment and development companies.

Many years ago, Peter Harris received the gift of a great mentor in his career and in his every day life, who guided and encouraged him to always get out of his comfort zone and play a bigger game. Mentoring one-on-one or to hundreds at a time around the nation is Peter's way of giving back and imparting the message of hope and faith in the dynamic and rewarding world of real estate. Even though Peter's first career was a physicist, holding several U.S. patents on outer space simulation, the school of hard knocks was where he got his real education in the business world.

Besides his business life, Peter's passions include hanging out with his son PJ, serving at his church, smiley faces, and riding his bike hundreds of miles at a time. Peter Harris lives in the heart of San Francisco with his son, PJ.

You can e-mail the authors at mentor@mentorfinancialgroup.com, or you can call them at 800-952-9585.

A Free Gift from the Authors: Your Bonus Commercial Quick Start Training Package

Here's your chance to join the authors for over six hours of training that just wouldn't fit in the book so that you can hit the ground running with your commercial real estate investing. You'll get to listen in, watch, and respond as they guide you in putting together highly profitable commercial deals.

Here's what you get:

- ✔ Over 6 hours of audio and video commercial investing training sessions
- ✔ Special form "Addendum A," which gives you up to 90 days to decide if you want a deal or not
- ✔ A Quick Start exclusive: The Money Raising Workshop
- ✔ Audio interviews with leading commercial real estate investing experts

You'll discover:

- ✔ The fastest way to get started investing in commercial real estate
- ✔ How to retire in five years or less
- ✔ Insider secrets to finding deals
- ✔ How to buy commercial real estate with no money
- ✔ Three steps to quickly fund even the biggest deal
- ✔ How to explode your net worth with land development

You'll also receive this special report: "The 3 Best Places to Buy Commercial Property Today"

Get your Commercial Quick Start Training Package (a $299 value) by registering your copy of this book at www.commercialquickstart.com. Enter code **CFD101**.

Dedication

Peter Conti: This book is dedicated to Peter Harris. You are an incredible blessing in my life.

Peter Harris: I dedicate this book to God first and foremost. I thank Him for His faithfulness, His love and grace, and for all of the amazing people He blesses me with. I also thank my great mentor, a great man named Nick Tsujimoto. Thank you, Nick, for your wisdom and love, for our many "closed door" sessions, and for helping me set and achieve awesomely scary goals. Lastly, I want to thank my partner Peter Conti for being the man and friend that he is and always will be. And to everyone else: The best is yet to come!

Authors' Acknowledgments

From both authors:

To every one of our Commercial Mentoring Program students. This book, along with all of the fun we've had and all of the properties we've bought together, would not be possible without you. Your courage motivates us every day. To Tim Gallan and Mike Lewis at Wiley publishing, we don't know how you do it. Thanks for giving us a little breathing room.

From Peter Harris:

To PJ, for always hanging in there with Dad. You are the greatest son a father could ever ask for. I love you, dude.

To Steve, Gary, Abe, Marge, June, Beck, Lela, Stone, Steph, and wonder boy Kyle, for always cheering for me.

To Da' Girls, you know who you are! Thanks for being warriors in your lives and mine. I am the wealthiest man on earth because of who and what we share together. The best is yet to come!

From Peter Conti:

This book wouldn't have happened without the awesome changes I've seen in my life over the past few years. Thank you, God, for such a great life and especially for surrounding me with so many wonderful people. Joanna, I love you. I miss you girls. You grew up so fast. Son, our time together is precious to me.

To everyone at MentorFinancialGroup.com: Marilyn, Angela, and Jeff. Wow! You are the most incredible and fun people I've ever had the privilege to work with. To Deb, Elizabeth, Kevin, Elaine, and Molly, you are the backbone of the Mentor Family. All of you have proven that nothing is impossible for the man who doesn't have to make it happen.

To all of our coaches, Peter Harris, Cheryl, Rob, Stephen, Emily, Juli, Cleve, Jeff, Matt, and David. Your daily support and encouragement for our Mentorship students is changing the world.

To Mr. X in one of the southern states. Your passion for helping all of our students to profit from every single deal they do with us is the keystone of the Mentor System. You deserve the credit even though you wish to remain anonymous.

To my friends in Christ: Brett, Rob, Peter, Baden, Tom, Thomas, Stephen, and Robb. Thank you for your leadership and guidance. And Rob, that praying over your wife thing you taught me is awesome!

To Mom, Dad, Lisa, Debbie, Linda, John, Paul, and Matthew, I love you.

Publisher's Acknowledgments

We're proud of this book; please send us your comments through our Dummies online registration form located at www.dummies.com/register/

Some of the people who helped bring this book to market include the following:

Acquisitions, Editorial, and Media Development

Senior Project Editor: Tim Gallan

Acquisitions Editor: Michael Lewis

Copy Editor: Jessica Smith

Editorial Manager: Michelle Hacker

Editorial Assistants: Joe Niesen, Leeann Harney, David Lutton

Cartoons: Rich Tennant
(www.the5thwave.com)

Composition Services

Project Coordinator: Kristie Rees

Layout and Graphics: Reuben W. Davis, Alissa D. Ellet, Brooke Graczyk, Christine Williams

Anniversary Logo Design: Richard Pacifico

Proofreaders: Cynthia Fields, John Greenough, Bonnie Mikkelson

Indexer: Steve Rath

Special Help
Elizabeth Kuball

Publishing and Editorial for Consumer Dummies

Diane Graves Steele, Vice President and Publisher, Consumer Dummies

Joyce Pepple, Acquisitions Director, Consumer Dummies

Kristin A. Cocks, Product Development Director, Consumer Dummies

Michael Spring, Vice President and Publisher, Travel

Kelly Regan, Editorial Director, Travel

Publishing for Technology Dummies

Andy Cummings, Vice President and Publisher, Dummies Technology/General User

Composition Services

Gerry Fahey, Vice President of Production Services

Debbie Stailey, Director of Composition Services

Contents at a Glance

Table of Contents

Part V: Kicking Your Investing into High Gear............241

Introduction

Welcome to *Commercial Real Estate Investing For Dummies!* We both love commercial real estate and are thrilled to be able to share our passion with you. In this book's chapters, we provide you guidance by showing you our experiences and the combined experience of thousands of our Mentorship students who have invested with us across the country since 1995.

Investing in commercial real estate allows you to:

- ✔ Make much larger amounts of money while putting in almost the same amount of work that smaller deals, such as single-family houses, require.
- ✔ Establish multiple streams of income that are generated by properties that almost run themselves. In fact, you discover how to be in command of everything right from your home office.
- ✔ Retire in five years or less. Sounds impossible, doesn't it? Well, it really isn't!

The downside of investing in commercial real estate is that it does take some time to get up to speed. Plan on getting a good education before you jump into your first deal. Oh, and if you're frightened by the prospect of making hundreds of thousands of dollars from just one deal, investing in commercial real estate is probably not the right path for you.

About This Book

This book is your complete how-to guide for investing in commercial real estate. You may want someone who's already investing to help you oversee your first deal or two, but our goal is to give you enough information so that you'll be able to go out and find, structure, and negotiate profitable, money-making deals on commercial properties.

In these pages, you have all the answers to complex issues broken down into an easy-to-read format. Start at the beginning, in the middle, or simply pick a section that interests you most. It doesn't matter where you start because the most important thing is that you begin today. You may have been looking for your opportunity to become your own boss, make more money than your stockbroker, or simply be able to retire fast by investing in commercial real estate. Now, with this book, you finally have the opportunity and the information you need to take charge.

We mention our students a lot in this book, and that's because we do 82 percent of our investing with our Commercial Mentoring students across the country. We hope that by sharing the success of others who are just like you, we'll be able to encourage you to do whatever it takes to live the life of your dreams.

Conventions Used in This Book

We include the following few conventions to help you make your way smoothly through this book:

- ✔ Important terms are shown in *italics,* with definitions following the terms.
- ✔ **Boldfaced** words highlight the keywords in bulleted lists and numbered steps.
- ✔ Web sites are printed in `monofont`.

When this book was printed, some Web addresses may have needed to break across two lines of text. If that happened, rest assured that we haven't put in any extra characters (such as hyphens) to indicate the break. So, when using one of these Web addresses, just type in exactly what you see in this book, pretending that the line break doesn't exist.

What You're Not to Read

If you're in a hurry as you read through this book, you can skip over some of the anecdotes and sidebars (the text in the gray boxes). These bits of text are interesting, but not essential to your understanding of the basics of commercial real estate investing. However, most of them contain interesting and helpful info that you'll likely want to go back and read when you get a chance.

Foolish Assumptions

When writing this book, we kept a few assumptions in mind about you:

- ✔ You're interested in real estate but you're probably not as rich as Donald Trump. However, we assume that you aren't broke and looking for money to make your next house payment either.
- ✔ You have some experience in business, management, or real estate investing, whether it is in commercial real estate or not.

✔ You're sharp enough to be investing in commercial real estate, so you aren't going to rely on us for legal, tax, or other professional advice. After all, one of us is a former auto mechanic, so you should take everything we share with you as our real-world experience. That means you need to combine that experience with the counsel from your own attorney and your tax professional.

How This Book Is Organized

The text of this book is organized into self-contained chapters that you can read in any order. Think of this book as a reference that you can pick up and read bits and pieces of whenever you have the time. (Of course, we'd love it even more if you read the thing from cover to cover.) The chapters are arranged in parts, and here's what each part covers.

Part I: Getting to Know Commercial Real Estate Investing

This part is where you might just fall in love with commercial real estate investing. Understanding what types of property make up commercial real estate and getting past some of the biggest myths about it will provide a strong foundation that you can use to support all the other in-depth information you get in this book. In this part, you also discover just how simple it is to quickly determine the value of any commercial property. After you understand this formula, you'll be able to confidently hold your own while negotiating your way to your newfound fortune.

Part II: Getting Started Making Deals

In this part, you discover the four essential steps to every commercial deal you put together. For instance, you find out where the best sources of brokers, sellers, and properties can be found. Then we jump into some serious deal making by sharing with you our Instant Offer System, which shows you how to make successful offers. And because all big commercial deals need to be checked out before you make the final move to buy them, you need to understand how to use due diligence and the closing process to uncover hidden problems, negotiate prices down, or determine when the best deal for you is *not* to buy. We end this part, appropriately enough, by showing you how to close a deal.

Part III: Funding Your Deals: Financing and Lending

Okay, so you've hooked a big deal and are reeling it in. Making sure that you have all the funding you need is critical at this point. In this part, you find out how to get approved for conventional financing. Or, if you like the idea of getting creative and buying commercial real estate without using any of your cash or credit, check out Chapter 9. We close out this part with a chapter in which you discover the secrets of raising private capital from outside investors. In it we also show you how to put together profitable partnerships.

Part IV: Day-to-Day Ownership and Operations

Now that you have bought a property, who's going to mind the ship? You may be amazed to find out that it isn't always going to be you! In this part, we cover important points such as how to pick commercial properties that can afford to pay for outside management. And we help you keep tabs on your important investments by revealing our simple "manage the manger" process. In this part, you also uncover the secrets of protecting your assets. Unfortunately in today's world it isn't what you make but what you keep that really counts. Finally, you get an insider's look at something you won't find in most investing books: the reasons why some properties fail and how you can avoid making the same mistakes.

Part V: Kicking Your Investing into High Gear

When you start feeling like a pro and you're ready to jump into the fast lane, this is the part for you. These are the chapters where we really get you up to speed. For instance, we introduce you to commercial fixer-uppers. We also help you discover the insider secrets to taking a piece of land through the approval process so that it can be developed. Owning commercial real estate combined with the ideas Chapter 16 can save you tens of thousands of dollars in taxes every single year. Finally, in this part you find out how to jump into a commercial real estate career for extra income or to get an insider's edge on the deals you're putting together.

Part VI: The Part of Tens

In this traditional *For Dummies* part, you quickly discover some important information. For example, we provide the top ten ways to increase the value of your commercial properties. We also include ten great organizations that you should consider joining.

Icons Used in This Book

In this book, we highlight certain types of information with icons so you can find what you're looking for fast. Here are the icons we use and what they mean:

The text highlighted by this icon usually consists of helpful ideas and strategies to make your investing easier.

This icon highlights important points that are essential to your successful investing.

Investing is fun but it also has pitfalls that you need to watch out for, so this icon does the job.

When we attach this icon to text, you know that you can be sure to get the real-world scoop from stories and investing ideas that come from Mentorship students and our own deals.

This icon reminds you to do more research, hire an inspector, or consult with an attorney or tax advisor.

Where to Go from Here

This book is written so that you can jump into the shallow end or you can go off the high dive, depending on your experience level. You can begin anywhere you want — none of the chapters need to be read before any of the others. So, if you need a refresher course, start with Part I. If you're more experienced and want to kick your investing into high gear, check out Part V.

Otherwise, simply peruse the table of contents or the index to find what you're looking for. To understand what commercial investing can do for you, check out Chapter 1. Whatever you do, don't let this book get out of your hands without reading Chapter 15, which is all about land development. In this chapter, you can find out how some of our most passionate students have made millions — yes, that's millions of dollars — doing big land development deals.

Part I
Getting to Know Commercial Real Estate Investing

The 5th Wave   By Rich Tennant

"I'd like to invest in some commercial real estate, but this one comes with more risk than I'm comfortable with."

In this part . . .

In this part, we help you understand what types of property make up commercial real estate and also help you get past some of the biggest myths about it. We present information that will enable you to simply and quickly determine the value of any commercial property. After you understand this formula, you'll be able to confidently hold your own while negotiating your way to your newfound fortune.

Chapter 1

Just Imagine . . . Commercial Real Estate and You!

. . . .

. . . .

Can you imagine yourself in the world of commercial real estate investing? Imagine yourself walking through the lobby of your 100-unit apartment complex. What would it look like and feel like to be pulling into the parking lot of a neighborhood shopping center that's all yours? Maybe you can imagine that you're watching your construction crew break ground on your luxury home land development project. What if this project leads to a life where you can live a life of luxury and balance? You'd be able to do things such as drive your kids or grandkids to school every day, maybe even in your pajamas, with a big smile on your face because you've invested wisely. Okay, here's one more scenario that may get you excited: Imagine yourself impacting the lives of hundreds or thousands of kids here and around the world who benefit from your charities, all funded by wealth-building skills and invaluable relationships developed from your commercial real estate investing.

We have two purposes for writing this book. The first is to introduce you to commercial real estate investing. We want to share with you that anyone can learn how to successfully find, research, negotiate, finance, and buy commercial real estate of any type. In this book, we do our best to break down powerful investing concepts that were once thought to be too complex for most people. Our second purpose for this book is to give you the confidence to go after what you really want in life instead of shying away from the true potential that you've always known is somewhere inside of you. To make this jump as easy as possible, you even get a free Commercial Quick Start Training Package, which will allow you to quickly implement the moneymaking ideas in this book. See the About the Authors section at the front of the book for details.

Creating the wealth that allows you to follow your real passion is what's waiting for you whether you're an investor, real estate agent, or lender. Commercial real estate will accelerate your financial freedom, and in the process our hope is that you'll find the true meaning of the "why" in your life. That alone makes this book worth diving into.

What Is Commercial Real Estate?

Commercial real estate is many things. It's office buildings, apartment complexes, shopping centers, warehouses, industrial parks, hotels, motels, resorts, and the list goes on and on. It's where businesses are conducted and where many people live together. Commercial real estate is everywhere. (Jump to Chapter 2 for a journey through all the different types of commercial real estate that are available.)

Commercial real estate is also a means of building long-lasting wealth for the investor. To us, long-lasting wealth is an investment that pays you every month. It's also one in which the value increases every year. Compare this to other types of investments that may allow you to draw a monthly payment, but the balance goes down year by year until the pot's empty. Sound familiar? That's not true wealth at all. In this book, we show you how commercial real estate has the ability to generate sizable cash flow every month as well as increase in value every year (and to be tax free!). We challenge anyone to find a better way out of the rat race than to invest in commercial real estate.

Commercial real estate can afford you a wonderful and fulfilling professional career that's second to none. And besides being enjoyable, commercial real estate investors are among the highest paid professionals in the nation. In fact, it isn't uncommon for a commercial investor's check from just one closing to equal one year's salary of an engineer. We see it all the time. We also get to hang out with and see the changes our Commercial Mentorship students are going through. Many of them have joined "The Quitters Club" by saying goodbye to their 9 to 5 jobs. These friends of ours absolutely love what they do and can't dream of doing anything else.

Every ultrasuccessful investor or high-income-generating professional we know in this business knows the secret — it's relationships. Commercial real estate is at its core a relationship business. For instance, big deals, huge fees, and long-lasting and fulfilling careers can all be created through the relationships you make. We talk more about relationships later on in this book.

As you're out and about, start looking around at all the commercial real estate that you see. When you go to the shopping center, notice what space is leased out. What buildings aren't fully leased? Why might that property be having trouble? After you realize that an investor owns every building, it's difficult to not think about owning your own commercial properties someday. To get started investing now, try out the free bonus that's waiting for you at www.commercialquickstart.com. As a reader of this book, you get three online training courses and a one-on-one strategic coaching session.

What to Think About As You Get Started

When choosing to make an investment in anything, you have to take several things into consideration, right? Why am I doing this? How much does it cost? Am I doing this at the right time? Well, the same applies for commercial real estate. In fact, you may find that you have too many choices simply because there are so many different ways to profit in this field. The following sections go over some of the most common questions you may have when deciding which part of commercial real estate is right for you.

Can I make money at commercial real estate investing?

This is one question that we have a definitive answer for: Yes! We know that you can make money investing in commercial real estate for three reasons:

- ✔ If we can do it, you certainly can too. Both of us started from modest beginnings and we aren't special by any means. In fact, coauthor Peter Conti used to be an auto mechanic. Coauthor Peter Harris was an introverted engineer.

- ✔ We are blessed to be surrounded by our Commercial Mentoring Program students who for the most part have started with little or no experience in commercial real estate. Every time a Mentorship student gets another deal they prove that it really is possible.

- ✔ If you look at the most successful investors out there you'll find that they all have a pattern in common: They've typically started out by investing in homes, running a business, or working in a fairly well-paying profession. The next step is to begin investing in smaller commercial properties such as apartment buildings. At some point the successful investors all move up to either big commercial deals or land development.

Coauthor Peter Harris started out investing in real estate by purchasing single-family homes. He did quite well in it, but one day he was daydreaming and said to himself, "What if I could combine all my rental homes under one roof?" He felt that would make managing the properties a lot easier because he wouldn't have to drive around the city chasing rents. In fact, he realized that he could make better use of the time that he saved by investing even more! When he woke up from his daydream, he realized that he had just described an apartment complex. To make a long story short, he sold all of his rental homes and bought large apartment complexes. And the rest is history. His cash flow went from hundreds per month to thousands per month in only two years.

If he can make it starting out where he did as an introverted engineer, and now he's buying commercial properties worth millions, you certainly can too. You see, Peter is simply an average person who applied the ideas in this book to change his life. If he can do it, anyone can use commercial real estate investing to transform his or her life.

Throughout this book, we show you what "good real estate" looks like, and we tell you how to time the real estate market, what markets to stay away from, and how to know a good deal from a bad deal Then we set you up with some powerful guiding principles of investment and some free ongoing training to help move you forward.

What type of investor am I?

You can fall into one of two basic types of commercial real estate investors. The first is the *cash-flow investor,* and the second is the *long-term hold investor.* Both make excellent cases for fantastic wealth building and both can do well in an up or down market. Read on for details.

Cash-flow investor

Cash-flow investors purchase properties for the purpose of putting monthly income into their pockets. And they buy commercial real estate just like you would buy a business. In other words, if you were buying a ready-made business, you would do whatever it takes to make sure that the business is a proven moneymaker, right? You would thoroughly check the financial records to prove that it could stand on its own every month. Well, cash-flow investors do the same. They take every measure to make sure they're investing in a property that produces nice monthly cash flow.

Also, cash-flow investors don't solely rely on appreciation as a way to get wealthy. They know that appreciation is only a bonus, a gift. If it's present, great. If it isn't, that's okay, because the focus is on income. Cash-flow investors know that relying on appreciation is a form of gambling and doesn't make good business sense. In Chapter 3, we show you how to easily evaluate and calculate cash flow for any income-producing property just like the experts do.

Another plus for cash-flow investors that's frequently overlooked is the ability to weather the storm in a down market. In down markets where sales are slow and prices are falling, people who normally would buy homes to live in aren't buying homes due to fear. These folks eventually become tenants for your multiunit commercial properties. This helps cash-flow investors to actually make more money in a down market.

Long-term "hold" investor

Unlike cash-flow investors, long-term "hold" investors rely on appreciation for wealth building, but they do so in a more conservative real-world fashion. They also benefit equity wise from paying down the loan amount over a number of years.

The long-term hold investor's goals are simple: They want deals with an upside, like the ability to increase the value by improving the cash flow of the property. For example, some of the wealthiest investors we know are our mentors, who are older gentlemen who bought their pieces of commercial real estate decades ago. One of them bought land and another bought apartments. Their philosophy was "Good real estate will always have a higher value over many years if I wait long enough." It's a too-simple strategy that has worked incredibly well for many patient investors. Both of these gentlemen held onto their properties in three separate down market cycles over the years. Both have properties that are debt free, and they have made millions of dollars since.

In this book, we cover the basic foundational strategies such as "buy good real estate and wait" (Chapter 8) along with many of the more creative, accelerated wealth building strategies just in case you're in a hurry (Chapter 9).

Do I have to be a genius to crunch the numbers?

Honestly, the only requirement needed to crunch numbers is to be able to count to ten with your fingers (or at least be able to use a calculator). What you'll find is that any type of income-producing property can be analyzed by simply splitting up the deal into three parts:

- ✔ Income
- ✔ Expenses
- ✔ Debt (mortgage payment)

The process for figuring out the cash flow for a 30-unit apartment complex is the same as the process for a single-family home. For instance, say you bought a three-bedroom, two-bath home and you're renting it for $1,200 per month. As the landlord, you're responsible for property taxes, insurance, and a landscaper. All those expenses total $300 per month. You also pay $800 per month for your mortgage. The tenant pays all other expenses. Here's a quick formula for figuring out cash flow per month:

Income − expenses − debt = cash flow per month

Using the numbers from the previous single-family home example, here's the formula in action:

$1,200 (income) − $300 (expenses) − $800 (debt) = $100 (cash flow)

Wasn't too difficult, was it? Now, here's an example for a 30-unit apartment building. You have 30 two-bedroom units renting for $500 per month. That totals $15,000 per month in income. Total expenses for the 30 units are $6,000 per month (which includes taxes, insurance, maintenance, and property management costs). The mortgage payment is $5,000 per month. Here's how the formula works to find the cash flow per month:

$15,000 (income) − $6,000 (expenses) − $5,000 (debt) = $4,000 (cash flow)

This concept applies for office buildings and shopping centers as well. Just remember that for any property you want to analyze, you need to get the income first, the expenses second, and the debt payment third. From there, you can see whether the property makes any money. In this book, we go through this concept in much more detail. In fact, after going through the real-life examples that we provide, your confidence level should be incredibly high.

What investing opportunities are available?

Gee, where do we begin to discuss how many types of opportunities you have to choose from when investing in commercial real estate? It may sound cliché, but there's something for everyone. If you like the cash flowing dynamics of the apartment business, there are exciting times ahead for you. How about making huge chunks of money developing land? What about the stability of owning office buildings? Consider also the endless growth of shopping centers.

Throughout this book, we explain how to find deals and how to spot the gems as well as how to tell the difference between a good, bad, or average deal. As examples, we give you simple and practical guidelines to follow as well as real deals.

When investing in a property, you have two choices:

- ✔ You can invest in a property that's "ready to go" with no necessary repairs, problems, or other hiccups.

- ✔ You can invest in properties that have lots of problems and need to be fixed up. Commercial fixer-upper opportunities are in every city. Just like you can do with a residential property, you can fix up, flip, and profit with commercial property.

Big investment returns await you if you take the time to study the fixer-upper how-tos shown in Chapter 14. We like the commercial fixer-uppers because after the rehab is complete, most times you can hold for cash flow, hold for long-term wealth generation, or flip for 'instant" profits that you once thought would take years and years of hard work to earn.

How does financing work?

Are there differences between obtaining a loan for a single-family home and a neighborhood shopping center? The answer is yes, of course, but the differences may surprise you. Pretty much all you need to get a home loan is a good credit score, and then you have to make enough money to pay the mortgage. When you get a loan for a commercial property, the lender is often interested more in how the property performs than she is in your credit score. For commercial real estate, getting a loan is based on the following three main qualifications:

- ✔ Does the property produce enough income to cover the expenses and mortgage?
- ✔ What is the condition of the property?
- ✔ What is the financial strength of the borrower?

In commercial real estate financing, the borrower (the investor), is number three on the priority list. In other words, a strong cash flowing property in good condition will almost always outweigh the poor credit (or no credit) of the borrower. (Flip to Chapter 8 to discover how to get your lender to say "yes" to your deal, what lenders like and dislike in deals, and tips on choosing the best loan for your deal.)

Understanding the Risks of Commercial Real Estate

Is commercial real estate risky? You bet it is. One of our mentors always said, "Anything you go after of great worth has great risk." Commercial real estate investing involves big dollars and lots of people. And whenever you have lots of money and people working together closely, trouble is right around the corner. But risk is a facet of doing business — any business. You can't avoid it. The best thing you can do to protect yourself is to understand all the risks that are possible, and then get your advisors involved to help you figure out how to avoid them. Don't skimp on getting the best advisors you can hire either. As the saying goes, "It's expensive being cheap."

But here's the good news: Risks can be managed to levels of great certainty. Being successful in commercial real estate nearly always means taking calculated risks. Are you willing to risk some of your time and money to be financially free? What if you could secure your family's financial future? There are risks with everything you do in life. You may have heard of people who spend their whole lives trying to avoid taking any risks, and in the process they accomplish nothing. What a shame. The point is that sooner or later you'll probably have to step out of your comfort zone to free yourself from the rat race.

Will you consider taking only a little bit of risk? If so, you may want to start out with a smaller multifamily building. Or maybe you want to roll the dice big time. In this case, check out Chapter 15 for more on land development, which can satisfy the riskiest adventurer.

One of the risks of real estate investing is that if you aren't careful the property can fail. We include a whole chapter in this book (Chapter 13) on why properties fail, because real estate investing and the decisions we make don't always turn out well. Sometimes you just make a bad deal. And sometimes you may hire the wrong property management company. And other times the market may take a turn for the worse and send you in a downward spiral. Chapter 13 may be the most important chapter you read because understanding why properties fail can enable you to spot where your property needs some help. Or, if you're looking at a deal, knowing why properties fail helps you analyze why the property is in its current condition. And don't forget that understanding why properties fail can put you in a great negotiating position and assist you in solving property problems.

Avoiding lawsuits, the most feared risk

The most feared risk in commercial real estate investing is getting sued. Every tenant you have can be a potential lawsuit. You can also be sued by contractors, city personnel, and the list goes on and on. How do you protect yourself? Here are two lines of defense:

- ✔ Obtain property liability and hazard insurance.
- ✔ Choose a protective form of ownership or holding, such as a limited liability company.

Limited liability companies (LLCs) are by far the most popular form of ownership used today to hold commercial real estate. ***Warning:*** The worst possible method of holding title is to hold it individually in your name. This way, you have zero liability protection and absolutely no privacy. In Chapter 12, we offer many tips and strategies for holding and protecting your property and assets. Your goal should be to build a "legal fortress" with the right experts.

Risk-proofing your investment plan

In our years of investing and watching numerous successful and not-so-successful investors go at it, we have come up with several fail-safe measures (we call them common-sense measures!) for risk-proofing your investing. Here they are:

✔ **Do proper due diligence.** *Due diligence* is the process you go through when verifying the financial documents of the property, performing a physical inspection, and checking out the legal pieces of the property, such as the title. Ninety percent of all deals die during due diligence. So, if you don't do a thorough job, the consequences can be costly. You may end up buying a property that's a money pit. However, when done properly, due diligence can actually help you make your sweet deal even sweeter. Reading Chapter 6, which provides the ins and outs of due diligence, may save you millions of dollars.

✔ **Don't overpay.** Overpaying is common among new investors. Don't be the investor in a deal where the agent sets a record price on selling a property! If you're buying apartments, make sure that you're aware of what price you're paying per unit. If you're buying a shopping center, make sure you know how much you're paying per square foot. In both cases, see what the recent market closings value your property at. Paying too much will lock up the property's cash flow for a long time. (See Chapter 3 for more on pricing your prospective properties.)

✔ **Have expert market knowledge.** Knowing your market like the back of your hand sets you up for success. Before you close on your deal, make sure you know the following:

• How competitive your rents are with other similar local properties

• When and if there's a "slow season" for rentals so you can plan ahead

• Whether there's rent control in your city, which would inhibit you from raising rents as you thought you could

---

Getting extra help

Why go it alone when we're here to help you? As a reader of this book, you get additional free material and training at www.commercialquickstart.com. At this site, you'll get your Commercial Quick Start Training Package which includes six hours of audio with your authors Peter and Peter, video training sessions, free commercial analysis software, and more! See the About the Authors section at the front of the book for details.

We also like to inquire on crime statistics on the property in question by calling the local police department.

✔ **Hold your goals loosely.** What we mean is that you should keep your investment's exit strategy flexible at all times. In fact, have several exit strategies ready at any given time. Market conditions change. Your personal circumstances can change rapidly as well. So, don't get wrapped up in executing just one exit strategy, because it may no longer apply.

✔ **Know where you are in the real estate cycle.** There are four parts to any real estate cycle: expansion, contraction, recession, and recovery. By reading Chapter 2, you can figure out where your particular city is in the cycle and you can determine when to buy, sell, hold, or bail. Each part of the cycle demands that you pay detailed attention to your investment decisions. Understanding real estate cycles helps you take the correct actions with the best timing. There's nothing like timing the market like a pro!

You can discover more about controlling the risk in your commercial investments as you go through this book. You may have thought that risk-proofing was impossible, but you'd be surprised at what a little knowledge can do to your investment portfolio.

Chapter 2

A Crash Course in Commercial Real Estate Investing

In This Chapter

▶ Understanding the basics of commercial real estate

▶ Surveying the types of investments available

▶ Discovering the tools you need to get started

▶ Debunking the myths of investing in commercial real estate

▶ Keeping timing in mind when selling, buying, and holding

*W*hat comes to mind when you think of commercial real estate? Downtown skyscrapers? Corner strip malls? Apartment complexes? Okay, that's a good start. But have you thought about being the owner of one? Too complex you say? Too expensive you think? Jumping into commercial real estate investing could be the wisest and most lucrative investment you ever make. To us, the benefits outweigh the risks. But find out for yourself.

In this chapter, you find out what commercial real estate is, and you discover the different types available. We break down the big world of commercial investing into easy-to-follow categories so that you can pick and choose your favorites. We also uncover the five biggest myths that stop people from investing and understanding commercial real estate.

Because the value of commercial real estate depends on the cash flow that it produces, we show you how cash flow is made on a monthly basis, and we help you discover the steps to building long-term wealth. We also tell you when it's the most profitable time to buy, hold, sell, or bail (we even share with you ways of predicting the future!). By the end of this chapter, you're sure to be convinced that commercial real estate is, by far, the best way to produce true and lasting wealth.

How Is Commercial Real Estate Different from Residential Real Estate?

Here's our definition of commercial real estate: It's any piece of real estate that's bigger than one house on one lot. So, commercial real estate includes everything from small apartment buildings (five or more units) and large office buildings to shopping centers, to industrial parks, and even land development.

The three biggest differences between commercial real estate and residential real estate include the following:

- ✓ **Commercial real estate projects are passive investments only after they're up and running.** Remember that unless you have a ton of money and don't care about getting huge returns, commercial real estate will take a lot of your time and effort to get started. After all, you have to deal with many things, including the learning process, finding the right mentors or teachers, searching for the right deal, financing your investment, picking management teams, protecting it from lawsuits, and overseeing the project.

  The good news is that after you have a commercial project off the ground, it's usually big enough that it allows you to pay other people to take care of it. So it won't take much of your time at all — and that's why it's called a *passive investment*. Compare this to a single-family home that may require collecting rents and making repairs for many years to come.

- ✓ **Commercial real estate has the potential to make you rich with just one deal.** Doing one commercial deal the right way can generate you a profit several times your yearly salary in addition to providing you sizable monthly income as long as you own the property. Residential real estate can produce a sizable profit as well, but it will not generate anywhere near the cash flow that a commercial property will. You'll receive one check per month from a single-family residence, but you can receive several hundred checks per month from a commercial property.

  If you don't believe us, consider these numbers: When several of our Commercial Mentoring Program clients were sharing how they got started in commercial real estate, we found out that one of them is in a project that already has a profit of $10 million or more. Another one bought a piece of land near his home for $1.5 million, and it has jumped in value over the past two years to $9 million (and he didn't even have to use his own money).

- ✓ **The people that you meet who invest in commercial real estate are all big thinkers.** They're people who have decided that they want to think big, live big, and hang around other people who are just as passionate about life as they are. Until you get involved, it's difficult to really understand just what your life could look like. Investors of residential real estate think of one monthly check and one tenant, they wait for appreciation (which may never come), and they're limited in ways of creating massive value for their property.

Why Invest in Commercial Real Estate?

We think commercial real estate investing is a great way to generate wealth, and the main reason we like it so much can be boiled down to one word: leverage. Leverage is what allows you to use a small amount of your time and money to bring you a magnified return. Commercial properties are usually bigger and more valuable than other types of real estate, such as houses. What this means to you is that after you figure out how to find, negotiate, and buy commercial property without using much of your own money, you'll be able to sit back and watch the magic of leverage work wonders for your financial future. Your family will thank you for generations to come.

When people get started with their investing, most of them dream of creating a six-figure annual income stream so that they can quit the rat race. However, deep down many of them have doubts that they can actually make it happen. But never fear. The goal of this book is to give you the starting steps and specific know-how to help you realize that you really can live the life of your dreams. And we want you to do it in a way that creates the lifestyle you want without years of hard work. We've helped other clients do it, and we know you can do it too.

Understand that there are still going to be naysayers out there who say you can't invest in commercial real estate in today's market, in today's economy, or in today's cosmic layering of celestial occurrences. But you have a choice. You can either buy into what these financially stressed-out individuals are desperately clinging to, or you can let go of everything that's been holding you back and go after the future that you want and deserve.

Let us be clear: Commercial real estate allows you to make whopping piles of money. With commercial real estate you can make anywhere from $20,000 to $50,000 on a little deal. And, you can make $10 million or more from a bigger property. Sound interesting? Does it take work? Sure it does. But a $100,000 commercial deal doesn't take anywhere near ten times the work that a $10,000 residential deal takes. So what you're doing is working at a higher level that rewards you with the opportunity to make a lot more money with just a little more effort.

What Types of Investments Are Available?

Most people think commercial real estate is all about apartment rentals. Even though residential properties *are* a big part of commercial real estate investing, other types of properties make for excellent investment opportunities as well. For instance, commercial real estate includes offices and warehouses, retail centers, and even undeveloped land.

We define commercial real estate as any real estate that's bigger than one house on one lot. So even if people live in the property, it's still commercial as long as it's bigger than one house. Some people would argue that a little property like a duplex or a four-unit isn't really commercial. That's ok. We like keeping our definitions simple. Actually, five or more units in an apartment building is considered commercial, but who's counting? We explain each of the different types of commercial property in the following sections.

Apartment buildings (also known as residential properties)

The commercial properties that are in the residential category include everything from small apartment properties (five or more units) to huge apartment building projects that cover several city blocks. You drive by thousands of commercial properties like this every day (or you may even live in one). Every single building you see is owned by a commercial investor who's in the game to make money. (Now anytime you see a nice apartment building, you won't be able to stop thinking about getting into commercial real estate investing.) What we find great about investing in apartments is that they're easy to find, banks love to lend on them, and they're great cash flow generators.

The advantage of starting off with residential properties is that they're a great way to jump into the exciting world of commercial real estate investing. We both started off investing in small- to medium-sized multiunit properties. This was a great experience because it allowed us to make the jump to get started. For most people, getting started is the hardest part. However, after you've started investing in commercial real estate, you'll have a difficult time going back to the old grind of the rat race that so many others find themselves trapped in.

Offices and warehouses

After you get the itch to invest in commercial real estate, you'll never walk into an office building again without thinking, "somebody owns this building. Why couldn't it be me?"

ANECDOTE

How a college dropout turned $4,000 into a $120,000 profit in 60 days

Tom was the kind of teenager in high school who thought that he didn't need anyone else because he had all the answers. Too "smart" to go to college, Tom worked a variety of jobs until he found himself working as a bouncer in a bar and surviving on 69 cent cans of beans. Well, you can probably imagine where Tom ended up: He found himself at age 22 with no real friends and a pretty bleak-looking future.

For some reason, Tom had the wild idea that he could somehow make money investing in real estate. So, he drove around town talking to agents and looking at properties. One day he saw a sign on an empty lot that said "Exxon Corporation Land for Sale." Tom didn't know much about land, but after looking at the county records he figured that the property might be worth about $200,000.

After calling and meeting with the agent, he was able to put a contract in place to buy the land for $160,000. But now Tom had a big problem because the agent was calling about the $4,000 earnest money deposit that Tom had promised to give to him. So he went down to the bank and talked them into lending him the $4,000 based on the value of his car, which was the only real asset that he had.

Now Tom was faced with the problem of having to close the deal in 120 days or he would lose his deposit and perhaps his car too. So, he went back to the county office and looked at all the other parcels of land around his piece that he had under contract. He saw that there was a larger lot behind his property that could have its access restricted depending on how he developed his property.

With the help of an architect, Tom put together two sets of plans. One set showed a larger commercial shopping center that restricted access to the lot behind it. He also put together another set of plans with another smaller building designed as a gateway to the property behind it. Tom's next step took a straight face. He marched into a meeting with the owner of the property that was behind his property and dropped both sets of plans down. He told the owner (in a nice way) that he had a choice: He could either buy his property for $320,000 so the owner could develop it with the gateway, or if the owner didn't want to buy it, Tom was going to develop it himself and restrict his access.

Tom was scared stiff at this point because he knew that he didn't have any way to close the deal himself. Fortunately the owner agreed to buy the property for $320,000 — and after they went through the due diligence, the price dropped down to $290,000. Tom walked away with $130,000 in profit (after paying the land owner his $160,000) and for two reasons: One was that he found himself in a place in life where he didn't have a lot of choices. Either he was going to go for it and make it in life, or he wasn't. The second reason that Tom was successful is because he had guts. Guts boil down to a willingness to move ahead even though you've never done it before and even though you're scared to death.

As our populations expand, more and more office and warehouse buildings are being constructed. Offices and warehouses are great for investing because they have what we call *triple net leases*. This type of lease is one where the tenants in the property pay you the rent plus they also pay for the following:

> ✔ All maintenance and repairs
> ✔ The insurance on the property
> ✔ The real estate taxes

Bingo! It's called *passive income* for a reason. After you get your office building rented out you can sit back and watch the cash flow come rolling in. Heck, you can even hire a property management company to lease it out for you. Then your only obligation is to sit on the beach.

Triple net leases are so called because the tenants in your office building pay for all three categories of expenses. Tenants pay all three of these costs so that the rent you get is a net amount that you don't have to pay expenses out of. So after the tenants pay for all the expenses and you pay the mortgage, the rest goes into your pocket. It's quite typical for a triple net lease to be 5 to 20 years in duration with rent increases every couple of years. But that can be a disadvantage as well and here's why: Let's say that the lease is for ten years. If your neighborhood experiences explosive growth over the next three to five years, you won't be able to charge higher rents or capitalize on what's happening because you're locked into a ten-year lease agreement. But overall, triple net lease investments are very much sought after.

Retail centers

Retail centers, also known as shopping centers or malls, are at the heart of most of the towns and cities in our country. These are the places where people come to shop, eat, and meet with friends. And retail centers are one of the commercial property asset types that you can invest in. Most investors like retail centers because, like office and warehouse properties, many retail properties are leased out on a long-term triple net lease basis where the tenants pay for all the expenses. The upside to this as an investor is that your rates of return won't go down over time as the taxes and expenses go up. In fact, as rents go up over time, your returns just keep getting better and better. And as in most triple net lease agreements, rent increases are built into the agreement with the tenant.

Hotels and resorts

This asset type isn't our recommendation as the place to get started, but many experienced investors have found it to be a fun and highly profitable area to focus on. Of course, other investors have also lost their shirts (and sometimes their trousers too), so make sure that you know what you're doing before jumping in.

To get started in this niche, we suggest that you invest in the property and then lease it out to another company that will operate the hotel or resort. Why? After you go beyond simply owning the real estate and start running the business, you've just stepped out of the wonderful world of commercial real estate investing and entered into the world of running a business.

Land development

Land development is one of the most exciting types of commercial real estate. However, it can also be an area that will teach you to some quick and painful lessons if you jump in without knowing what you're doing.

By taking some land that isn't yet fit for building and taking it through the approval process, you can dramatically increase the value. Commercial real estate investors call this "taking it to the map."

Remember that it also makes sense to start small and work your way up with land development. For example, most of our Commercial Mentoring Program clients get up to speed as quickly as possible by taking on initial land development deals in the range of $500,000. Starting off small allows them to get comfortable with the land development process before going out to raise millions of dollars.

When Stephen, one of our Commercial Mentoring Program coaches, was getting started with land development, he found a heavily populated area with a 5-acre lot in his town that had not yet been developed. You may hear some people refer to a piece of land like this as an *infill project*. Stephen's goal was to get the land under contract, and then he wanted to get the zoning changed and everything else approved so that the land was ready to have houses built on it.

Stephen was able to get a contract to purchase the land for $400,000. This wasn't too difficult to do because its zoning was agricultural which, by the way, is less desirable than being zoned for residential. After the 5 acres was taken through the entitlement process and was approved for building homes on, it would be worth $1.2 million. If you're thinking, "Wow, that sounds like a good deal!" you just had a little taste of why so many people are excited about land development.

With land development, the investor usually has a "free look" period — often 90 days or so — after the property is under contract to talk to the town planners and officials to see how likely approval is. To leverage and control the risk on this, you can bring in an outside investor who can fund the down payment.

What You Need to Get Started

What's the secret ingredient that allows someone to make it big in commercial real estate? If we told you, how long would it take for you to jump up, bolt out the door, and go find your first commercial deal? Well, you're about to find out, so put on your running shoes. The secret ingredient is none other than *desire*. Yes, desire! If you were expecting some fancy formula, we're really sorry. But, in the end, it really boils down to how bad you want it.

If you have a strong enough desire, you'll find a way. But, now that you know the secret, you still need to be familiar with the tools, techniques, and guidance that help you along the way. We explain them in the following sections.

No real estate license required

A lot of investors don't have a real estate license, and they often wonder if not having a license poses a problem. Our answer is no. Not having a license will not hinder you nor has it hindered many of our successful friends and clients who invest full time or part time.

Even one of your humble authors doesn't currently have a license. The fact is that as long as you're a principal in the transaction, you don't need to be licensed. A *principal* is someone who buys property to make a profit. *Agents* and *brokers,* on the other hand, are those who help an investor buy or sell, and they're the ones who get a commission as compensation. The duties they perform require a license. As long you don't receive compensation or represent yourself or someone else in the transaction, you don't need one.

A couple of advantages that we can see for having a license are having access to the multiple listing service (MLS), which allows you to see everything a sales agent sees, and getting paid commissions when buying or selling your own properties.

The disadvantage of having a license is that you'll be under a lot more scrutiny if one of your deals goes sour. You're held to higher standard when you're licensed, and rightfully so. And that means your liability is greater.

Some people think that you can give someone who isn't licensed a commission as long as you don't call it a commission. You may have heard things like "just put it down as a consulting fee on the closing statement." But, remember, if you're going to play, you need to play straight. Funny talk and alternative wording is what gets people in trouble. And with so many opportunities to make money playing by the rules, why would anyone want to bend them?

A few technical skills

Investing in commercial real estate requires a handful of skills. You don't need to understand differential equations or know how to rebuild a transmission. However, the skills in the following sections are a must.

Easily meeting people and making new friends

Are you able to talk and connect with people easily? Do you like meeting new friends and finding out more about how they view the world? If so, you'll do well at creating a stash of contacts. It's important to network with the people who will be investing in your commercial real estate deals because they hold the "pot of gold." People that you meet will eventually be your advisors, investors, and partners, and they'll send deals to you and connect you with wealth-building resources.

If you're the shy type, we're betting that you'll sooner or later get over your shyness after you see all the money that's being made by other investors who love having a network of colleagues and friends. If you're the shy, quiet type like one of your coauthors, then you'll have to gradually come out of your shell.

Doing simple math

Can you look at a fax and properly enter some numbers into a simple spreadsheet? And are you capable of using a calculator? These skills help you determine what a commercial property is worth, what you should pay for it, and what your payday will be. If you need some pointers and guidance when it comes to numbers, a course in business math is sure to get you up to speed.

Accounting and collecting

We believe that if you're going to be in business, you're going to need to be comfortable asking other people to pay you the money that they owe you (in rents). The neat part is that you can hire a property management company to do all the collecting for you. And, if you're starting small, you need to get a good handle on accounting and other business essentials. Why? Because throughout this book, we emphasize that investing in commercial real estate is like investing in a real business where you have to pay bills, hire employees, deal with contractors, and know how to read simple financial reports.

Your coauthor Peter Conti started his first business more than 22 years ago. One of the first books he read to bone up on accounting was *Small Time Operator* by Bernard B. Kamoroff. To find out where to get this book, and to discover other business-building tips, visit www.petercontiblog.com.

Myths and Questions about Investing in Commercial Real Estate

Like any complicated business, commercial real estate investing has its share of myths and questions. Knowing this information brings forth some valuable truths that will rescue you from the trappings of confusion.

The following are some pretty common misconceptions about investing in commercial real estate:

- ✔ **You must start off in residential real estate to get into commercial real estate.** There's no rule, rhyme, or reason stating that you must first invest in residential real estate in order to make the leap into commercial real estate investing. These fields are two different animals, two different languages, and two different consumers. It's like comparing apples to oranges.

- ✔ **Only the rich need apply.** As you can probably imagine, this myth is just that: a myth. It isn't true that you have to be rich to get involved with commercial real estate investing. You can be as creative in your financing here as you can be when investing in homes.

If you don't believe us, here's an example: Donald, a mentoring student of ours, recently purchased a 24-unit apartment building. The purchase price was $750,000. The owner carried a second mortgage of $100,000 for Donald. That left him $50,000 for a down payment. Donald negotiated $30,000 for repair credits at closing. That left him with an out-of-pocket cost of $20,000, which he funded from a refinance from another property. Donald proves you only need to be rich in desire and creativity.

- ✔ **This game is only for big-time players.** In commercial real estate it doesn't matter where you start, and it doesn't matter if you only want to devote part of your time to do it. Having a full-time job or being a single-parent doesn't matter either.

Coauthor Peter Harris started his career by buying small commercial properties. His first was a cheap seven-unit apartment building. His second was a small and quaint self-storage building used by the plumbers in town. He did this part time while holding a full-time day job and raising a small family. It all started from there and grew to owning and operating large community properties around the country.

- ✔ **Commercial real estate investing is riskier.** To this we say, "Compared to what?" If you compare it to stocks, do you have control over the companies you own stock in — in areas such as income, expense, debt, management, and insurance? We bet not. However, you do have these five controls in commercial real estate investing. If you compare it to residential real estate investing, what happens if you rent out your single-family home and the tenant moves out? What's your monthly income then? The answer: Nada. If, on the other hand, you own a 24-unit apartment building and one tenant moves out, what's your monthly income? Answer: 23 paying tenants worth of rent! What's more risky? We rest our case.

✔ **Commercial real estate is too complex for simple folks.** Again, this isn't true. Remember when you got your new PDA cellphone? You had no idea how to use it. It seemed too complicated, and it had entirely too many buttons. But there was a manual to get you started. After that, through repetition and practice, what seemed much like a puzzle is now fully understood and appropriately used. Getting to know commercial real estate investing is the same concept. You have quite a few things to master, but it isn't rocket science. We have taken students from knowing nothing to making offers in a few weeks. They're walking proof that it can be done.

Real estate, like the rest of life, does have risks. If it didn't, it probably wouldn't be as fun. And it surely wouldn't pay off with the incredibly strong rates of return that it does.

Timing the Commercial Real Estate Market

Wouldn't it be great if you could time the commercial real estate market precisely? For instance, what if you could predict what the office building market would do five years from now in your town? Imagine if you had a process and procedure for knowing the perfect time to buy in a certain market. Well, here's a secret: None of this exists. Sorry for bursting your bubble! But if we could predict such things, we'd be living on our own islands off of Tahiti.

But here's the good news. Remember the old adage, "Buy low and sell high?" Believe it or not, this truly is how you get wealthy in real estate over time. It's a tried-and-true method. And here's another secret (and this time we're serious): A tool exists that helps you buy low and sell high in any market anywhere in the United States. That tool is the _real estate cycle_. And when you pair this cycle with some knowledge of trends, you're sure to be successful. Pay close attention; we explain everything you need to know in the following sections.

Knowing whether to buy, hold, or bottom-fish

Real estate cycles are like traffic lights. When you see a green light, you go. When you see a yellow light, you go, but you proceed with caution. When you see a red light, you stop. The trick, however, is knowing when you're facing green, yellow, or red lights. Here are some examples:

- ✔ A green light in commercial real estate investing may be spotted when you notice upcoming job growth due to a factory expansion. Or when the demand to build exceeds the supply of available properties. Most likely, you'll also see a lot of undeveloped land sales activity.

- ✔ A yellow light may be indicated by interest rates creeping up suddenly and causing you to examine your costs of new money to borrow. Or it could be when you see vacancies and "lease specials" increase. Or how about reading in the local paper about the many struggling businesses in an area? That has yellow light written all over it.

- ✔ A red light may be revealed by a halt in new construction, which may be caused by overbuilding in the area. An increase in foreclosures and a decrease in property values is a sure red light.

Making big money in commercial real estate is all about managing risks. Understanding and gaining knowledge of real estate cycles helps you lower your risk. Even though predicting real estate cycles is largely a game of luck, it gets downright dangerous if you know nothing about the trends in the market in which you're investing. The following is an outline of the typical commercial real estate cycle. This cycle can help you determine the best time to buy, sell, or go bottom-fishing. Here are the phases of the cycle, which are depicted in Figure 2-1:

- ✔ **Expansion phase:** During this phase, population increases, incomes rise, employment is good, vacancies are decreasing, and rents are rising. New buildings are planned. The human emotion here is excitement.

- ✔ **Peak phase:** This is the time to sell for maximum profit. This is a seller's market, and in this phase you see new building projects increasing and bidding wars between investors. Listings are on the market for only a short period of time. The human emotion here is sheer confidence.

- ✔ **Contraction phase:** Most likely, you'll see a bunch of new projects on the market now, and you may see evidence of overbuilding. Inflation is up, interest rates are increasing, vacancy rates begin to creep up, and prices begin to level. Foreclosures generally grow during this time. The human emotion here ranges from mere concern and denial to utter shock.

- ✔ **Recession phase:** Real estate in this phase is becoming more difficult to sell, and so properties stay on the market for longer periods of time. Property values decrease, interest rates are high, and landlords are competing for tenants because of overbuilding. Foreclosures are usually rampant. The human emotion here is complete panic.

✔ **Bottom phase:** This is the best time to buy. However, this is the scariest phase there is: Unemployment and inflation are high, and the demand for apartments is decreasing. This phase separates the men from the boys, the women from the girls, and the true investor from the stock market refugee. The human emotion here is plain old depression for most folks.

✔ **Recovery phase:** This phase is the breath of fresh air. The local economy shows signs of life, vacancies decrease, rents level off and start to trickle upward, speculation starts again, and money begins to flow back into market. The human emotion here is pride, because you've waited out the storm.

If you can recognize the cycles of your local economy, three obvious questions come to mind, and answering them will determine whether or not you're a successful investor:

✔ **When is the best time to buy?** The truthful answer is that it depends. If you're a smart investor, you should buy in the bottom or middle of the expansion cycle. That way, you're buying on trends and following the market and other investors. You'll likely feel safe because you're following what everyone else is doing.

✔ **When is it the best time to sell?** The answer is at the peak phase, right at the top of the market. And the biggest problem with selling here is knowing exactly where the top is. Here are two clues that have never failed us yet: Watch the rents and vacancy rates separately. After rents level off and become flat for three straight months or more, you've reached the top. Or for another indication you've reached the top: After vacancy rates are at a three- to five-year low, you've reached the top. It's that simple.

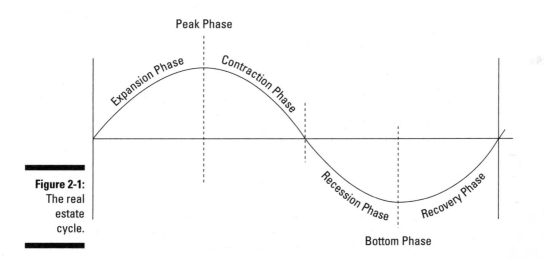

Figure 2-1:
The real
estate
cycle.

Peak Phase

Expansion Phase

Contraction Phase

Recession Phase

Recovery Phase

Bottom Phase

✔ **When is it the best time to go bottom-fishing?** If you aren't a bold risk taker, you may find this advice uncomfortable (so consider yourself fore-warned!). Maverick investors buy at the bottom phase or at the front end of the recovery phase. This is called "bottom-fishing" for deals. This is where the big, big money is made. Maverick investors are brave and courageous trendsetters. They're usually the first investors in the worst part of town, and they're usually banking on the area to come back big time. If they play their cards right, they come out on top, and if they don't, they simply walk away with an "aw, shucks." Now that's bravery!

Trends are your friends

True friends are always around when you call on them, and they won't ever let you down. And economic and demographic trends are your true friends in commercial real estate investing. And best of all, these trends aren't terribly complex or difficult to determine. Here are the three trends that are plainly fundamental when investing in any commercial real estate:

✔ **Job growth:** This trend makes perfect sense: Where the jobs are, people are. And where the people are, demand exists for apartment rentals, office space, and consumer goods. Job growth is an excellent indicator of a healthy real estate market.

The best place to start in researching job growth is to contact your local economic development department or chamber of commerce and ask for historical and current job growth data.

✔ **Development:** This trend is all about supply and demand. After all, if a shortage of office space or apartment housing is evident, you clearly have a demand for new development. On the other hand, if you see that the city is overbuilding, it's an indication for you hold off and reassess.

✔ **In the path of progress:** It isn't too difficult to spot this trend with your own eyes. Whenever new building and development is either coming your way or surrounds your property, you're in the thankful path of eco-nomic development. You can feel the "buzz" of prosperity around you.

Chapter 3

Evaluating Commercial
Real Estate

There's a myth going around town that you need to be an accountant with an Ivy League degree to evaluate and analyze office buildings, retail centers, and apartment complexes. Don't believe the hype. If you can count and do some basic math, you'll have no problem figuring out what your cash flow and return on investment are for any piece of commercial property. In fact, we guarantee that after you read this chapter and follow along with the examples, you'll be able to figure out what a commercial property is worth just like those sophisticated investor guys you see with their pocket protectors and fancy spreadsheets.

This chapter explains what creates value in a property, shows you how to analyze an apartment building and a shopping center like a pro, explains how to know a good deal from a bad deal, and provides invaluable guiding principles of investment that will keep bad properties out of your portfolio — guaranteed.

Talking the Talk: Terms You Need to Know

Throughout this chapter, we use some terminology that you need to be familiar with. Having these terms under your belt is crucial on two fronts:

✔ We presume you're reading this book because you want to invest in commercial real estate. Most likely, you'll be using a real estate broker to help you locate and close the deal. Real estate brokers know — and use — most of the terms mentioned here. Gaining thorough understanding of the terms levels the playing field. If you can speak their language, you gain instant credibility and a relationship advantage over someone without your knowledge and understanding.

✔ Just by increasing your word power, you gain increased confidence, which enables you to make sound, efficient investment decisions, and gives you an increased ability to hold your position, especially in negotiations.

Here are the words you need to know to navigate this chapter and talk the talk:

✔ **Capitalization rate:** Your *capitalization rate* is your net operating income divided by the sales price. Also known as the *cap rate,* it's the measure of profitability of an investment. Cap rates tell you how much you'd make on an investment if you paid all cash for it; financing and taxation aren't included:

> Cap rate = net operating income ÷ sales price

✔ **Cash flow:** Your *annual cash flow* is net operating income minus debt service. You can also figure *monthly cash flow* by dividing your annual cash flow by 12:

> Annual cash flow = net operating income – debt service

> Monthly cash flow = annual cash flow ÷ 12

✔ **Cash-on-cash return:** To find your *cash-on-cash return,* divide your annual cash flow by the down payment amount:

> Cash-on-cash return = annual cash flow ÷ down payment

✔ **Debt service:** *Debt service* is calculated by multiplying your monthly mortgage amount by 12 months:

> Debt service = monthly mortgage amount × 12

✔ **Effective gross income:** You can find your *effective gross income* by subtracting vacancy from gross income:

> Effective gross income = income – (vacancy rate % × income)

✔ **Gross income:** *Gross income* is all of your income, including rents, laundry or vending machine income, and late fees. It can be monthly or annual.

✔ **Net operating income (NOI):** Your *net operating income* is your effective gross income minus operating expenses:

> Net operating income = effective gross income – operating expenses

- ✔ **Operating expenses:** Your *annual operating expenses* of the property typically include taxes, insurance, utilities, management fees, payroll, landscaping, maintenance, supplies, and repairs. This category doesn't include mortgage payments or interest expense.

- ✔ **Vacancy:** A *vacancy* is any unit that's left unoccupied and isn't producing income. *Remember:* A unit that's vacated and rerented in the same month isn't considered a vacancy; it's considered a *turnover.*

- ✔ **Vacancy rate:** Your *vacancy rate* is the number of vacancies divided by the number of units:

Vacancy rate = number of vacancies ÷ number of units

Figuring Out What a Property Is Worth

When you first hear the word *analysis,* you may freak out — especially if you aren't a spreadsheet guru. We were intimidated by that word when we first started out, too. But through the years, we've come to look at property analysis more simply. The dictionary definition of the word *analysis* is "a separation of the whole into its component parts." So, we break down *any* property analysis into its component parts: income, expense, and debt. That's it. We take a look at the income information. Then we take a look at the expenses. And finally, we add a loan or mortgage to the overall picture. We combine them to come to a conclusion as to whether this deal makes money. Analysis made simple.

The size or complexity of the deal doesn't matter. Separate the deal into its three component parts: Analyze and compile the income part; analyze and compile the expense part; and analyze and compile the debt part. Any deal can be broken up into these parts. When you have these parts, you can calculate the net operating income, cash flow, cash-on-cash return, and cap rate. It's that simple.

Before you can figure out what a property is worth, you have to decide what you really want from the property. You may want a stream of passive income every month. Or you may want to hold a property long term to build your wealth. Or you may want to buy it, rehab it, and sell it for a profit.

Not-so-obvious tips on analyzing

When you're analyzing any property, keep the following in mind:

- ✔ **Be leery of broker proformas.** *Proformas* are brokers' presentations of data on the property that reflect a best-case scenario or even a perfect-world situation. For example, even though the property may have eight

The technical meaning behind the numbers

Cap rate, cash flow, cash-on-cash return, and *net operating income* are investment terms that we show you how to use in this chapter, but what do they really *mean* to you as an investor? Here's the in-depth explanation:

✔ **Capitalization rate:** A cap rate is used as a measure of a property's performance without considering the mortgage financing. If you paid all cash for the investment, how much money would it make? What's the return on your cash outlay? Cap rate is a standard used industrywide, and it's used many different ways. For example, a high cap rate usually typifies a higher risk investment and a low sales price. High cap rate investments are typically found in poor, low-income regions. A low cap rate usually typifies a lower-risk investment and a high sales price. Low cap rates are typically found in middle-class to upper income regions. Therefore, neighborhoods within cities have "stamped" on them their assigned cap rates.

That said, if you know what the NOI is, and you know the given cap rate, you can estimate what the sales price should be: sales price = NOI ÷ cap rate. For example, if the NOI is $57,230 and you want to make investments into 9 percent cap properties, the price you'll offer will be $635,889 (57,230 ÷ 9 percent). This is a good way to come up with your first offer price — at the very least, it's a starting point.

✔ **Cash flow:** Positive cash flow is king, and it's one of your primary objectives in investing. Positive cash flow creates and maintains your investments' momentum. When purchasing an apartment building containing more than five units (considered commercial), a bank's basis for lending is the property's cash-flow capabilities. Your credit score is a lower priority than the cash-flow potential. An apartment building with poor cash flow will almost always appraise much lower than its comparables for the area. Finally, positive cash flow keeps you sleeping at night when property values drop, because your bills and mortgage will still be paid.

✔ **Cash-on-cash return:** This is the velocity of your money. In other words, how long does it take for your down payment to come back to you? If your down payment were $20,000, how soon would your monthly cash flow add up to $20,000? If your cash flow added up to $20,000 in one year, your cash-on-cash return would be 100 percent. If it takes two years, your cash-on-cash would be 50 percent. If it takes three years, it would be 33 percent.

Commercial real estate investing can produce phenomenal returns. Cash-on-cash returns of over 100 percent aren't uncommon. Now, if you were to go to your local bank and deposit $20,000 into its most aggressive CD investment for one to three years, what type of cash-on-cash return could you expect? Maybe 2 percent or 4 percent? You need to put an emphasis on cash-on-cash return when you invest simply because you need to know how fast you can get your down payment back so you can invest it again — and again.

✔ **Net operating income (NOI):** This term is one of the most important ones when analyzing any deal. The net operating income is the dollar amount that's left over after you collect all your income and pay out your operating expenses. This amount is what's used to pay the mortgage with. And what's left after you pay the mortgage is what goes into your pocket — your cash flow.

Always keep your eye on the NOI and look for ways to increase it by either raising rents or reducing expenses. As the NOI increases, so will the value of your property. In fact, if you're in an 8 percent cap neighborhood, for every $100 that the NOI increases, your property value will increase by $1,250. Is that a good return for your efforts or what?

You know that cap rate = NOI ÷ sales price, but you can also flip the calculation: sales price (or value) = NOI ÷ cap rate. Therefore, you can figure a new value by dividing your new NOI or increase of NOI by the going cap rate. So $100 ÷ 8 percent = $1,250. Now, if you can increase your NOI by $20,000, your property value will have gone up by $250,000 ($20,000 ÷ 8 percent = $250,000).

unrentable vacant units, the broker proforma will reflect those units as if they were producing income. So, be careful in your analysis when you see the word *proforma*. It isn't how the property is actually performing. Here's the bottom line: Never make offers based on proforma data.

✔ **Look deeper into the price.** When analyzing apartments, always look at sales price per door or price per unit. Get information on what local apartments have sold for recently on a price-per-unit basis. For example, if you know for a fact that the last three sales of apartments on the same street sold for $45,000 per unit, then you know in your analysis that paying $65,000 per unit may be too much. Knowing your price per unit allows you to make quick decisions if the real estate agent is asking too much or if you're getting a steal of a deal.

✔ **Not knowing expenses can cost you.** One of the most understated and misunderstood aspects of property analysis is expenses. Of course, plugging actual and true operating expenses into your analysis isn't easy, because often that data isn't available.

You'll get your most reliable expense data from your property manager or from a professional property manager who manages similar properties, not from the broker. Look at property expenses three different ways:

- Look at it in expenses per unit. Basically, divide the total expenses by the number of units.

- Look at expenses as a percentage of the income. For example, as a general rule, for apartment sizes that are greater than 50 units, we take expenses to be at least 50 percent of the income.

- Look at expenses in the form of expenses per square foot. You get this number by dividing the total expenses by the total square footage of the living space.

✔ **Don't forget about the taxes.** Be wary of property taxes stated in your analysis or given to you by the broker. Brokers who present property data rarely have the *new* property taxes in their spreadsheets. *New taxes* refer to what your new tax bill would be upon transfer of ownership. For example, the current owner may have owned the property for 30 years and his property taxes may have increased only slightly in those years. But when you take over, the tax assessor will reassess the property value, most times based on your sales price. So it's quite possible that your taxes may increase three to five times from what the previous owner paid. Do your research by calling the property tax assessor's office and ask how property taxes are reassessed upon transfer of ownership.

✔ **Verify your analysis.** When we're analyzing a deal in which the broker feels that we can either raise the rents or decrease the expenses after we take over, we always verify the broker's projections. To verify whether raising the rent is possible, we call properties in the area and do our own rent survey; it only takes a few minutes to do and the information is invaluable. To verify whether we can reduce expenses, we call our property manager or contact another professional property manager and run the expense scenario by him; easy to do — with results worth their weight in gold.

✔ **Get a thumbs up from your money guy or gal.** When we get excited about a deal during our analysis, we send it to our lender. He looks at it from his point of view: Are the numbers good enough to get a good loan on it? We may run our cash-flow projections based on a 15 percent down payment, but he may spot something in the financials that may only qualify the property for a 25 percent down payment. If your lender won't do this for you, get another lender.

✔ **Keep in mind that concessions may penalize your future.** When you're presented with information about the tenants, ask about any move-in specials given to the current tenants. Those specials are called *rent concessions,* and concessions are given when the market is weak and tenants need to be enticed to move in or renew their leases. Usually, the tenants are given one month rent free and it's usually the 13th month of a 12-month lease. The problem with this is that if you're acquiring the property, you won't receive rent from that tenant on the 13th month of the lease. And this gets worse if 50 percent of your tenants have this concession, especially if their 13th month is the same month — this means that 50 percent of the tenants will not be paying you rent that month. Ouch!

Breakeven analysis

When analyzing property, we always want to know what our breakeven point is. The *breakeven point* is the point at which occupancy income is equal to our mortgage payments. In other words, if we know that our breakeven point is 70 percent occupancy, we know we're able to at least pay our expenses plus mortgage without going into a negative cash-flow position. So for a property that's highly leveraged or has a large mortgage payment, its break-even point is higher than usual — meaning, you have more risk if you're negative in cash flow.

To calculate your breakeven point, add up all your property's operating expenses and annual mortgage payments and divide by the gross potential income. *Gross potential income* is what the income of the property would be if it were 100 percent occupied with paying tenants. Here's the equation:

Breakeven point (%) = operating expenses + annual mortgage payments ÷ gross potential income

Here's a quick example: Let's say your operating expenses are $75,000, your annual mortgage payments are $35,000, and your gross potential income is $200,000. To find your breakeven point percentage, here are the calculations:

$75,000 + $35,000 ÷ $200,000 = 55%

This means that at 55 percent occupancy, we're breaking even when it comes to cash flow (see Figure 3-1). Anything over 55 percent occupancy sends us to cash-flow positive. Conversely, if we drop below 55 percent occupancy, we're in negative cash flow.

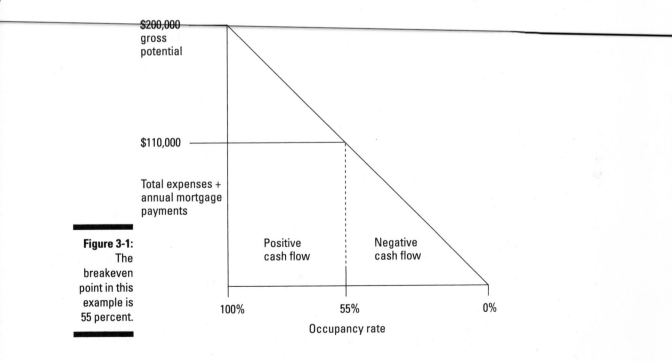

$200,000
gross
potential

$110,000

Total expenses +
annual mortgage
payments

Figure 3-1:
The
breakeven
point in this
example is
55 percent.

Positive
cash flow

Negative
cash flow

100%   55%   0%

Occupancy rate

Establishing and following guiding principles

When you're looking at any types of income properties and analyzing them, you need to have a set of guiding principles for investment. We've established some starting guiding principles for you. These principles will set the standards for your investments and help you set working goals moving forward. Without them, you'll wander aimlessly in the real estate investment game.

We've used these standards for years ourselves and with our clients, and we've saved many people, including ourselves, from passing up that great once-in-a-lifetime deal or buying that deal that really stunk. Your guiding principles are basically fail-safe measures to guide you into cash-flowing, wealth-building investments and to keep you out of negative cash-flowing ones.

Here are our guiding principles:

- ✔ **Make sure that you have a positive cash flow.** We believe that having positive cash flow keeps your momentum going. Positive cash flow allows you to leave your day job if that's your goal. Positive cash flow allows you to invest more money, and it opens doors for the next investment to flow right in.

- ✔ **Have a cash-on-cash return of 10 percent or greater.** A good cash-on-cash return puts velocity on your money. It keeps your cash flow positive when you have those not-so-good months. A good cash-on-cash return allows you to brag to your investor buddies about what a well-run property you have.

- ✔ **Have a cap rate of 8 percent or greater.** A great cap rate means your NOI is healthy. A healthy NOI is stable and growing, which means your property value is doing the same. A great cap rate also gets you the best loan terms.

These are only *starting* guiding principles of investment. You have to start someplace, right? You may be thinking, "But you won't find any 8 caps in my city!" And you may even believe that it's impossible to find double-digit cash-on-cash returns. Or you may be convinced that it's impossible to cash flow positively unless you put down 50 percent. Well, our reply to that type of thinking is this: Sooner or later, you'll be convinced and support the theory that at any one time, there are great deals out there waiting for you.

Running the Numbers on Some Properties

Now that you have some basic commercial property investment terms and principles under your belt, we want to walk you through analyzing two properties. This is where it gets fun!

Be sure to follow these tips when analyzing your own retail property deal:

✔ **Look at the price per square foot.** When analyzing retail, one of the first things we look at is the price per square foot. It's an easy way to compare apples to apples and oranges to oranges. It's also a way to get a reality check to see if you're paying too much for the property compared to other recent sales.

✔ **Be conservative in your number crunching.** What you'll find when you own a few retail centers is that incomes given to you by either the broker or seller are overstated and expenses are understated. Really take a hard look at each item given and then take a conservative approach when running your numbers.

✔ **Replace your reserves.** One of the most overlooked expenses when analyzing retail is the replacement reserve. *Replacement reserve* is an amount set aside every month to pay for property items that wear out and need to be replaced, such as roofs, siding, sidewalks, parking lots, heating/air-conditioning equipment, and so on. When these items come up for repair or replacement three to five years after you take ownership, the money has to come from somewhere — refinancing, your pockets, your partner's pockets, or a reserve account you cleverly set up ahead of time.

✔ **Look at the parking ratio.** The parking ratio for your retail center is more important than you think. The standard to begin with is four spaces per 1,000 square feet. If you don't have enough parking, it can create a problem down the road.

✔ **Consider class.** All commercial properties fall under classifications — A, B, C, or maybe even D. Class A properties are newer, have top-of-the-line features, are in the best locations, and attract the highest-quality tenants. As you go into the lower classes, location, age, and construction become less desirable. Pay attention to what class property you're evaluating because as classes differ, so do location, price, rent, and occupancy.

✔ **Match rent rolls to estoppels.** The *rent roll* is a list of tenant names showing what they pay in rent, in addition to when the lease agreement expires. *Estoppels* are letters sent to the tenant by someone other than the landlord to confirm in writing the terms of the lease, including rent amount, lease expirations, and any other options they have agreed on.

Estoppels are used because the tenant may not be paying the landlord in rent what she has agreed to for whatever reason, or the landlord may have made a side agreement with the tenant that can't be confirmed or enforced by new owners. When the tenant-signed estoppels are received, you can compare them to the rent rolls and actual signed leases for income verification.

✔ **Check in with your money guy or gal early.** Before digging too deep into your analysis, call up your lender buddy and present the rent roll, the type of tenants, and financials to her. Have the lender review this deal from her perspective. Some lenders may not like certain businesses. For example, securing a loan for a shopping center with a dry cleaner or automotive repair place has been more difficult lately because of environmental concerns, and movie theater chains and video stores chains have come under scrutiny because of recent national bankruptcies.

Analyzing an apartment deal

Here's the deal: Cool Heights Apartments is offered at $550,000. It's a well-maintained 20-unit (all 2-bed/1-bath) complex located in an up-and-coming area one block from City Hall. Each unit is rented for $525 per month and the building is currently 100 percent occupied. The owner has spent over $100,000 in rehab and upgrades in the last 12 months. All new furnaces and air conditioners were installed. The owner is retiring to Florida with his family, and that's his reason for selling. Professional property management is in place and the building is managed very well. It has a good rental history. Covered parking is included. Tenants are responsible for their own electric and heat utility bills; the owner pays for the property's water and garbage removal. The total building square footage is 22,160 square feet.

The following financial data was given for yearly operating expenses:

- Insurance: $4,500
- Real estate taxes: $9,610
- Maintenance: $14,900
- Electrical (common area): $1,300
- Water/sewer: $9,400
- Property management (5 percent): $6,210
- Garbage removal: $1,150
- Supplies: $2,700
- Reserves: $6,000
- Accounting: $1,400

So, adding that up, the total operating expenses are $57,170.

Now, separate this whole deal into its three simple components of income, expenses, and debt. Here's the income breakdown:

Gross income = $525 × 20 units × 12 months = $126,000 per year

Vacancy rate = $126,000 per year × 10 percent (assumption) = $12,600

Effective gross income = $126,000 − $12,600 = $113,400 per year

Here's the expense breakdown:

Total operating expenses = $57,170

To figure out the debt breakdown, we're going to assume that the interest rate is 6.5 percent today with a 30-year amortization period:

Asking price = $550,000

Down payment = 20 percent of asking price, which is $110,000

Loan amount (principal) = $550,000 – $110,000 = $440,000

Loan payment per month = $2,781 (we used a mortgage calculator for this figure)

Loan payments per year (debt service) = $2,781 × 12 months = $33,372

Now, you have everything you need to figure out whether this deal makes money or not, using these four easy steps:

1. **Calculate the net operating income (NOI).**

   Net operating income = effective gross income – operating expenses

   $113,400 – $57,170 = $56,230

2. **Calculate the annual cash flow.**

   Annual cash flow = net operating income – debt service

   $56,230 – $33,372 = $22,858

3. **Calculate the cash-on-cash return.**

   Cash-on-cash return = annual cash flow ÷ down payment

   $22,858 ÷ $110,000 = 21 percent

4. **Calculate the cap rate.**

   Cap rate = net operating income ÷ sales price

   $56,230 ÷ $550,000 = 10.2 percent

So, in a nutshell, you're putting down $110,000 to earn $22,858 per year in cash flow, or approximately 21 percent return on your $110,000. That's pretty darn good.

Analyzing a retail shopping center

One of the most important items to understand when analyzing retail investments is the lease. A *lease* is a written legal agreement between the landlord (called the *lessor*) and the tenant (called the *lessee*) that establishes how much the tenant will pay in rent; how long the tenant is legally committed to stay; any additional payments by the tenant for taxes, insurance, or maintenance; rent increases; renewal clauses and options; and all rights, privileges, and responsibilities of the tenant and landlord.

Following are types of leases you'll run into in the course of looking into investing in retail shopping centers. Each has its own wrinkles and stipulations, so pay attention to the small differences:

✔ **Gross lease:** The landlord agrees to pay all operating expenses and charges the tenant a rent that's over and above the operating expenses. The types of expenses covered include taxes, insurance, management, maintenance, and any other costs associated with operating the property.

✔ **Modified gross lease:** This lease is slightly different from the standard gross lease in that some of the operating expenses — such as maintenance, insurance, or utilities — aren't paid for by the landlord and are passed on to the tenant. These expenses are called *pass-through expenses* because they're passed through to the tenant. Many office-type buildings use a modified gross lease.

✔ **Net lease:** In a net lease, the tenants pay the operating expenses of the property and the landlord gets to net a certain amount every month by charging rent over and above the total operating expenses. This lease is favorable in many ways: It's favorable to the landlord because she isn't responsible for any operational expenses of the property. It's favorable to the tenant because he gets to fix up his store as he sees fit and do his own maintenance and cleaning. Net leases are typically customized to fit tenant needs.

This type of lease is used mainly by retailers. The landlord takes care of the common area maintenance, and the expense of that is spread among the tenants and billed back to them.

There are several different levels and types of net leases:

- **Single net lease (N):** In a *single net lease,* the tenant agrees to pay property taxes. The landlord pays for all other expenses in the operation.

- **Double net lease (NN):** In a *double net lease,* the tenant agrees to pay property taxes and insurance. The landlord pays for all other expenses in the operation.

- **Triple net lease (NNN):** A *triple net lease* is most favorable for landlords and is one of the most popular today. The tenants agree to pay the landlord rent plus all other property-related expenses including taxes, insurance, and maintenance. The landlord gets a true net payment. Banks, fast-food restaurants, and *anchor tenants* typically use triple net leases.

Anchor tenants are major tenants, usually the tenant occupying the most space. Anchor tenants are critical in giving value and security to a retail shopping center investor. Their signs are usually the largest and stand out. Major retail chain stores typically are anchor tenants and are called so because they attract other businesses to the shopping center location. They "anchor" the shopping center so to speak.

A common clause used in net leases is the *expense stop clause,* which states that any amount over a certain fixed expense will be charged to the tenant. The fixed expense is a dollar amount agreed on by the tenant and landlord.

A great income generator for landlords is to build into the lease a clause called *percentage of sales.* With this clause, the landlord gets an additional payment from the tenant if and when the tenant reaches a certain sales volume or profitability. For example, say a burger restaurant has agreed to pay an additional 3 percent of its gross sales after its sales reach a certain level. The landlord would be paid the 3 percent in addition to the normal lease payment.

Even though retail leases are long term — say, 5 to 15 years in length — it's common for leases to have rental increases or rent escalations in the middle of the leasing years. For example, you could have a rent escalation of 5 percent once every five years until the lease expires.

Now that you have all that info on leases down, it's time to analyze a deal. Here's the deal: Kimo's Landing, a 36,000-square-foot retail center anchored by a major chain pharmacy is in the center of town, right in the path of progress. It's on 3 acres of land. The retail center is composed of eight stores of various types, ranging from a bagel shop to a U.S. post office. Table 3-1 provides the square footage and yearly rent of each unit.

Table 3-1	Square Footage and Yearly Rent for Kimo's Landing		
Lessees	*Square Footage*	*Rent Per Square Foot*	*Yearly Rent*
Pharmacy	10,000	$10	$100,000
Bank	8,000	$8	$64,000
Bagel shop	1,500	$5	$7,500
Express photo shop	1,500	$5	$7,500
Electronics shop	1,000	$6	$6,000
Beauty store	2,000	$6	$12,000

(continued)

Table 3-1 *(continued)*			
Lessees	*Square Footage*	*Rent Per Square Foot*	*Yearly Rent*
Clothing store	6,000	$7	$42,000
U.S. post office	6,000	$8	$48,000
Total	**36,000**	—	**$287,000**

All leases are triple net (NNN), with the owner charging the tenants for common area maintenance (CAM). The CAM expense for the owner is $3,000 per month and includes landscaping, parking lot, hallways, and restrooms.

Now, you need to separate this whole deal into its three simple components of income, expenses, and debt. Here's the income breakdown:

Gross income = $287,000

For the expense breakdown, because this is a triple net lease, the tenants pay all property operating expenses. The landlord takes care of all common area maintenance expenses, and then bills back to the tenants. But this is billed back to and divided among the tenants. So, there's no hard expense to use here.

To figure the debt breakdown, you need to figure out what the yearly loan payments would be. We're going to assume that the interest rate is 6.5 percent today with a 30-year amortization period:

Asking price = $3,100,000

Down payment = 20 percent of asking price, which is $620,000

Loan amount (principal) = $3,100,000 – $620,000 = $2,480,000

Loan payment per month = $15,675 (we used a mortgage calculator for this figure)

Loan payments per year (debt service) = $15,675 × 12 months = $188,100

Now, you have everything you need to figure out whether this deal makes money, using these four easy steps:

1. **Calculate the net operating income (NOI).**

   Net operating income = effective gross income – operating expenses

   $287,000 – $0 = $287,000

2. **Calculate the cash flow.**

   Annual cash flow = net operating income – debt service

$287,000 − $188,100 = $98,900

3. **Calculate the cash-on-cash return.**

Cash-on-cash return = annual cash flow ÷ down payment

$98,900 ÷ $620,000 = 16 percent

4. **Calculate the cap rate.**

Cap rate = net operating income ÷ sales price

$287,000 ÷ $3,100,000 = 9.3 percent

A pretty decent return on your investment that's pretty hands-off compared to being involved with managing a property every day.

The Professional Approach to Valuing Properties

Professional property evaluators, commonly called *real estate appraisers,* have the awesome responsibility of estimating or giving an opinion of a value on commercial properties. It makes sense for you to understand how appraisers value commercial real estate so you can apply their techniques to our methods of estimating value.

Approach #1: Comparable sales

The first and easiest method in commercial property evaluation is called the *comparable sales approach.* Remember when you bought your first house and the bank had an appraiser go out and give the property a value that you hoped at least equaled your purchase price? Well, the same applies here for commercial property. The commercial appraiser goes out and compares prices of recently sold local properties that are similar in form and function to the property he's appraising. The comparison will produce an average price and that price is what your property will be valued at. But in commercial comparables, instead of looking at just overall sales price, the sales price per square foot of the building is also considered one of the main factors.

Here's a quick example:

Property A, a 10,000-square-foot building, sold last spring for $65 per square foot. Doing the simple math to compute the sales price, you calculate 10,000 square feet × $65 per square foot = $650,000.

Property B, a 9,000-square-foot building, sold three months ago for $68 per square foot. Again, doing the math, 9,000 square feet × $68 per square foot = $712,000.

Property C, the property you want to figure a price for, is similar to Property A and Property B and is 11,000 square feet in size. If you average out the price per square foot on both Property A and Property B, the average comes out to $66.50 per square foot. Use that price per square foot as your number to evaluate Property C. Doing the math, you get 11,000 square feet × $66.50 = $731,500 as the value for Property C.

When attempting to value apartment complexes, price per unit or price per door is used more often than price per square foot. Much like the preceding example, price per unit is calculated from previous apartment sales. When you have an average of price per unit for several complexes, you can estimate a value of another complex.

Even though the comparable sales approach is the easiest method for figuring out a value for a commercial property, we've run into two problems when using this approach:

✔ When a market isn't stabilized, or values go up or down, this can nullify the use of the comparable sales approach.

✔ In some small-town markets, there are no comparable sales because of the lack of overall sales.

Approach #2: Income

When you get out into the real world of commercial real estate, you'll discover that commercial properties are chiefly valued by the amount of income they bring in. Actually, to be more precise, it's the net operating income that's most important.

When accurate financial and operating data are available on the property, the *income approach* of valuing a property can be used. This approach is based on the capitalization rate being calculated for a property. To calculate the cap rate, you must know the property's net operating income and sales price.

After you calculate the cap rate of a property, the next step is to compare the cap rate to similar properties' cap rates. Every area in your city that has commercial properties has a cap rate stamped on it. Your job is to find those other properties and their cap rates and get the average. That average cap rate percentage is what you use in calculating property value when you know the net operating income.

Here's an example to follow: Let's say you want to value a 50-unit apartment building. You've calculated the net operating income to be $180,000. Your research from previous apartment sales tells you that the going cap rate for the neighborhood in which the property is located is 8 percent. Now, if you know the net operating income and the cap rate, you can figure out the sales price. Here's how:

> Cap rate = net operating income ÷ sale price
>
> 8 percent = $180,000 ÷ sale price
>
> Sale price = 180,000 ÷ 8 percent = $2,250,000

Therefore, the property should be valued at or estimated to be $2,225,000, based on average cap rates in the area and the property's net operating income.

Every investor who wants to find out how to estimate values of income-producing properties should know and understand the basics of the income approach. It's an indispensable tool that's very commonly used by investors, real estate agents, and lenders.

Approach #3: Cost to replace the property

The third approach to figuring out what a property is worth is the *cost approach,* which is seldom used these days by appraisers. The theory behind it is this: The value of a property is whatever it costs to construct a new one in addition to the cost of the land.

The cost approach is best when the property is new or almost new. For older properties, this approach isn't used because of several issues — primarily, depreciation.

To apply the cost approach in valuing a building, you must first figure out what the value of its land would be. This is typically done via a sales comparison approach (see the section "Approach #1: Comparable sales," earlier in this chapter). Then you have to determine what it will cost to construct, reproduce, or replace the building in question as if you were doing it from scratch. Be sure to allow for accrued depreciation and obsolescence of the building.

You end up with a property value calculation of:

> Land value + building cost – depreciation = estimated property value

Understanding What Creates Value

What is it that really creates value in commercial real estate? Well, in residential real estate, such as single-family homes, what creates value is location. Location, location, location is the saying that you always hear. The most expensive homes are in the best of neighborhoods, right? But location isn't the only factor that creates value in commercial real estate. In fact, there are two factors that are actually *more* important than location: use and the lease. We cover these in the following sections.

Use: How the property is used gives value

How a property is used is probably the most important factor in understanding values in commercial real estate. Here's why: Let's say that you have a 5-acre lot directly across the street from a brand-new luxury apartment complex that has a three-month waiting list for new tenants. Common sense says that you should develop it into another apartment complex because there's great demand. It appears big money awaits you.

But upon further research, you find out that the city says that your 5-acre lot can only be used for agricultural purposes. Where is there greater investment value — in a high-rent luxury apartment complex or a tomato farm? Exactly — the luxury apartment complex! Therefore, how a property can be used determines its value.

How a piece of land or property can be used is, for the most part, controlled by the city's local planning department. The planning department keeps control of this through zoning. *Zoning* specifies which type of property may be built in specific areas. Zoning is a governmental system in regulating land use and is typically master planned by the city. In the preceding example, the city has zoned that particular piece of land, the 5 acres, as agricultural use. This means that it can only be used for agricultural purposes and can't be used to build apartments, retail centers, office buildings, or industrial parks. The 5 acres would achieve its highest investment value if it were zoned for apartments or even retail — but the planning department may have other development plans for the area.

Here's a quick example showing how use can have a significant impact on property value: Let's say you go ahead and decide to farm and grow tomatoes on your 5 acres. You can produce a thousand 25-pound cartons of tomatoes per 5 acres. You can sell them for $2 per pound, which produces an income of $50,000. After you deduct a production cost of 30 percent, you're left with $35,000 of income over 5 acres. So, you end up with $7,000 per acre. If you were to capitalize that at 8 percent, here's what it would look like: $7,000 ÷ 8 percent = $87,500 per acre. And here's how to get the estimated value over the 5 acres: 5 acres × $87,500 = $437,500.

Now, let's say that the 5 acres was approved for use as an apartment building. On your 5-acre lot, you can fit 2 acres of living space. Each acre is 43,560 square feet. So, 2 acres equals 87,120 total square feet of living space. It's reasonable to say that apartment sales are going for $50 per square foot. Therefore, 87,120 square feet × $50 per square foot = $4,356,000, which is the estimated value for the apartment building.

Wow, how exciting! This is what commercial real estate is all about — finding opportunity, creating a product that betters humankind, and then reaping the rewards. The challenge in front of you in this example is to get the zoning changed on the 5 acres to allow an apartment building. To find out more on zoning and land development, flip to Chapter 15.

Leases: As the lease goes, so goes the value

A *lease* is a written legal agreement between the lessor (the landlord) and the lessee (the tenant) whereby the lessee compensates the lessor (by paying rent) for the use of the property for a specific time period. There's no such thing as a typical commercial lease, but here are a few main differences between a lease for a commercial property and a residential property (an apartment unit, for example):

- ✔ A commercial lease is a lot tougher to get out of than a residential lease.
- ✔ A commercial lease tends to last a lot longer, sometimes for 20 years.
- ✔ Because no standard commercial lease exists, parties can be as flexible and creative as they want.
- ✔ A commercial lease has significantly less consumer protection (for the tenant) than a residential lease does.

When you buy a commercial property, you're buying the leases, and the property comes for free. That's how important the actual lease is to the value of the property. Simply put, if the lease is weak, your property value is weak. And conversely, if the property has a strong lease, the property value is going to be strong.

As you may imagine, leases are the number-one killer of deals. They're the lifelines of income to the property. If the lifeline is tethered and weak, then your income is weak as well. And who wants to invest big dollars in a not-so-sure income stream? The lender won't and you shouldn't either. In fact, if a business in one of the shopping center's stores has a lease agreement with one year left, the income from that store isn't even counted by the lender when making a loan decision — maybe you shouldn't count it in your initial analysis either.

Here's how you, the investor, or a lender would look at a property's lease in connection to the value it creates for the property: Say you've been sent a great deal from your broker. It's for a 5,000-square-foot, single-tenant property that's occupied by the successful family-run and family-owned Grandma's Corner Groceries. The rent is $7 per square foot, or $35,000 per year and that includes taxes, insurance, and maintenance. The current lease has five years remaining.

Say also that you've been sent another deal for a 5,000-square-foot property that has a Starbucks as its tenant. Starbucks pays $6 per square foot, or $30,000 per year, which also includes taxes, insurance, and maintenance. The current lease has five years remaining.

The question is this: Which is the better investment? Grandma's Corner Groceries or Starbucks? Which one is a lower risk? Which one allows you to predict that you'll be paid every month for the next five years? Which one is less likely to go out of business? Which one will allow you to sleep at night knowing that your investment dollars are in good hands?

Starbucks is the obvious answer, even though you have higher income on the grocery store. Starbucks is a highly rated company and is publicly traded on the NASDAQ. Its financials are open to the public. It has a responsibility to its shareholders to make a profit. Even if it decides to close up shop there and abandon the property, it must make good on the lease and pay the lease off in its entirety. On the other hand, Grandma's Corner Groceries is backed by who knows what. If it goes out of business for some reason — fire, theft, infighting — your options for financial recourse don't favor your breaking even. So, the property with the Starbucks lease will command a greater value because of its lower risk.

Here are a handful of things to watch for when reviewing a lease agreement as an investor:

- ✔ Rent amount
- ✔ Lease term or how long the lease is for
- ✔ Additional costs that the landlord and tenant may be responsible for
- ✔ Subleasing
- ✔ Whether you need to do any improvements to the property before you move in
- ✔ How much your security deposit is to move in and how you ensure getting it back after your lease expires and you move out

Read the leases thoroughly many times so that you don't miss a thing. If you don't believe us, check out this example about our friend who missed a very important clause in the lease: He purchased a shopping center and his largest tenant, which took up one-third of the total space, had a clause in the lease that said if the store didn't produce $600,000 in gross sales per year, it could back out of the lease. Two years into the lease, the sales volume dropped below $600,000 and the tenant opted out of the lease.

Location: The unchangeable factor

As we mention earlier, location is a key factor in understanding what creates value in commercial real estate. How does location create value? One way is job growth. If a city has gone out of its way to attract and entice employers to open up businesses there, that causes economic growth to occur. And economic growth affects real estate value in a positive way, just as a city with negative economic growth causes real estate values to fall.

Certain neighborhoods or districts are better bets than others for commercial real estate, especially if they're in the path of progress (see Chapter 15 for more on locating the path to progress in your city). New construction, revitalization, and gentrification are all associated with instilling new life into a neighborhood or district. If you witness an area undergoing any of these, you can bet the real estate values there will be impacted positively.

The success of a shopping center, for example, largely depends on its location. You can fix parking lots and physical appearance, but you can't fix poor location. A great location combined with well-selected stores equals long-term success and a superb investment.

Differentiating a Good Deal from a Bad Deal

What's a good deal? And how do you define a bad deal? Well, unfortunately, the answers can be a bit squishy. After all, what's good for us may be bad for you, and vice versa. It really depends on the purpose of your investment buys. The purpose behind your investment could be for cash flow, long-term hold, or short-term hold. In this section, we examine all three.

Cash-flow investors

Cash-flow investors invest to produce cash-in-your-pocket-every-month income. For the cash-flow investor, a good deal would be:

- A 95 percent to 100 percent occupied, well-maintained apartment complex with excellent professional property management

- An apartment complex that has a breakeven occupancy point of 70 percent or less

- A retail shopping center with a highly rated, credited tenant on a ten-year triple net lease with rent escalations every year

✔ A multistory office building that you own debt free and that's filled with great long-term tenants

For the cash-flow investor, a bad deal would be:

✔ Any type of property with lots of deferred maintenance

✔ Any property that's so highly leveraged with debt that if 10 percent of the tenants moved out, you'd be in a negative cash flow situation

✔ An apartment complex in an apartment-filled neighborhood in a soft rental market

Long-term investors

Long-term investors hold their investments over time and build wealth through appreciation and paying down the loan principal.

For the long-term investor, a good deal would be:

✔ A shopping center with a long-term triple net lease in a medium-sized town with an aggressive economy

✔ An apartment complex built in the path of progress of new construction and job growth

✔ Any commercial investment in an area that has had decreasing cap rates for the past few years

For the long-term investor, a bad deal would be:

✔ Overpaying in an area where cap rates are increasing

✔ Buying in an area where the economy has been sustained by one large employer

✔ An office building that's functionally obsolete today and new building projects are underway nearby

Short-term investors

Short-term investors hold their investments two years or less. Their goal is to buy, fix up, stabilize, and sell.

For the short-term investor, a good deal would be:

✔ Buying at a really low price by using ultraconservative resale figures

✔ Acquiring an "easy-fix" rehab property with little down payment and owner financing in a seller's market

For the short-term investor, a bad deal would be:

✔ Buying a rehab in a market that starts to decline right after your purchase

✔ Not doing a thorough enough analysis and due diligence and finding out that your rehab budget is actually off by double the amount

✔ Assuming a loan with a large prepay (early payoff) penalty over the next few years

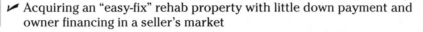

Supply and demand: Timing the market just right

When demand is high for certain commercial real estate, value goes up. Your job as the investor is to find out why. Why is demand high? What's driving the demand? Is it the influx of companies moving in or expanding in the area? Is it the explosion of retail shopping due to the influx of young families and professionals? Find out what's going on.

See where you are in the real estate cycle. Are you in a rising market, at the top of the market, or in a down market? If you're in a rising market, values will increase. Ride it to the top, and then make a decision to sell or wait for the inevitable downward trend. The downward trend is absolutely okay if the property sustains itself and cash flows well. If you find yourself on the downward trend, get out before you lose too much value or weather the storm and think long term.

Keep in mind that supply and demand come in cycles. And because of this, property values will be cyclical as well. (Study the real estate cycle in Chapter 2 — it will help you see where your market is currently and how values are affected by supply-and-demand situations.) How can you time the market to ride the wave of increasing value? Here's how:

✔ **Watch prices.** If the downward trend has stopped, you've reached bottom or almost bottom. It's time to buy and ride the wave back up.

✔ **Watch job reports.** When job growth is positive, it's time to ride the wave.

✔ **Watch investors.** When you see other investors come in and start investing heavily early, it's time to jump in with them.

However, there are pitfalls to valuing the market by watching rising prices, positive job growth, and outside investors. Here are some of those pitfalls:

✔ **You waited too long.** Determining exactly when the upward wave starts isn't easy. If you wait for signs that are too obvious, you can miss the wave entirely.

✔ **You misjudged the wave.** What you thought was a wave, was just a ripple. Oops.

✔ **You got greedy.** People tend to get overly confident when the market just keeps going up and up and up. But what goes up must come down at some point. So, if you wait too long, you may miss your run at the profits.

Part II

Getting Started Making Deals

The 5th Wave   By Rich Tennant

In this part . . .

Here we present the four essential steps to every commercial deal you put together. Then we jump into some serious deal making by sharing with you our Instant Offer System, which shows you how to make successful offers. And because all big commercial deals need to be checked out before you make the final move to buy them, you need to understand how to use due diligence and the closing process to uncover hidden problems, negotiate prices down, or determine when the best deal for you is *not* to buy. We end this part by showing you how to close a deal.

Chapter 4

On Your Mark, Get Set, Go Find Deals

. . . .

. . . .

So you want to know where you can find bargain commercial properties. Well, you've come to the right place. In this chapter, we discuss just that: finding deals in the commercial world. By connecting and getting to know some of the right people and players, you can pull in some pretty big fish (and maybe find a commercial deal or two!). We share with you useful tools that may come in handy in your search. We tell you who to talk to, where to go, and why you should go there. Always buying in your own town can get boring and costly, so we also talk about how to go big-time and invest in commercial properties in other cities across the country.

Discovering the Secret to Finding Great Deals

Let's face it: Finding *great* commercial properties is difficult to do. So what's the big secret to being successful? The secret is that there is no secret. Finding great commercial deals is a matter of having multiple fishing lines in the water and being willing to put in the work upfront, knowing the real payoff comes down the road when you find that incredible "once-in-a lifetime" deal. It's also a matter of performing a variety of different tasks, including creating relationships, sending out mailings, and focusing on the ponds that are most likely to have the big fish — those profitable, cash-flowing commercial properties that you're trolling for.

To get the hang of all this, you need to spend time with other successful commercial investors. The fastest way that you can discover what's possible is by being in a group of people who are finding and investing in commercial properties that make sense. That way, when you run into the sellers who want too much, a part of you will get angry and say, "Wait a minute. There must be a way to have this commercial property purchase work. I know from watching other in my peer group that there are great deals out there."

One of the most important things you need to do is to know and believe through to the core of your being that you can find great commercial deals. You need a burning passion and unstoppable desire to overcome and blast through any obstacles that inevitably get in your way (no matter how impossible it may seem). It's incredibly important to have the mind-set that great commercial properties will come into your life because of the actions you take each and every day.

If this sounds like it's too much to overcome, rest assured. We're here to lay out a proven path to those big streams of potential deals. When combined with your powerful determination, our suggested path will allow you to catch those big fish.

Defining your property search

What type of properties are you looking for? You need to think through your ultimate goals to make sure that you're fishing in the right ponds. It doesn't make sense, for example, to be looking at only Class A properties (the mostly new, beautiful properties in really nice areas) if you want to get your career started by leveraging your way into a property. Oftentimes it's the owners of Class C or D properties who are most open to using creative financing.

Many beginning commercial investors typically start out looking for commercial multiunit properties with anywhere from 5 to 50 units. Creative financing, including nothing-down deals, is possible in this market segment because it can be difficult for owners to get conventional financing. The reason is because lenders who make loans on commercial properties would much rather put together a loan on a 300-unit apartment building than they would on a 20-unit apartment building. It's basically the same amount of work, and the lender makes much more on the larger property.

Aim to know enough about office buildings, small shopping and retail centers, and other types of commercial properties so that you can quickly analyze any deal you run across, even if it isn't exactly the type of commercial property that you're looking for. After you've spotted a good deal and have it under contract, you can pass the deal along to another commercial investor you network with.

Developing relationships

After you've decided on the type of properties you want, the next step is to think through all the different ways that you may be able to connect with either the owner of the property or someone who knows the owner of the property. Perhaps it's someone who's aware of some of the life challenges that the owner may be facing. It's unfortunate, but even commercial property owners end up getting divorced or having medical issues. Or maybe the property is having challenges that the owner himself can't resolve.

How can you get to know people who are aware of the challenges that may come up with the property itself? Did you think of property managers? Good job if you did. What about county health department officials? These folks will know about commercial properties that are in trouble because necessary repairs have not been made. Don't forget about everyone else who's involved in the real estate process, including commercial real estate brokers, residential real estate brokers, title agents, mortgage brokers, bankers, bankruptcy attorneys, and eviction services.

You get the idea here. There are lots of ways you can either get to know or find out about the owner of a property. In fact, our favorite method of buying a property is sitting down directly with the owner to find out what the owner wants. After you know this, you can often put together a great deal that meets the seller's needs, yet still allows you to make a big profit.

Never, ever attempt to "go around" a real estate broker. Even if you put a deal together directly with the owner, make sure that the real estate broker earns a commission, whether or not that broker is involved directly in helping put the deal together. Commercial real estate is a small world and you can bet that word gets around how you "stole" a client from a broker to get a deal. If you get "stamped" with that reputation, other brokers will avoid you like the plague.

The relationships you create with other investors, with commercial brokers, with property owners, and everyone else in your life will be the lifeblood of your commercial real estate investing business. It will also be the difference between living a life that focuses only on material wealth compared with the wealth of living a life that also embraces your ability to create lasting connections with other people.

Getting Leads on Commercial Property Investments

When finding commercial property leads, it's like fishing in an ocean rather than a pond. A pond has a few varieties of fish, but oceans have many different fish and about just as many ways to catch them. It's important to have an open mind when doing this because there is no "best way" to get commercial leads. We share some of our favorite methods in this section.

Newspaper ads and publications

You can often find owners of commercial properties who want to sell by looking at newspaper classified ads. *The Wall Street Journal* and *The New York Times* are good places to get started, especially if you're looking to buy in an area that isn't necessarily close to you. And we like these publications because they list properties from all across the United States.

Your local newspapers and even some trade journals can be good resources as well. Our local newspaper has a huge real estate section on Sundays as do most large cities. Trade journals are good sources, but most of the good properties listed are taken, so we mainly use them as potential relationship sources. Who knows, maybe the seller has other properties she planned to sell. You may be able to purchase them before they're listed.

Internet sites of commercial real estate

A number of good Web sites can lead you to potential commercial real estate deals. The most well known is www.loopnet.com, which is sort of a multiple listing service for commercial real estate properties. Another well-known online resource is CoStar.com (www.costar.com).

Or, why not go direct to the source: national commercial real estate brokerage firms. They have their own Web sites with listings and valuable market reports. The beauty of Internet sites is that if the property that we find there is no longer available, we count it as all good because we have just made a valuable contact. We can either sign up for property availability alerts or we keep in touch with the realtor we made contact with. In many cases, we found that the property we checked on was no longer available, but we ended up buying another property that was soon to be listed.

Government agencies

Due to various guarantee and support programs, the federal government ends up owning thousands of properties that they want you to buy. While most of these are single-family homes, you can also find great commercial deals from time to time by using this resource — as long as you know how to find them.

The Office of Property Disposal sells government-owned commercial properties to the public. Check it out by going to www.homesales.gov, and then clicking on the Buildings and Land tab. Or try the U.S. Department of Agriculture (USDA) — Rural Development Real Estate for Sale (www.resales.usda.gov). Its Web site has for sale government-owned real estate and potential foreclosure sales for multifamily housing.

When a taxpayer defaults on his or her income taxes, the Internal Revenue Service (IRS) can file a lien against property owned by the taxpayer. At that point, the taxpayer can't sell or refinance the property without first settling their debt with the IRS. If a property like this is foreclosed on, the IRS has 180 days after the foreclosure sale to redeem the property. *Redeeming* the property means that the IRS comes up with all the money to pay off the amount paid for the house at the auction. After the 180-day period, the IRS will lose its rights if it doesn't redeem the property.

The Government Services Administration, better known as GSA, and the IRS have come up with a program where investors can provide the funds to redeem the property. Here's a rundown of this process: The investor gives the IRS a minimum bid, and if the IRS is happy with the amount, it accepts the bid. Then the GSA puts the property up for public sale. The investor who put up the bid is automatically the first bidder for the GSA sale. As long as no one else outbids the investor at the sale, the investor gets to purchase the property for the amount of the bid that he or she put up.

Realtors and brokers

When looking for deals, you're looking for commercial real estate firms that sell commercial properties as their specialty. The Realtors and brokers that you get to know can be incredible sources of commercial properties for you over time. You want to focus on getting to know commercial brokers, but it's also important to understand that everyone in your network who may know of a commercial property for sale is a potential source of another deal.

You can also connect with residential agents who have good relationships with clients who have used the agents for buying and selling homes and who also own commercial property. Some of our best commercial deals have come from residential agents! You're typically looking for the residential brokers who have a client who owns just one or two commercial properties. When you find a property this way, you have the added advantage of being able to negotiate the price and terms with the owner before a commercial broker simply overinflates the owner's expectations by saying, "I can get you $10 million, no problem. Just give me the listing."

How do you know when you've found the right real estate agent to work with? Our answer? You never find *one* right real estate agent! Commercial brokers earn their commissions by bringing you good commercial deals, so you should never limit yourself to working with just one real estate agent. You want to keep your options open. Commercial real estate is too big to limit yourself. There's no way that one agent can bring you all of your deals.

You'll find agents who suggest that you work only with them. When you do, don't take the bait. Your response should sound something like this: "Mrs. Agent, I will definitely work diligently with you to take a close look at any commercial property you bring to my attention. Obviously, to meet the needs of my investors, I need to be looking at properties in many areas and from many different sources in a way that will protect my interests. I'll work strictly with you on anything that you provide me so you can make a commission at closing, but I'll do the same thing with other agents and brokers in my network. I'll also do my best to make sure that you don't spend significant amounts of time on a property that I have no intention of buying. Is that fair enough?"

Property owner associations

Join both the local and national chapters of any commercial property owner or manager associations, as well as any other associations that may include commercial property owners or brokers. Consider joining the National Association of Apartment Owners (www.naahq.org) and finding a local chapter to network with. You should also consider the Institute of Real Estate Management (www.irem.org) because it focuses primarily on owners of managers. Or if your interest lies in office buildings, join the Building Owners and Managers Association (www.boma.org). There are 92 local chapters nationwide. And for you shopping center lovers, take a look at the International Council of Shopping Centers (www.icsc.org). They're known for deal making among themselves. Join the party.

After you join an association, how do you get the word out? Well, you can run either a small display or classified ad in the association's newsletter. You can also stand up in meetings and announce your intentions, or just informally tell other members what you're looking for. We suggest that you do more than the average investor would; that's what it takes to get the great deals.

To get the most out of any association you belong to, try the following:

✔ **Become a leader in the association.** This means volunteering to be on the board and stepping up to help produce events. In other words, find a role in which you can be visible to the group.

Often the best way to become known is by volunteering to be the membership chairperson or an officer of some sort; it isn't a popular job, but it's one that allows you to get in front of the group at every meeting. As you speak to the members in the audience, they'll see you as a credible authority and someone they'd like to get to know.

✔ **Find ways to meet key people throughout the association.** This doesn't mean that you simply exchange business cards. Doing so doesn't work to create the relationships that lead to profitable commercial deals falling into your lap. Instead, make time to develop a connection so that when you call these key folks, they already know who you are and have some respect for you.

Real estate investment clubs

Most of the bigger cities in the United States have a number of local real estate investment clubs. These groups provide great opportunities to network and meet with other investors who have a similar interest in commercial property. The members typically include just about everyone: beginning investors, those interested in investing in homes, commercial investors, real estate brokers, real estate attorneys, title company officers, appraisers, and others who make their living from the various real estate investing professions. Most of these associations meet once a month to discuss current events, share information, and have an expert speak to the group. The meetings are actually very educational to attend.

We first heard of these clubs years ago through word of mouth. After we started to attend their meetings regularly, we heard of other existing clubs as well as new clubs that we just starting. These days, to find clubs in your city, enter "real estate investment club" into your Internet search engine. Or try going onto the National Real Estate Investor Association Web site (www.nationalreia.com) and search your area for the nearest club.

To get the most out of an investment group, we suggest starting a subgroup for commercial real estate investing. Typically the group's leadership will provide support for this type of group because it's an extra benefit to group members. However, don't forget to check with a group's leaders before announcing the subgroup's start. But rest assured that because you're running it, the leaders will likely be okay with it (after all, they don't have to put any extra effort into it).

As the group's leader, you can pick the meeting topics and either have group discussions on these topics or invite someone, such as a commercial lender or commercial broker, to give you their view on the marketplace. You'll find that there's no shortage of people who are willing to come and share their expertise, because most folks know that they're going to end up getting clients as the group gets to know them.

Getting leads through friends

From Peter Conti: As a father of four kids, it's difficult for me to avoid talking about my children. I've found that, when I'm getting to know someone, I enjoy finding out about other people's kids as well. Earlier in my career, I got to know a real state broker named Jesse whose son was born the same month as mine. We got together at times for a business lunch and at other times for dinner with our families. After getting to know Jesse informally over the course of a year and a half, I suggested trading all the names in my property owners' database for all the names in Jesse's database. By doing this, both of us were able to increase the number and accuracy of the commercial property owner contact information we could access.

As a result of expanding my database, I was able to make numerous offers to owners that previously weren't accessible to me. In just one of these offers, I used creative financing to purchase a medium-sized commercial property, using none of my own money. This property is still in my portfolio, steadily bringing in a passive stream of cash flow each and every month year in and year out.

Some of the best deals that I have found came my way simply because of a relationship that was started for reasons beyond real estate. When you operate this way you'll discover many people who you can now call friends. You, too, can use commercial real estate to meet great people, have fun, and of course make money.

Looking Locally and Nationwide

As you become an investor, you need to decide whether you want to limit yourself to investing locally or whether you want to open yourself to the possibility of investing across the nation or even in other countries. We explain everything you need to know in the following sections.

Surveying the pros and cons of local investing

How do you decide whether to venture out and invest in another state or whether you should stay local? Well, each strategy has its ups and downs.

If you're investing locally, you can work the relationships that you build locally because it's easier to have a cup of coffee or lunch as you get to know those in your network. Depending on how much of the work you plan to do yourself, you'll be nearby and able to oversee the work of contractors and vendors. You may even find it possible to manage a smaller property on your own when you're just starting out.

The main downside to investing locally, however, is that you're limited to just the commercial properties in your area. What if you can't find a good deal close by? What if properties are too expensive? And why would you want to limit yourself to just investing locally when you can pick from any of the thousands of commercial properties available across the entire United States? Another disadvantage to investing locally is that you're likely to be tempted to stop by, give your advice, and stick your nose into situations that should have been outsourced to a property management company (check out Chapter 11 for more on property management).

Many of our Commercial Mentoring students struggle with this disadvantage at first. They want to find that perfect commercial property right down the street so they can drive by and monitor it. Of course, unless there's a tornado, real estate — whether it's in Kansas City, Chicago, or San Francisco — isn't going anywhere.

To get through this struggle, we encourage our students to focus on buying properties that are so big that, even if they did want to manage them themselves, they couldn't. With a big property, you need a team of people to help you manage. Ideally, you'll have a quality management team in place. This may be a different way of looking at things, but if you're going for the big life, why not go about it with gusto.

Investing outside of your community

Many of us who live in big cities have had to go out of our states to find commercial properties that meet our investment objectives. And this is because sale prices in big cities have increased so much that our investment returns have shrunk to almost nothing. Going out of your community, you'll find the kind of great deals that were in your city years ago. In most cases, it's just a matter of time before that community will be out of your price range too. If you live in the city, consider going to the suburbs to look for deals. Go to the outskirts of your community, to "sleepy" towns and undiscovered areas, to find your next great deal. You may find lower prices, great investment returns, and greater growth than you would in an already matured big city.

Secondary investment markets are markets outside of big city markets that are much smaller and less developed. These are potentially great places to begin investing because you're entering a market that has yet to fully mature. You are basically getting in on the bottom. Properties found in secondary markets have lower prices and rents that aren't too far off the levels of big city markets.

Tertiary markets are even smaller than secondary markets and can be quite scary to invest into because of this. We've invested in some of these markets before where the population was only 15,000. That's scary for most folks, but the town had everything going for it that we liked — growing population, stable job growth, a vibrant local economy, and a demand for what we're investing into. It made sense for us, we saw it as good risk, and in the end we're still being rewarded.

Determining your location with demographics

If you could peek into the boardroom at Wal-Mart as the leaders were deciding where to put their newest stores, do you think they'd be throwing darts at a map of cities and neighborhoods? No, of course not. Those Wal-Mart leaders are going to examine demographic and market indicators to know what's going on before making an investment to add a store in another location.

The study of demographics allows you, as a commercial real estate investor, to pick the areas of the country that are most likely to have the conditions that make commercial property a successful investment. *Demographics* include the following:

- ✔ Finding out about the population trends and knowing how likely it is that those trends will continue
- ✔ Determining who's moving where and when, and then figuring out why
- ✔ Discovering how many people are moving into an area
- ✔ Figuring out what factors attract people to an area and understanding how stable these factors are

It's true that when talking about what makes a good real estate location, good economic times and prosperity are a big piece of the puzzle. So, when you're looking for the market in which to buy your commercial property, find markets where jobs are increasing, where median income is rising, and where companies are relocating and hiring people.

As an area develops, you'll see that some of the businesses that come in will look at what's going on there and they'll find a bigger business that depends on similar demographics as their own. Then they'll wait until the bigger business does the research and casts in the same waters, only tagging along after that business is successful. As you get to know these patterns, you can hit on an area where the demographics are right for development.

With commercial real estate, it's all about being in the path of progress or going into a marketplace that's really at the point of taking off because of the people moving in and businesses growing to support them. If you have a strip mall in this area and suddenly a lot of new apartment buildings go up and people come into the area, your rents in the strip mall will likely increase.

And with higher rents from a commercial property, you get increased property values and, of course, a boost in cash flow.

Here are a couple of tips to keep in mind:

✔ Large retail chain stores, also known as *big box retailers,* spend millions of dollars every year on demographic studies on where to build their next stores. Wal-Mart and Home Depot are a couple of typical examples. So why not save your time and money and start investing where you see those folks break ground for new stores? They've already done their research and have decided to invest tens of millions of dollars in that location. We suggest that you find out what's in demand there and follow right behind them.

✔ Another way to recognize growth that's right around the corner is to watch the Department of Transportation. When you see freeways being built and on and off ramps being constructed, you better believe that it's happening for a reason. The government is planning for and expects growth in that area. Hop on the bandwagon by asking the city's chamber of commerce or the city's department of economic development what their master plan is. These are the best places to get specific demographic information quickly. You may want to buy up land nearby and wait for developers to approach you. Or you may want to start buying commercial property nearby before anyone else discovers what's going on.

Locking Down Deals: Don't Leave Home without These Tools

As a commercial real estate investor, you should never leave home without the tools you need to buy commercial properties. You never know when you might stumble upon an excellent deal that you need to quickly analyze and get under contract. Here's a list of the essentials:

✔ **A good cellphone that allows you to talk, send and receive e-mail, and take pictures of properties:** Also, look for the voice memo feature so that you can record notes about properties or ideas when you're out and about.

✔ **An addendum template that you can attach to any commercial real estate contract:** This addendum should include the escape clauses and other language that allows you to lock up a property under contract while still retaining the ability to get out of the deal if you don't like it.

✔ **An outside third party or mentor:** You need a mentor that you can talk to or run a deal by to make sure that you aren't getting caught up in the emotions of the deal. Mentors are also great for reassuring you that you're making good decisions.

We also feel that you need to understand the three Rs of commercial real estate investing. Knowing these Rs can help you avoid wasting time on marginal commercial deals:

- ✔ **Risk:** How much of my money would be at risk? Would I be personally liable for debt that's used to fund the deal? How could this deal negatively affect my life's goals and relationships? How much time will it take?

- ✔ **Reward:** How much profit is in the deal? When would I see that money (cash at closing from a refinance, cash flow over time, or long-term equity I'd tap into in a few years, for example)? How certain am I of realizing that profit? In other words, what has to happen for me to end up with cash in hand?

  We also look for any "deal sweeteners" we can easily use to bump up the cash flow or value from the property. And we look for ways to structure the financing to increase cash flow or cash-on-cash return.

- ✔ **Roll out:** Is this a one-shot deal or can I replicate it with another property? Can I use my learning and effort from this deal as a template for later deals? What contacts and relationships will this deal bring me that will be valuable for me to do more deals in future? Can I expand and leverage this deal into a much larger opportunity?

Allowing the Great Deals to Find You

We know of investors out there who are true deal magnets. Every time we hear from them or see them in person, they're always telling us about the deal that just happened to fall into their laps. Of course, that's what it appears like to us. But we know better. These folks have set up brilliant and fun systems of having deals find them. Read on and see how to rev up a system like theirs for yourself.

Attracting owners with reports

Rather than trying to chase down all the commercial property owners and hoping to approach them at just the right time — when they're ready to talk about selling their property — here's a better way: Create systems that allow commercial property owners to be attracted to you.

For example, one thing we have done is to create a special report called "Three Little Known Ways to Increase the Value of Your Commercial Property." We tell commercial property owners that we have this valuable report available and that they can have it for free; all they need to do is provide their contact information. In the past, we sent the special reports through the mail. Mailing these reports not only took lots of time, but it also used up a lot of envelopes and stamps. A better way of getting commercial property owners to respond is by going to your Web site after you send them a postcard or perhaps you place an ad in the property owners' association newsletter. The ad would look something like what you see in Figure 4-1.

Figure 4-1:
A sample ad to spark interest from property owners.

Recent Market Changes Affect Commercial Property Values

To get your copy of this free special report called

'Th ree Little Known Ways to Increase the Value of Your Commercial Property"

go to www.HowToIncreaseValue.com

An ad like the one shown in Figure 4-1 encourages the commercial property owner to visit your one-page Web site that provides more information about the special report. After all, commercial property owners will want to get this report in their hands right away. All they need to do is enter their name and e-mail address on the Web site and they'll get the special report instantly.

The great thing about this process is that you acquire their contact info, which allows you a way of contacting these owners in the future. You also hope that it will allow the owners to get to know more about you and for you to get to know more about them.

Making unsolicited offers

Properties that aren't listed for sale that you make offers on are *unsolicited offers*. This is a superb way to add commercial properties to your portfolio. Here's what we did, and you can do the same: We went to a title company and got a copy of all large (50-plus units) apartment owners' names and addresses in a certain city. We sent letters to every one of them telling them that we are interested in purchasing their property. On half of the properties, we had enough bare property info to send purchase contracts via certified mail. We got a much higher response from the owners that received contracts than just letters of interest. The most interesting thing we found was that nearly all the owners who responded to us had additional properties they wanted to sell. You can do the same on shopping centers, office buildings, or warehouses.

Discovering properties that have been relisted

One of the biggest frustrations for commercial investors looking for great deals is talking to the brokers or owners way too early in the process. Often the owner may list the property at a certain price, and either because of the owner's false expectations or because the broker has misjudged the market, the property has been priced too high and the numbers don't make sense — even if you did get great terms.

If you run into this type of situation, wait it out and let the marketplace bring the owner's expectations down to earth. When the owner of the property is ready to relist the property for the second or third time, he usually becomes more realistic about where the asking price should really be.

Because commercial properties don' t have a multiple listing service like residential properties do, some of the best deals come from those properties that have been relisted at a new price, but the new price hasn't been announced in the marketplace.

To take advantage of a deal like this, you need to find a way to keep in touch with the broker and preferably with the owner of any property of interest that you run across. Contact the owner by using e-mail, by sending out a reminder postcard, or by simply leaving a quick message over the phone. The following are some examples of how you can word the messages. After the owner comes down to earth on the pricing, make contact directly.

Here's a sample e-mail to an owner of an overpriced property:

> Subject: I'd still like to buy your commercial property.
>
> Hey there,
>
> This is Peter Conti, and a while back, we took a look at purchasing the commercial property that you had available. We like the property itself, but were not able to have the numbers make sense at the price you were asking at that time.
>
> If you should ever decide to make a significant drop in the price or other concessions that you feel would make this property attractive to us again, please contact me at 303-233-2233.
>
> Sincerely,
>
> Peter Conti

Here's a sample postcard to an owner of an overpriced property:

> If you really want to sell, I'd really like to buy your property located at 123 Main Street. Let's have coffee together when you're ready to make a deal.

Call Peter Conti at 800-952-9585

Here's a sample message left on voicemail for an owner of an overpriced property:

> Hey, this is Peter Conti. I'm calling about your property at 123 Main Street. You may remember me. I looked at the property several months ago, and I really wanted to buy it. The problem was that I just couldn't make the numbers work with the price being so high. When you're ready, call me because we can close in 30 days if needed. My phone number is 303-233-2233. Thanks for your time.

Unlisted properties: Hidden fish in the streams

We suggest talking to property owners who don't currently have their properties listed. With this tactic, you're looking for the property owners who have thought of selling, but who aren't actively marketing their property for sale.

How can you find these commercial property owners? One way is to run a simple "property wanted" ad in your local newspaper. Here's some language that worked for coauthor Peter Conti:

> *Private investor wants commercial property. Will look at all, any condition. Call Peter at 303-233-2233.*

You can also send direct-mail flyers or postcards to commercial property owners. To do so, you first need to create a list of the names and addresses of the commercial property owners in the areas that you're interested in. Look for companies that provide these lists online. These companies put together lists after purchasing information from the county recorder's office. They put information into their databases, and then sell specific lists to investors and other users. To find a list company in your area, ask other investors at your local investors' association. If you don't have success there, take a trip to your county recorder's office; there you can ask about the companies that purchase information to make it available for resale.

Many of the addresses that you get for commercial properties end up at property management companies or other entities. They may either fail to pass your interest along to the owner or deliberately keep you from contacting the owner. If you're unable to come up with an address that goes directly to a property owner, you may have to do additional research to get the appropriate contact info. Some property owner associations also have directories that provide names and addresses of commercial property owners who are members. However, if you use this as a resource, make sure that you don't violate any of the guidelines the association may have about marketing to other members.

Chapter 5

Strategies for Making Offers and Negotiating

So maybe you've found what you *think* could be a great deal. It's okay if you're unsure about the deal's strength because in this chapter you discover how and why the seasoned pros constantly make offers to buy commercial property without needing to know all the important facts about whether a property might be successful or not.

This chapter explores how you can increase your chances of actually getting a deal accepted and what to do after your offer has been accepted. We also give you tips on successfully dealing with sellers, paperwork, and contracts. After you understand how easy it is to sign up a deal — including using a special escape clause that makes it risk free — you'll be doing it all the time.

Increasing Your Chances of Getting Your Offer Accepted

The best investors have discovered that they must conserve their time and energy when looking at properties and making offers. If you aren't careful you can waste all your time on deals that aren't worth buying. So, follow these three rules to increase your chances of getting an offer accepted:

✔ Use a qualifying system so that you're focusing only on the leads that have a high probability of turning into deals.

✔ Know the strategies that will make a deal work and direct the negotiation toward a winning deal right from the start.

✔ Use a systematic method to negotiate and put the deal together instead of relying on gut feelings or some other nonrepeatable process.

Starting with the end in mind

To increase the chances of getting your offer accepted, you need to understand some of the games that are played in the commercial real estate arena. Making offers used to sound something like this: Offer a low price or great terms and be willing to negotiate up from there.

Now it's oftentimes a matter of getting the ball rolling by using an initial offer that gets the broker's or seller's attention and with not too much back and forth so that your offer quickly becomes a signed contract. Then it's a matter of ethically negotiating down to a purchase agreement that allows you to have the return on investment and cash flow you need to make the deal work.

One of the biggest mistakes you can make is writing up every offer as a winning deal for you right from the start. You probably won't close on a deal unless it's a win for you, but due to the competition in the marketplace and the games that brokers play, we often (as crazy as it sounds) make offers that we know contain terms or conditions that we can't meet, just to get the ball rolling.

Sizing up the sellers and what they really want

Putting together great deals involves finding out what the seller really wants to accomplish, and then finding a way to structure the deal where you give the seller what he absolutely needs, while keeping enough of the benefits in the deal over on your side of the table to make it a huge win for you as well.

We understand that when most folks start investing, they may not have tons of cash laying around to put into deals. So, if you fall into this category, instead of sitting around moaning about it, focus on those commercial property owners who don't need or want cash right now. These sellers are found in three groups:

✔ Owners who are ready to sell but don't want to pay capital gains tax

✔ Property owners who prefer to get a secure cash flow each month rather than a big chunk of cash all at once

✔ Owners who have made tons of money by investing in commercial properties and simply want to see someone who's passionate about their property become the new owner

The single most-important skill you have as an investor is your ability to connect emotionally with people. This skill will help you create trust and rapport with the seller, which in turn helps you get the seller to open up about his real reasons for selling. Master this skill and you'll never really be "negotiating a deal." Rather, you'll be helping the seller to come up with a solution that is an acceptable win for the seller, and that is a great deal for you too.

Compare this to how most investors negotiate: Many commercial investors use what we like to call the "big stick" method of negotiation. These investors go in and negotiate with hardball tactics. And for some this works. However, we've found that it isn't a good fit for us, and so we don't recommend it.

In fact, we've discovered that most investors we've worked with just don't feel good going in and beating up the broker or seller. Plus, we've found that hardball tactics aren't an effective way to get a good deal. Sure, if you're simply negotiating a low-ball cash price for the property, these tactics may work, but we still believe there are better ways to get a low cash price. However, when you're looking not just to get a good price on the property, but to also negotiate great terms, it's essential to negotiate with people in such a way that you maintain your connection and rapport with them.

For instance, we won't ask you to give a broker a "take it or leave it" last offer. And we won't ask you to fight with the seller over a price. Instead, we suggest that you use simple questions worded with powerful language patterns. Following this system will do much of the negotiating work for you.

So, you don't need to have a magnetic personality to persuade sellers to sell to you. What you need instead is a supply of sincere care for the other person and the willingness not just to listen to them but to really hear what they are telling you. By using these powerful negotiating tools, you'll become unstoppable. And the better you get at connecting with people, the wealthier you'll become. Not only will you end up with more commercial real estate, but you'll also probably be happier, have more friends, and even communicate better with your family.

Sealing Deals: The Instant Offer System

Okay, so you've found what you think may be a great deal. As we note earlier in this chapter, getting the deal you want isn't about writing up the perfect offer as much as it is about finding a way to connect with the other parties and discover what they really want. The way to do this is by using the Instant Offer System.

Here are the five steps of the Instant Offer System:

1. **Build rapport with the broker or seller.**

2. **Establish an upfront agreement.**

3. **Build the broker's or seller's motivation level for selling.**

4. **Determine the financial details of the deal (also known as the "Money Step").**

5. **Find the critical pieces to a winning deal (also known as the "What-If Step").**

One of the easiest and hardest things to do is play the role of the reluctant buyer. It's easy because the concept is so simple. You just have to make sure that you appear more reluctant to move ahead on the deal than the seller or broker. On the other hand, the reason it can be so difficult is that when a deal looks like it's going to come together, it's hard not showing your excitement and even harder to appear reluctant.

Step 1: Build rapport with the broker or seller

Rapport is a fancy word that means "connected like friends." Connecting with people (in this case brokers and sellers) is easy when you follow these steps:

1. **Listen and be 100-percent present.** These days no one is ever fully present. When you give your full, undivided attention to someone, they are going to love it.

2. **Notice and briefly point out those things that you have in common with someone else.**

   This technique works because people like others who are similar to them. Get them to talk about their interests and you've connected on a common ground.

3. **Continue to listen to them instead of talking too much yourself. Make sure you remain 100-percent present.**

To initially create rapport with a seller, find or create an environment where you have the time and quiet space to spend two or three hours if needed in getting to know the broker or seller. Being in an office environment with interrupting phone calls or in a room with the TV blaring isn't going to work. When creating the proper space to connect, look for a place where you feel comfortable having a cup of coffee or a glass of juice while you hang out for a few hours.

After the seller starts to relax, she will feel more comfortable around you and will (hopefully) start to like you. When people like you, they will also tend to open up and trust you more — which is one of your goals when trying to get a great deal on a property.

One of the most important things to master is building an emotional connection with the broker or seller of the commercial property. As part of putting together winning deals, you need to get comfortable with helping the broker open up enough so that you can fully understand the seller's situation and motivation. No matter how you plan on structuring a purchase, you'll always fare better if you can work collaboratively with the broker or seller instead of working like it's you against her. Maintaining a high level of rapport with the broker and the seller is the glue that holds this connection together.

After you've built an initial rapport with a broker or seller, make sure to continue the rapport all the way through the negotiation. We like to refer to important connection points, such as a sport or hobby that the seller is interested in. For example, you might say, "Even if you had to settle for $6 million, at least you'd be done with this and able to go sailing every day." Here are some items to focus on to keep the connection going:

- **Things that you have in common with the broker or seller:** If you know that the broker likes football, make sure that you know enough about the recent games to chat about the results from the weekend when you call to check up on a listing at the beginning of the week.

    Ideally (and even though it may sound a little creepy), you may want to use a database to help you keep track of the broker's and seller's interests. Otherwise, you'll never be able to remember which of your clients likes football and music and which one enjoys horseback riding and tennis.

- **Things that you may not have in common but that the broker or seller is passionate about:** One of the perks of investing in real estate is the number of interesting people you get to meet. When you really get to know someone, one of the benefits is that they share details about their passions and areas of interest. The critical key is that you have an interest in what is important to them, even if you don't have it in common. So, you get to make a friend and also find out all about a new sport, business, or other passion that you may not have known much about prior to meeting this person.

Here's the upside to all of this: Because people love to talk about themselves and their interests, the more you can get the broker or owner to share with you, the more connected both of you are going to feel with each other.

Step 2: Establish an upfront agreement

An *upfront agreement* is an understanding between you and the broker or seller that each time you invest your time in talking about a deal you'll both tell each other exactly where you stand at the end of your discussion. Having this agreement helps you avoid spending enormous amounts of time trying to make a deal work that isn't ever going to meet the other party's needs.

In its simplest form, the upfront agreement that we use with commercial properties sounds something like this:

> **Investor:** Mr. Broker, if you end up hating the ideas we talk through today, are you okay with letting me know that you don't like any of the ideas we came up with together?
>
> **Broker:** Sure.
>
> **Investor:** And I understand that, until we get to the point where we might be including the seller directly in our conversations, you can't answer for the seller. On the other hand, if you do feel that any of the ideas we come up with may get us all to the closing table, are you okay sharing that with me as well?
>
> **Broker:** Yes, I am.
>
> **Investor:** Great, I appreciate that. Now I'll be doing the same thing. If I don't feel that this property is a good fit for our group, I'll let you know. And if I do think that what we talk through today is a fit, I'll let you know. I want to be respectful of your time and my time, so at the end I'll let you know exactly where we stand — either yes it is a fit or no it isn't. And understanding that you have limitations until the seller is here with us directly, I would appreciate the same courtesy from you. Is that fair?
>
> **Broker:** Sure, no problem.

Step 3: Build the broker's or seller's motivation level for selling

It is part of human nature that someone who has owned a commercial property for a period of time is probably going to have an inflated idea of the type of offers they may be getting. After all, one of the nice things about owning a property that gives you a passive stream of cash flow is daydreaming about exactly how much your little "gold mine" is going to be worth some day. So, make sure that you use this step to bring the seller's motivation into the equation.

Another problem you may run into is that sometimes brokers let sellers retain the idea that their properties are worth more than it is simply to get the property listed. The broker knows that over time there's a good chance that he can get the seller to either lower the asking price or counter to a lower offer so that the sale actually happens.

By mastering the motivation step (which really is the most important step of the Instant Offer System), you can get the broker and seller to open up with you so that you know enough about the seller's real needs while still being profitable from your end. This is why during the four-day training we do with our Commercial Mentoring Program students, we invest a good portion of one day to mastering this step.

Your goal in Step 3 of the Instant Offer System is to help both the broker and the seller to:

✔ Understand their respective motivations for getting the deal done.

✔ Share with you the opportunities for you to improve the net income from the property. It's important for the broker and the seller to recognize that because you profit by improving properties, this commercial property isn't for you if it's "perfect."

For a real-life example of how the motivation step works, let's "listen in" to a conference call with one of our Commercial Mentoring clients named Lisa. In this script, Lisa is the investor and Rob is the Commercial Mentoring coach:

Lisa: Hi Rob, I've got a deal I'm really excited about.

Rob: Hi Lisa, I've been looking through the Platinum Form you submitted into the online system, and this looks like it could be a nice deal. I see that the cash-on-cash return is just over 12 percent.

Lisa: Yeah, but that percentage is based on the numbers from the broker. I met with the seller yesterday, and he didn't seem to want to tell me much other than "It's a great deal."

Rob: Okay. How long has it been for sale?

Lisa: About nine months now.

Rob: So, if it's such a great deal, why hasn't someone else bought it?

Lisa: I was wondering the same thing. That's why I need you to help me figure out what to do here.

Rob: What did it sound like when you went through the motivation step?

Lisa: I found out that the seller wants to buy a small shopping center rather than this apartment building.

Rob: That's it?

Lisa: Well, yes. I guess I should have spent more time on the motivation step, huh?

Rob: Try this with the seller. Say to him "The good thing for you is that most people would stay awake at night worrying about an apartment building like this. You seem to be pretty well rested. It's nice that you're able to avoid thinking about this building 24 hours a day." Lisa, you need to spend some time here and get the seller to open up. Let's face it, a motivated seller isn't going to step right up and say, "I'm desperate." So, I want you to go back to see the seller and find out how much time you can spend in the motivation step. Then I or one of the other coaches will help you to move ahead with the next steps.

Lisa: I can do that!

Other investors can almost always see ways to improve a deal that you're involved in. The reason is that all of us get too close to the deals that we're working on. Another investor can help to point out things that are usually obvious. Find a group of supportive investors who have goals and values that are similar to yours. If you want to listen to a conference call where we help our clients in the Commercial Mentoring Program get better at using the motivation step, call 800-551-5993. It's a recording so you can listen 24 hours a day.

Step 4: Determine the financial details of the deal (The Money Step)

After you've discovered the seller's motivation, move on and get all the financial details onto the table so you can start working with the seller to create a deal that meets his most important needs and has a fair profit for you. When done well, this step helps you lower the seller's expectations of what the commercial property is worth so that you can get a good buy on the property.

Make sure that you follow all the steps of the Instant Offer System in the order described. The first three steps are critical and need to happen prior to the Money Step. In this step, you use three simple techniques to help lower the seller's or broker's expectations. We explain these techniques in the following sections.

Money Step technique 1: Realistic expectations

With this technique, you look at the broker or seller with that insider glint in your eye that says, "Hey, come on now. We both know that you might be asking $4.5 million for the property, but you don't really expect to get that much do you?" This technique usually gets the price down by 3 to 10 percent. Here's what you say: "So, how much do you *realistically* expect to get?"

When you say this phrase, make sure you do these three things to make it even more powerful:

1. **"Mark" the word "realistically" by using just your voice.**

   You can do this by putting a very slight pause right before and right after the word that you're "marking."

2. **Scrunch up your face by moving your mouth as close as possible to your nose.**

   Try scrunching now. Good job. Now do the scrunch and mark the word "realistically" as you ask the question. See how much better you sound already?

3. **Lower the pitch of your voice while saying the word "realistically."**

   Say "realistically," making sure you take your pitch down as you say the word. Why do you do this? Because it works. When your voice goes down, you're sending a subliminal signal that the price should also be going down.

What happens if the broker or seller doesn't come down at all? At this point, don't fight with him about it. You haven't lost anything by asking, and you still have more techniques to use.

Money Step technique 2: The range

Turn the lowest price that the broker gives you into a range with his number as the high end of the range. It sounds like this:

> **You** (starting off with the realistic expectations technique): So how much did you *realistically* expect to get?
>
> **Broker:** Well it's listed at $7.5 million, but between you and me, I think the seller just might accept an offer of $7 million.
>
> **You** (here you're going to use the range technique): Wow, that much? $6.5 to $7 million?

If the broker doesn't object, he has just clued you in to the low end of the range as the new point from which you'll negotiate. If the broker defends the $7 million price, simply shrink your range and feed it back to the broker again. It sounds like this:

> **Broker:** No, I said $7 million.
>
> **You:** Oh, okay. I get it . . . $6.8 to $7 million.

This is sort of a question, but not one you want the broker to answer. Instead, you want to simply state the range (all the while nodding your head ever so slightly up and down indicating agreement. Think of how you'd nod to a friend as you say, "It's a nice day out today, isn't it?" When you reach a point where the broker or seller stops correcting you, you've just moved the amount you're negotiating down another notch.

It's important here to nod your head in agreement and give out all the non-verbal cues that you're agreeing with the broker even though you're subtly changing his answer in a way that fits for you.

The range you should use depends on your local real estate market. If you're in a slow market, be aggressive in your choice of opening ranges by shooting for a much lower number. If you're investing in a hot market, use a smaller opening range.

This technique, just like everything else in this book, only works if you use it. Don't be afraid if the seller does object to your range. This technique lets you test the water and find out where the broker's and seller's real limits are. You can shrink your range two or three times until you find the point where the other party is comfortable.

Money Step technique 3: The fictitious buyer

With this technique, you introduce a fictitious buyer through a real estate agent to help knock 3 to 6 percent off the price. However, remember that this technique won't work unless you're talking directly with a seller who hasn't listed his property.

You'll discover that this is a fun technique to use. Why? Consider this: If the seller would accept an offer through a real estate agent, he would have to pay commission to the real estate agent. So, in essence, he's saying that the price would be lower by 2 percent to as much as 5 or 6 percent to cover the commission. Some sellers will point out that they would be willing to pay for a buyer's agent commission but not for a listing commission. In this case, they're saying that they're willing to knock 2 or 3 percent off the purchase price. Here's a sample script you can use:

> **Investor:** So, if a broker came in here and told you that he could have this commercial property completely sold, done, and handled at that $4 million price, and you really believed that he could get it done within 60 days, you'd probably tell him to take a hike . . . huh?
>
> **Seller:** No, I'd be crazy not to take that.
>
> **Investor:** Okay, so help me figure this out. Five percent of $4 million is . . . .

The two key points with this technique are for you to use the negative phrasing as shown in the sample script and to make sure that you do the math slowly to ensure that the seller feels comfortable with the final answer.

After you've used the three Money Step techniques to talk the seller's price from, say, $4.5 million down to $3.8 million, does this make $3.8 million the final price? No, it simply means that $3.8 million is the starting point of what the seller wants. If, during the Money Step, you're writing notes on a scratch pad in front of the seller, don't write any number down until you get to the lowest number after using all three techniques. Then when you write this number down, you're legitimizing it as the "full amount" that the seller will get. Depending on the terms you negotiate, you may go ahead and give the seller this "full amount," or you may feel that you still need to negotiate to get it lower. At the very least, you have just discovered how to simply and easily decrease the price by at least 8 to 10 percent or more from the original asking price.

Step 5: Find the critical pieces to a winning deal (The What-If Step)

During this final step of the Instant Offer System, your goal is to close the deal. The What-If step allows you to get the broker or seller to agree to an offer before you ever make one. In fact, wouldn't it be nice to make offers only to sellers you know would say yes? Well, you can! You're going to do it by using the two most powerful words in any negotiation: "what if." This is a powerful phrase because it commits you to nothing and commits the other side to everything.

For example, imagine that you're negotiating to purchase a 20-acre piece of land. You've done most of your negotiating, and you're in the final stages of closing the deal. Instead of making an offer such as "Mrs. Seller, I'll pay you $8 million dollars for your land," ask a what-if question. This question would sound something like this:

> *Mrs. Seller, I don't know if I can do this, but what if I were able to pay you $7 to maybe as much as $8 million for your land? Is that something that's even worth taking the time to talk about . . . or probably not?"*

Notice the subtle difference between these two ways of making your offer: When you make a formal offer, you give all control over the deal to the other party. You've made an offer; the seller gets to say yes or no. When you qualify your offer by using the what-if phrasing, you aren't really making a formal offer. However, after the seller agrees to your what-if offer, the seller has committed herself to saying yes! This technique is your way of never making an offer until the seller has agreed to at least being open to it.

This technique is your way of never making an offer until the seller has agreed to at least being open to it. Only when the seller says, "Yes, let's talk about your offer," do you actually move ahead with it. If the seller isn't up for your what-if offer, simply move on to another until you find one that she agrees to. Then you can see whether you can put a deal together based on this acceptable what-if offer.

How to Meet the Seller When Submitting Your Offer

As a real estate investor, you've probably run into the following statement from a broker too many times to count: "I'm sorry but I can't let you meet the seller." You may have tried to get around this by insisting to be present when your offer is submitted. The challenge with this tactic, however, is that if the agent allows you to be there but he downplays your offer both before and after you're in the room, then you are sunk?

We stress throughout this chapter that to put together great commercial deals you need to not only meet the seller, but you also need to get to know him. You need to become friends with him. You need to take the time to really listen so that you have the best possible chance of putting together a deal that works for the seller and for you.

Here are a few ways to meet directly with the seller:

- ✔ **Limit your offers and negotiations only to for-sale-by-owner property that isn't listed with an agent.** This is the simplest way to make sure that you connect directly with the seller (and a method we've used extensively when guiding our mentorship students to buy single-family houses), but we don't recommend it as the only method. Why? Because most of the commercial properties that you'd want to buy are probably going to be listed with a real estate agent.

- ✔ **Make an offer on the property knowing that after you've written up a serious offer, you're in a much better position to ask for a meeting face to face with the seller.** We use this choice on a regular basis by suggesting to the broker that a meeting may very well lead to a commission for the broker.

The last option in the preceding list sounds something like this (with you speaking to the broker):

> Thanks for all of your help with this. I've found that <u>the deals I'm able to take to a closing quickly</u> usually result from a quick meeting where all of us — you, me, and the seller — get together to answer each other's questions and find the best way to <u>get this deal put to bed.</u> Does that make any sense to you at all, or should I just figure that this deal is going to take months of back and forth before it finally dies?

Notice the language (underlined) that subtly reminds the broker of the closing, which is when the broker gets paid. If the broker doesn't give in, try saying this:

So, I'm getting the feeling that perhaps I should just pass on this deal and spend my time on one of the other commercial properties that I'm considering with another agent.

No matter which method you use to connect with the seller, make sure that both the seller and the broker know that you insist on the broker receiving her real estate commission. We regularly meet directly with sellers and take the extra step of reassuring the seller and the broker that the broker's commission will be paid no matter how the deal comes together.

Writing Up the Offer

If you've met directly with the broker or seller, and have put together a winning deal, then you'll probably just write up a contract on the spot. What about the properties that are in another state or that you want to make an offer on as a way of opening the door to further negotiations? Do you send a simple one-page letter of intent or do you need to send a formal purchase contract? The answer is really one of preference.

Some of our Commercial Mentoring students insist that a letter of intent saves time, is easy to send out, and tells you whether you and the seller are in the same ballpark prior to putting the efforts into negotiating or writing up long agreements. Other investors insist that the best way is to send out complete offers. They feel as if brokers and sellers appreciate seeing a "real" offer and that it's worth the extra effort to write up a formal agreement instead of using a letter of intent.

Coauthor Peter Harris likes to use letters of intent. Almost all of his deals come from the nationwide network of relationships and connections that he has. He feels that if it can't be put on one page (to start with), it isn't worth his time.

Coauthor Peter Conti, on the other hand, tends to use formal agreements with an incredibly long addendum that asks for everything under the sun. If the addendum comes back completely deleted, Peter knows that the seller isn't motivated. When the seller or broker comes back negotiating to remove some of the outlandish claims that Peter makes in his addendums, he knows that he has a potential deal brewing.

Letter of intent

A letter of intent should tell the broker and/or owner that you're a real buyer who's ready to close at the price and terms that you've spelled out — provided you can work through the details. Make sure to include this important clause in your letter of intent:

While this letter of intent, once signed, does not legally bind the buyer or seller, it is expected that both parties will move forward in good faith toward completing details and signing a Commercial Contract to Buy and Sell real estate within 10 days of the date this letter is signed.

This clause lets everyone know that your letter of intent is a serious offer and should be treated as such. The parties are agreeing to move forward toward completing details. We call this "getting the ball rolling." Your letter of intent is like a starter's gun for the negotiation and agreement process. To see samples of letters of intent for the various commercial asset types, go to investorforms.com.

The advantage of using the letter of intent is that it's a simple, time-efficient way to get the basic points of a deal down. Besides, a one-page document is easier to get a seller to agree to right at the time you strike up the deal. The disadvantage is that you don't have the property under contract until you've written up a formal agreement. So with all your killer deals, make sure you write up the official contract pronto!

Commercial contract to buy and sell real estate

Your commercial broker should have the standard state-approved contract form that's commonly used to buy and sell commercial properties. On this form, which is many pages long, you'll find all kinds of clauses to cover every possible situation that might ever come up with your deal. Ask your broker to give you a copy of this form so that you can get familiar with it.

It's important that you use the proper state-approved commercial contract to buy and sell real estate because brokers and agents will be used to seeing it and will be comfortable with it. Writing up your commercial offer on a form that brokers aren't used to seeing is a surefire way to cause a listing broker to immediately question the seriousness of your offer.

There are certain disadvantages that come up when you use your state-approved form, however. The biggest drawback is that the approved form probably has a number of clauses that you don't necessarily want to have as part of your deal. Don't worry, though. You can use a simple addendum to remove or change any of the language to make it sound exactly like you want it to. The secret is to put the addendum at the end of the standard contract so that you can make your changes after the broker and the seller have gone all the way through all the good, official-sounding stuff. Then at that point they get to see your addendum that includes a statement like this:

In the event that any of the provisions in this addendum conflict with the attached commercial contract then in that event the provisions of this addendum shall prevail . . .

This language allows you to put whatever you want in the addendum. For instance, if the official contract says that your agreement isn't assignable, you simply add a quick paragraph that says it's fully assignable to whomever you want. Pretty cool, huh? Look for addendums you can use at www. investorforms.com.

You can also use addendums to provide the "outs" in your agreement. This allows you to tie up a commercial property yet still have time to look it over, do your due diligence, and make sure it's a deal that you're comfortable moving ahead with.

Another disadvantage of commercial contracts is that they can be fairly large and may be a little bit intimidating for new investors and sometimes for sellers. Most serious investors use a computer program to fill out their offers so that they don't end up with writer's cramp. (Check out www.commercial investingsoftware.com for details on investing software.)

Liquidated damages clause

When you're looking through your state contract, the most important thing to do is to find out whether there is a *liquidated damages clause* and whether it is written in a way that will protect you (as the investor) in the event that you don't close on the property. Here's what a typical liquidated damages clause says:

> *If the buyer fails to perform any of the covenants of this contract, all money paid to Seller by Buyer as aforesaid shall be retained by or for the account of the Seller as consideration for the execution of this contract and as agreed liquidated damages and in full settlement of any and all claims for damages.*

The liquidated damages clause says that in the event that you don't close on the property (which means that you've basically defaulted in your agreement to buy the property), the seller's only remedy for your failure to buy the property is to keep whatever money you've given to the seller so far.

The advantage of the liquidated damages clause is that it doesn't really look like an escape clause. This allows you to make quick close/cash offers with no obvious escape clauses that a seller may balk at. We use the liquidated damages clause as an "out" in the deal only in situations where we've tied up the property for a short period of time, such as 30 days or less. Why? We don't ever want a seller to feel as if we tied up his property for an unreasonable time — and then didn't close.

When we first started investing in commercial property, we used to think that when you signed an agreement to buy a property that you absolutely had to close. We soon realized that by using the liquidated damages clause you could make all kinds of offers, and the only downside was that you'd lose any money that you put into tying up each property. That's when we developed Addendum A, which provided clear language so that the sellers were never surprised when we decided not to close on a property. You can get a copy of The Addendum A that we use as part of your free Commercial Quick Start Training Package by registering at www.commercialquickstart.com.

Memorandum of agreement

After your deal is accepted, you'll want to take one extra step beyond keeping a copy of the signed agreement. We use a *memorandum of agreement* that's recorded at the courthouse, which lets everyone know that you have the property under contract. This prevents the seller from selling the property again. (Sounds crazy, but hey, it happens.) It also prevents another investor from trying to do an end run around you if you decide to sell your contract or flip the property.

Presenting Your Offer in the Best Light

At times, it seems that life is going 100 miles per hour. When you call a broker on the phone or visit her office, she may be racing along getting everything done that's on her to-do list. For some people, even when they stop and sit down with you, their minds can easily continue to race ahead, which means that you don't stand a chance of really connecting with them. And if you can't properly connect with your broker, you aren't able to create the rapport and other elements that are so critical to getting your deal accepted.

The way to break through to the quiet place of attention that you prefer is by using our scripts. For instance, here's what you can say if you're calling your broker on the phone: "Hi this is Peter Conti. I'm calling about the strip center on Elm St." Pause here for two to three seconds (it doesn't matter if you get a response or not), and then say "Sounds like I caught you in the middle of something." The broker will normally give some excuse like "No, it's okay. I'm just clearing off my desk." However, by calling the broker on her lack of attention, she'll likely stop what she's doing and give you her full attention.

 When presenting offers, it's important to convey a message that the brokers will understand. As part of becoming an expert commercial real estate investor, you need to be able to speak about "cap rates," "the mix," and "value added" deals. If you're new to the commercial real estate field, simply study and notice the words used by investors (many of which are in this book). It's also helpful to talk with your mentor, because chances are that he or she is already in the loop when it comes to talking like a pro investor. After you understand the lingo, you can start sprinkling the new "investor language" into your conversations with brokers.

The Five-Step Deal Filter

We don't want you banging your head against a wall trying to seal a deal that just isn't going to happen. Use the following five filters to make sure a deal is worth more of your time.

Filter 1: The five-minute test

To make it through this first step, one of the following things (all of which indicate a high probability of success) has to happen within the first five minutes of beginning to look at a deal:

- ✔ The seller or broker gives (or hints about) a compelling reason that's motivating the owner to sell the property quickly.

- ✔ Your number-crunching software tells you that based on the actual numbers (or the software's estimates) the property is priced at or below market value.

- ✔ You become aware of a big upside to the deal, such as knowing that the current rents are way below market value.

It may seem harsh to judge a deal this quickly, but you have to remember that there are thousands of opportunities to buy commercial properties. So, your time and energy must stay focused on deals with the highest probability of success.

Filter 2: Sign it up!

If the deal you're analyzing passes through the first filter, you should move quickly to get the deal under contract by using forms that will allow you to get out of the deal without any cost besides your time. Why do we encourage you to be in such a hurry to sign up the deal? Because good deals don't last. If it really is a good deal, you need to move on it before someone else snatches it up. The other reason is that getting a deal under contract — even if the price and terms aren't perfect — gives you the green light to move ahead with the next steps.

It seems that people are so afraid of risk that they hesitate to sign up a deal until they know for sure it's going to be a great deal. We're here to tell you that it's rare to find a deal that you know for sure will be great at sign up time. Great deals simply don't wait for you to process through days and days of analysis or contemplation.

One of the first things you need to have in your investing arsenal is a set of forms and contracts that you use on a consistent basis. This keeps you from having to spend hours of your time and from spending money with your attorney every time you negotiate a deal. In fact, you'll probably end up with your own version of agreements. These will likely be a combination of other investors' forms, your own changes, and your attorney's tweaks. Research www.investingforms.com to come up with a number of options to use.

When using escape clauses that allow you to get out of a deal, make sure you not only have the right language in your agreement, but that you also use the right language when talking to the broker and/or the owner. That way they aren't unpleasantly surprised when you exercise the rights that the contract gives you. Go to this book's companion Web site, www.CommercialQuick Start.com, to hear a podcast of a sample script that we use. With this sample, you can listen to the language, the tone, and the timing that we use so that sellers and brokers understand the escape clauses without being alarmed about them

Filter 3: The quick view

The quick view filter is designed to help you determine whether the property is worth the time it will take to do the real due diligence required in the next filter. *Remember:* We don't start this step until we have the property under contract. The quick view for commercial property requires you to check two important numbers:

- ✓ **Check the purchase price as it relates to the true market value of the property in its "as is" condition.** This view helps you determine whether you have equity.

  Using your connections with brokers and property managers in the area, find out and enter these variables into your number-crunching software to help determine the estimated value of the property:

  - The market cap rate

  - The average price per unit for apartments

  - The average price per square foot for land, office, or retail properties

- ✓ **Check the market rents for comparable properties in the area.** Doing so tells you whether the property value can be increased by raising rents over time.

You're doing a fast-and-dirty quick view in this step to see if the property has an upside. At this point, you aren't trying to see *exactly* what the property is worth. So expect to make some estimates and assumptions here with the comfort that this isn't the final filter for your deals. If the property looks like it may be priced under market, or the rents appear to be low, move to the next step.

Filter 4: The "realists" check

This filter is all about preparing for due diligence (flip to Chapter 6 for a full explanation of this important task.) This is the time to look at the deal from a fresh perspective to make sure that the numbers really do make sense. Be sure to begin this step after that first blush of initial excitement has worn off. You want to make sure that the deal really is a keeper.

Here are some questions to ask:

- ✔ Is the price really right?
- ✔ What assumptions am I making in my forecasts and projections?
- ✔ What realistically can go wrong with them?
- ✔ How will these setbacks affect me?
- ✔ How would I handle the setbacks?
- ✔ Can I build a safety mechanism into the deal to handle this contingency?
- ✔ If not, am I really willing to live with the risk?
- ✔ If I had no time in this deal and no psychological commitment to see this deal happen (and knowing what I know now), would I move forward in this deal?
- ✔ Can I handle the consequences of this deal not working out?

The bottom line is that this is your chance to check your assumptions and make sure that you're making an intelligent and balanced decision. After you're confident that you're making a rational decision to move ahead, you can start going through your due diligence checklist (checking the title to the property, ordering inspections, reviewing leases, and so on).

When you're going through the reality filter stage, the single most important thing you need to do is to neutralize your emotions and check your assumptions. You can neutralize your emotions by realizing that everyone makes decisions emotionally — everyone. Remember the old saying, "When emotions goes up, intelligence goes down." You just need to bring your emotional biases onto the table so that you're aware of them. Then examine the deal alongside these biases. You'll make a much better, more balanced decision by checking your assumptions against the facts.

Filter 5: End users determine the value

You can do all the fancy analysis you want. You can even create spreadsheet after to spreadsheet "proving" that the deal is a winner. But if you can't sell, hold long term, or flip your commercial property, the deal is a bust.

You need to get real data from real buyers and commercial tenants (the end users for the property). The only way to really know that you have real data — and not just fluff — is to ask prospective buyers if they're willing to buy or prospective tenants if they're willing to lease your property.

This may sound a bit crazy to be trying to sell or lease a property while you just have it under contract, but in the 27 combined years we've been investing, we've discovered that the very best way to know that you did a poor job negotiating a purchase is when you're struggling to resell or lease out the property. Why not find this out ahead of time?

Don't be guilty of the cardinal sin of waiting to market your property until you close on it. Immediately start aggressively marketing the property to see what kind of interest you can develop. Strong interest from willing buyers or commercial tenants is your best insurance that the deal is a keeper.

The Seller Has Accepted My Offer! Now What?

You're ecstatic: The seller accepted your offer and it's all that you wanted and more! What do you do now? Here are the five most important steps that you need to take after your offer is accepted (and you've celebrated!):

When the owner goes shopping with your offer

One of the reasons that you want to create a strong connection and rapport with the broker and the owner is to prevent them from unfairly "shopping" your offer. *Shopping* an offer occurs when a broker or owner calls all the other investors who have had any interest or made lower offers on the property and says "Hey, the property is about to go under contract unless you hurry and get us an offer." You may even run across situations where the other investors are allowed to know some of the elements of your offer. Here are two ways to prevent the seller from shopping your offer:

✔ **Make sure that you leave enough time for the seller to get your offer, but not much more.** For instance, we've made offers on a Thursday afternoon that expire on a Friday at 5 p.m.

✔ **Get an agreement from the broker that he won't share any details of your offer, including the fact that you have made an offer.** We use a one-page form called the "Confidentiality and Non-Disclosure Agreement" to prevent this. See www.investingforms.com for this form and others.

What's your exit strategy?

One of the biggest mistakes that investors make when involved in big deals is not creating the contingency plans needed to make money no matter what happens in a deal. In other words, understand this: The single most important way you can control risk in a deal is to have multiple, carefully planned-out exit strategies so that you make money no matter what.

For example, imagine that you're buying a 156-unit apartment building on the edge of a reviving downtown. You're buying the property with the intention of turning it into a rental property. But what happens if you find that the property is difficult to keep as rental property? What are your contingency plans?

One option would be to convert the units into condos and reap a huge premium over the next 12 to 24 months as you sold off the individual units to conventional cash buyers. This option would provide a maximum amount of cash to you in a short period of time. Or, if you had trouble selling enough of the units with conventional financing, you could offer 30 percent of the condos with seller financing in the form of a large seller second mortgage. You then help these buyers get a new loan for 75 to 90 percent of the purchase price (and because they're owner-occupied loans and in a lower price range, they should be easier to get.) You carry back the balance as a higher interest rate second mortgage with interest-only payments due monthly. Or you can let the interest accrue and compound.

The key is to make sure that you have thought through at least five solid exit strategies for how to handle the most likely contingencies before you move forward in the deal. This extra effort on your part will pay off handsomely not only in extra profits from deals, but also in the peace of mind you'll gain in knowing that you made smart decisions to buy a property.

1. Record a memorandum of agreement (which is covered earlier in the chapter).

2. Begin your due diligence (Chapter 6).

3. Come up with three to five exit strategies (see the nearby sidebar).

4. Move ahead with lining up the financing (Chapters 8–10).

Chapter 6

Due Diligence: Doing Your Homework

*O*kay, so you've a signed contract — now what? Well, we highly suggest that you get busy figuring out if the property is a good, bad, or average deal and whether you want to buy it. A signed contract usually contains a clause, called a *due diligence clause,* that allows you to check out the property for free for a period of time, usually 30 to 60 days. Let's face it, sometimes sellers and owners stretch the truth about their properties when it comes down to how much money they bring in, their monthly expenses, their prior repairs, the future repairs needed, and how well the properties have been operating. Luckily, the due diligence clause allows you the chance to do your homework and discover the nitty-gritty on a property so that you can make an informed decision on whether to buy or not.

In this chapter, you find out how to perform due diligence, what tools you need to do a good job, how to manage the whole process, what safeguards you need to protect yourself while under contract, what paperwork you need to verify, what to watch out for when you inspect the property, what to do if you find problems (and you will), and plenty more.

What Is Due Diligence?

Due diligence is the process of "doing your homework" on the property that you're thinking about buying as an investment. It's the process of checking, double-checking, and confirming any important information that was used to determine whether the property is a good, average, or bad deal.

Proper due diligence takes persistence and weeks to accomplish. And remember that due diligence isn't used as an excuse to back out of a deal; it's primarily a means to protect you financially and legally. In your typical purchase contract, you find a clause that says either "due diligence period" or "inspection period." What property items you'll be able to inspect and how many days of due diligence you have are stated in that contract clause as well.

During this time, you want to verify many different pieces of information, including the following:

- ✔ Rents, leases, and any other income
- ✔ Any and all expenses related to the property
- ✔ Any defects in the physical condition of the property's interior and exterior
- ✔ Possible environmental problems on or surrounding the property
- ✔ Building code violations
- ✔ Any service and vendor contracts
- ✔ Existing warranties
- ✔ Local police reports
- ✔ Any liens placed against the property, such as loans, back taxes, or judgments or anything else that stands in the way of transferring ownership

If, after digging into all this information, you find something wrong with the property, you should go back to the owner and renegotiate.

There's usually no charge for you to perform due diligence, but you'll likely have to hire either a professional inspection company or an accountant (or maybe both), and this expense can run several thousands of dollars. But before you spend any money, we suggest that you follow the tips in the later section, "The First Things You Need to Do."

Proper due diligence enables you to uncover potential problems with the property (or as we call them, "elephants underneath the carpet") before the deal is closed. These potential problems can be very costly and can quickly turn a good deal into a bad one. Any experienced real estate investor knows and understands the importance of completing due diligence tasks.

Making due diligence a team effort

In due diligence, you're the detective. You want the truth and nothing but the truth. And think about it: Detectives that solve cases usually have the best team of specialists to help them obtain information to build their cases. So it is with you, the investor, to build your case for the purchase of a property.

Due diligence can be broken up into three main specialized parts: physical, financial, and legal. We explain each of these parts in the following sections. And later in this chapter, we give you a detailed due diligence checklist that breaks out each specialized physical, financial, and legal task.

We suggest that you hire third-party companies and specialists to do the more complex tasks in your due diligence. In fact, you can hire companies that complete the entire due diligence process for you. Or you can hire the different specialists individually.

Physical inspection

For the physical part of due diligence, where you actually walk around and inspect outside and inside the property, you should hire a professional inspection company. We believe that the physical part is the most important of the three because these types of mistakes are the most costly to correct and are the most damaging to the property's long-term value.

The best way to find a property inspection specialist is through a referral by an individual or a company that has experience with this part of due diligence. You can also ask your local commercial real estate broker for a referral. If you have no luck there, try entering the key word "commercial property inspection" into your favorite search engine. A handful of sites is bound to pop up.

Financial investigation

When it comes to the financial part of due diligence, we suggest that you be advised by an accountant who has real estate investment experience. Accountants aren't all created equal. Qualify your accountant by verifying that he or she has commercial real estate accounting experience, not just single-family residence accounting experience or general business experience. In some cases, the investment you're considering may be one of your largest. Would you trust the advice of an accountant with little experience in one of your largest financial endeavors ever? We didn't think so. By far, the best way to find a qualified accountant is by referral. Call on one of your investment buddies and check out who they're using. And again, make sure that referral has commercial real estate accounting experience.

Here's a tip to stand on: Don't believe any financial information or books and records given to you by the seller. Double-check everything. Turn things inside out and hold each financial statement up to the light for proof. We recommend that you get deeply involved in the financial aspect of due diligence. Verify each dollar of income reportedly coming in and verify every dollar reportedly spent on the property by reviewing actual billing receipts.

Legal inquiries

The legal side of due diligence is most often done by an attorney and aided by a reputable title/escrow company. These folks look at things such as the following:

- Defects on the title and survey
- Any potential environmental problems
- Proper and improper special uses and encroachments that affect the property

These are all potential deal killers.

Be sure to have tenant leases thoroughly reviewed and audited. After all, when you buy a commercial property, you're essentially buying the leases and the property comes for free! Contracts imposed on the property, such as employment contracts, service contracts, and warranties, all need to be scoured over with a fine-toothed comb.

All attorneys are not created equal. Attorneys specialize in areas of law. Please don't have a family law attorney represent you when purchasing a large shopping center. That's like having a foot doctor give you an eye examination. Instead, hire a real estate attorney. The real estate attorney that you hire doesn't have to be local, but needs to be familiar with laws in the state in which the property is located.

As for selecting a title/escrow company, that's a little easier than selecting an attorney. Title and escrow companies, by law, are neutral parties; they can neither favor the buyer nor the seller (nor the real estate agent). If you enter the key words "commercial title companies" into your favorite search engine, you'll get a few to start with. We find it advantageous, however, to work with an office that's local and is familiar with closing practices of that city or state.

Getting to the truth about due diligence

Performing due diligence is about attaining and understanding the truth about an investment. It's more than just reviewing documents and walking through a building. Here are some truths to consider as you go through the due diligence process:

✓ **Due diligence is about more than just completing certain tasks (which we outline in the preceding section).** It's also about having the right attitude. Having a Type A personality (detailed, driven, and aggressive) during the due diligence process is a good thing.

✓ **Due diligence will cost you several thousands of dollars and could take several weeks (if not months) to thoroughly complete.** Don't be afraid to spend plenty of time and money during the due diligence process. Doing so allows you to really study the property and alleviate the butterflies that you get when jumping into a new deal. And remember the old adage that says, "It's expensive being cheap."

✓ **Deal making is glamorous; due diligence is not (so don't expect it to be).** Because due diligence is no fun and doesn't always feel like a worthwhile activity, you may have to force yourself to bite the bullet and dive in. Literally every document concerning the property and its operation must be examined. Rolling up your sleeves and staying up to the wee hours studying property statements is the norm — not the exception — when doing a thorough job with your due diligence.

✓ **Due diligence actually starts in contract negotiations.** Make sure the seller knows upfront exactly what you're going to be asking for. Otherwise, we guarantee that you'll have trouble getting to the closing table. Check out the due diligence checklists we provide in the later section, "Creating Checklists for Effective Due Diligence," and you'll understand why.

✓ **The seller is guilty until proven innocent.** Don't believe seller-provided information right off the bat. You have to cross-check it first. We would like to believe that most sellers are honest like us. But some sellers tell stories and stretch the truth.

✓ **Never use the inspection company that a seller recommends.** An inspector that gets business from the seller's side will likely be biased and will see to it that the deal goes through (that way they can get further referrals). The moral of this story? Find and hire your own property inspector.

✓ **Be wary of any tactic the seller uses to avoid inspections.** The seller may want to hurry you through your due diligence process. If the seller is pushing you, it may mean that he or she wants you to overlook something. Take your time. Also, don't fall for the seller-provided inspection report. Sellers use this as a way of "saving you time and money." Yeah right.

✓ **Be present.** What's the opposite of being present? Absent! The consequences of being absent during your due diligence are not good. Free yourself of distractions, late-night parties, and whatever else may keep you from focusing on due diligence tasks. One mistake can cost you dearly, so be in the moment and be present.

The First Things You Need to Do

In the case of commercial real estate investing, it's okay to shoot first and ask questions later. Before you go spending your time, money, and energy on due diligence, you first need to get control of the property by putting it under contract. Because thorough due diligence costs several thousands of dollars and involves many days of hard work, make sure it's a deal worth going after. The following are some things you can do *after* you're under contract but *before* you spend any money or significant amount of time:

- ✔ Scope out the property
- ✔ Get a title commitment
- ✔ Crunch the numbers

After you complete the tasks outlined in the next three sections, it's gut-check time. Based on the information you obtained from your initial check of the property, answer this question: "Is this deal still good enough for me to pull the trigger, get out my checkbook, and continue on to the next phase of due diligence? Or should I pull the plug and go back to the drawing board?"

Scope out the property

When we say scope out the property, we mean just that: Go look at it. Examine it to make sure that the property isn't falling down or in an undesirable location. In some cases, sellers may require you to put the property under contract before you can perform this run-through. These sellers may simply want you to show that you're serious about the property by putting your best foot forward with a contract. That's okay.

A more efficient way of checking out the property is to have a previously selected property manager perform a drive-by and report a "thumbs up" or "thumbs down" on the property's physical appearance and location. This way, you're using what we call "O.P.T." (other people's time).

Get a title commitment

After giving the property a quick once-over, present the property address to a title company and order a *title commitment*. Before issuing a title commitment, the title company will do a title search. This search will disclose if there are any ownership issues with the property such as liens, encumbrances, easements, access problems, or restrictions. Court orders, divorce decrees, and probate issues may even pop up. With the title commitment, you're making sure that the sellers can actually convey the property's title to you.

If the title commitment problems can't be overcome in a timely manner, you may want to pass and move on. Otherwise you may run into problems later on in the process. For example, with one of our apartment deals, we got to the day of closing only to find out that the seller wasn't authorized, by himself, to sell the property. He tried to sell the property without his family's approval.

Look at the property's numbers

Here's the fun part, where you get to see how much money you'll be making. The seller will provide you with the property's numbers on which you can base your investment objectives. Due diligence here will enable you to see if the property makes a ton of money or is a money pit. Crunch the property's numbers with the seller-provided income and expense statements (after they have been cross-checked, of course).

If you're just starting out, we suggest that you get the advice of a real-estate-savvy accountant. Or find someone who has been successful and is willing to show you the basics of number crunching. However, after going through a few deal evaluations, you can probably do this number crunching yourself. Chapter 3 tells you how the experts do it.

When you ask for the seller-provided info, you may get the following two sets of statements:

✔ **Proforma:** Most *proformas* will list the income, expenses, and cash flows. You should be quite leery of proforma statements because these are simply the seller's best-case scenario or "perfect-world" financial projections. These projections are often unattainable in the real world. In other words, these reports may stretch the truth a bit to shed a positive light on the property.

✔ **Actuals:** The *actuals* are the statements that you really want. This information tells how the property actually performed or is performing today. To get a true property performance indication, complete your financial evaluation based on these figures.

If the proforma evaluation is far from your actuals evaluation, ask yourself this question: "Can you reasonably bridge the gap between the two?" In other words, do you have the vision or capability to take the property from where it is today to where you would like it to be in the future. If the answer is yes, go ahead and proceed. If the answer is no, you may want to do further research and decide whether to continue.

Creating Checklists for Effective Due Diligence

In the earlier section, "Making due diligence a team effort," we break down the due diligence process into three specialized parts: physical, financial, and legal. In this section, we discuss the must-dos of each aspect.

The simple checklists that we provide in this section are going to be your very best friends when it comes to not missing a single step of your due diligence. The items on each of these checklists are to be asked for and obtained within your due diligence period. And remember that sometimes the most obvious things are the easiest to overlook. So don't just read through the lists and think that you can remember everything on them. Instead, use the lists we've created as a template for your own checklists that you can tweak and improve over time. Check them off as you complete them. We know from personal experience that you become sharper, if not more at ease with due diligence, as you examine more properties.

Physical due diligence checklist

When investors think of physical due diligence, they often only think of an actual walk-through of the property with an inspector. Walk-throughs are a part of physical due diligence, but only a tiny part of it. You have quite a bit more to think about and do. For instance, ask the seller for the following items:

- ✔ **Site plans and specifications:** This group of documents includes all the construction documents, building plans and schematics, floor plans, and land use documents. These docs provide a road map of the property's inspection for when it was first built, how it was built, and for what purpose.

- ✔ **Photos of the property:** Photos of the exteriors, interiors, and the surrounding land and structures should be taken. Digital aerial photography is widely available and aids in showing the placement of property within neighborhoods and in between highways. Having photos allows you to start putting together the pieces of the puzzle and knowing what's in your vicinity can only help you in determining what obstacles you may be facing now or in the future.

- ✔ **A structural inspection:** Inspect the walls, roofs, and foundation, and make sure there are implements in place for earthquake safety. This inspection counts as the exterior and interior inspection. Allow a professional inspection company to guide you in this inspection.

✓ **An interior systems inspection:** Inspect the interior of the property for wear and tear, including items such as doors, doorways, windows, and weatherproofing. Then inquire about the age of the roof, any building code violations, government compliance (such as physically impaired requirements), and site improvements.

✓ **A mechanical and electrical inspection:** Make sure that every mechanical and electrical system is inspected. Such systems include heating, ventilation, air conditioning, plumbing systems, and all electrical power systems and controls.

✓ **A list of capital improvements performed:** Obtain receipts and documentation of any capital improvements that were made over the last five years. This documentation will help with the clarity and assessment of the physical inspection and allow you to project when parts of the property may need repairing or replacement within the next few years.

✓ **A pest inspection:** On some types of buildings, an inspection for pests, such as termites, may take place. Most apartment buildings have this inspection done as part of a lender requirement. If termites are found, the building is chemically treated.

Hiring inspection professionals to undertake the engineering side of your due diligence requires some skill in itself. Hire from reputable companies that specifically inspect the type of property that you're considering. Check out their licenses and certifications as well. Get recent references from the company and look for happy and satisfied customers. You should interview at least three companies and ask for sample inspection reports from each before making a final decision. Enter "commercial property inspection" into your favorite search engine to find a few companies to get started.

Financial due diligence checklist

The financial aspect of due diligence focuses on why you're buying the property. It helps ensure that you make money by verifying the seller records of the property's financial performance. To perform thorough financial due diligence, be sure to obtain the following from the seller:

✓ **Income and expense statements:** These statements show what the seller has collected in income from the tenants as well as what the owner spent in operating the property. You should at least obtain annual income and expense statements for the past three years. Also, get all of last year's monthly profit and loss statements and review the balance sheet for the past three years. These documents can be obtained from the seller. After you have all this information, complete your financial evaluation on the property to ensure that it produces the type of returns that you expect or desire.

- **Rent rolls:** A *rent roll* is essentially an attendance sheet for all the tenants. It displays the tenant name, unit space or square footage, amount of rent paid, move-in date, lease expiration date, and security deposit. When you have the rent roll, verify the rent amounts with those given on the lease agreements. Also, add the total income of the rent rolls and compare that with the income and expense statements amount. If you notice any discrepancy here, put up a red flag and investigate further.

- **Tax returns:** Obtain the property's tax returns for the past three years. If there's a single owner, you only need to review that return. If the property is operating under a partnership agreement, you need to get every partner's tax return for the property. Add up all the income and expenses shown on the tax returns. These numbers should match those from the property's income and expense statements. If they don't, ask yourself a question: "Which would you believe? The IRS tax returns or documents that the seller produced?" Crunch your numbers again and see if the property still produces an acceptable return for you. If the discrepancy is in your favor, that's okay, but if it's not, you may have to renegotiate the terms of the deal to meet your objectives.

- **Lease agreements:** A lease agreement can be a complex legal document. We suggest allowing someone who has expertise with that type of lease do the auditing for you. If all the leases are the same, such as in an apartment building, have an attorney review the first few to make sure that they're valid. For every other category of commercial real estate, we suggest verifying the leases by using an *estoppel letter*. This letter confirms that the lease is true and accurate and is the only agreement that's made between the tenant and the owner.

  Pay strict attention to the expiration of the leases of each tenant. What if a good portion of the tenant leases expire next year? Do you have the financial strength to carry the property while it's being filled up again (which can take several months)? For the tenants that have upcoming expirations, do you have the right to renegotiate the leases even if you aren't the owner yet?

- **Utility bills:** Obtain the past two years' worth of actual utility bills for the property. These bills include electricity, gas, water, sewer, trash, telephone, cable, and Internet service bills. Compare the totals of each utility category to the seller's total given on the expense statements. If the numbers don't match, put up a red flag. Reevaluate the numbers and see if the deal is still worth making.

- **Property tax bills:** Obtain the past two years' worth of property tax bills. Verify the amounts with those given on the seller's expense statements. Again, if the numbers don't match, put up a red flag and investigate the discrepancy. Reevaluate to see if it's still a good deal. Also, call the tax assessor's office and find out how the property will be reassessed and how often after you become the owner. It's a good idea to figure this property tax increase into your expense calculations as the new owner. It also varies from state to state. For example, in California the tax rate is roughly 1 percent of the sales price, but in Texas, the tax rate is about 3 percent of 80 percent of the purchase price.

Getting assistance for the financial portion of your due diligence is critical if you're just starting out. As mentioned in the checklist, leases can be complex and they're extremely important. So, you can't be lax. Until your skill level increases at deciphering income and expense statements, we recommend having a more experienced investor or mentor review them along with you. And as for hiring an accountant to review any of the financial documents and tax plan for you, make sure he or she has relevant real estate work experience. A lot of times we discover that being book smart in crunching numbers and tax planning just doesn't cut it. Pay for good experienced help. You owe it to yourself and to your future with this property.

Legal due diligence checklist

Legal due diligence can be pretty extensive, and checking on the items in this list takes a team effort. But, from experience, we know that it gets easier as you go. When you begin to understand the importance of the many documents and the ins and outs of each, you can cut to the chase really quickly. Here are the items that you need to ask the seller for:

✔ **An environmental inspection:** The environmental inspection most often used is called a Phase I Environment Site Assessment. During this inspection, the inspector explores the past use of the property and the surrounding area, looking for onsite and offsite environmental problems and liabilities. Phase I reports cost in the thousands of dollars and are very involved timewise, so plan ahead if you want one or if the lender requires one. Keep in mind that every seller won't necessarily have one lying around either.

This inspection can help answer questions like these: Does the property contain any hazardous materials? Is the property close to any endangered or protected animals or wildlife? Has asbestos been used in any of the construction? Is there an underground storage tank? These environmental issues are expensive to cure and can be potential deal-killers, so be sure to schedule an inspection if needed.

Make sure you really take the time to read the environmental report. If you don't understand everything, find someone who does and ask him or her to explain it to you. Just because the lender is willing to loan you money doesn't mean that the property is free of potential problems. Find out now or pay later.

✔ **A survey and title inspection:** With this inspection, a title company can verify the property size and that the title report has the same description as the survey. With this inspection you'll also review any liens, judgements, easements, or encroachments on the property that could drastically affect its value and use. If the title has any issues, it must be delivered "clear" by the seller before closing.

✔ **An inspection for building code violations:** Some of the most common violations you might run into with this inspection include unauthorized construction, non-city approved improvements, or substandard electrical or plumbing work. If a violation occurs after a building is built, it may be considered a *nonconforming use* and is considered to be grandfathered in. Going to the city's planning department's records will clarify this.

✔ **The zoning code:** Every property has a specific use permitted. For example, a property can be zoned as residential or commercial. So, you need to review the city's zoning ordinances to make sure that the property's use complies with what it's legally zoned for. If it's used illegally, the property can be shut down. Lenders will not loan on a property that's being used for what it's not permitted for.

✔ **The insurance policy:** The property's insurance policy can be a treasure trove of information if you can get the claim history. The property's claim history will tell you if the property has experienced fires, flooding, lapses of coverage, or policy cancellations.

In addition to getting a copy of the policy from the seller, it's highly recommended to begin your own search for insurance quotes. It can take up to 30 days in some cases just to get quotes. Get at least three, and then shop and compare. Don't be afraid to negotiate for the best pricing either, as commercial insurance is a very competitive business.

✔ **Licenses, permits, or certificates:** Some of these items are necessary to operate a business, so make sure to get them from the seller. If not, check with the city to see what's required to operate your property. Oftentimes you're required to post business licenses, permits, or certificates. Make sure that you're proactive in notification of new ownership to avoid hefty fines.

✔ **Service and vendor contracts:** Review all service and vendor contracts to make sure that you have the right to choose or discontinue the services. These types of services may include, among others, maintenance, landscaping, or laundry. Review and keep records of any equipment warranties and guarantees.

✔ **A personal property inventory:** Obtain a list of all personal property items, such as equipment, tools, computers, furniture, supplies, and appliances that are to remain behind with you, the new owner. Document all these personal items in writing or consider them gone. In most transactions, you use a Bill of Sale form to document the personal property items to be transferred. Check your purchase contract as to how personal items are accounted for and transferred.

> ✓ **Any police reports:** Determine past and current police reports by call-
> ing the local police department. Review the type and frequency of calls
> to the property. Know what's going on before you buy. You should even
> do some of you own police work. Show up to the property at 9:00 p.m. and
> park your car in a spot with good visibility until 11:00 p.m. Observe what
> goes on for those 2 hours. Is it peaceful? Is it party time? Did you witness
> possible illegal activities? Know what's going on before you buy.

Managing the Whole Process

The due diligence process is a long one. It's like a tape measure that shows
stuff to do every inch along the way. Sometimes it can seem like it will never
end, and so it requires good time management and a great deal of focus. But
don't worry, when broken down into bite-sized pieces, the process can be
managed successfully. As for organizing the whole process, we recommend
that you organize yourself much like a project manager would — with project
task lists and project deadlines. We guide you in the following sections.

Opening an escrow

Let's say that you have a signed contract and you're ready to begin due diligence. The first thing you should do is open an escrow with an escrow company or title company. (In some states, an attorney will act as the escrow
holder and perform those duties as well.) The escrow company is an unbi-
ased and neutral party to the buyer and seller. It handles all the money and
relevant documents that pertain to the transferring of ownership and closing
of the deal.

To open an escrow, simply go to an escrow company (or an attorney that performs escrow services) and request that it handle your escrow for a property
sale. And don't forget to bring along your signed purchase contract. When
choosing a company to handle your escrow, ask a real estate broker or a
fellow investor for a referral. A seasoned and hardworking escrow officer can
make all the difference when things get hairy, especially during the last few
days of closing.

After you're set with your new escrow, you can expect the escrow company
to do the following tasks:

> ✓ **Prepare preliminary escrow instructions:** The escrow instructions tell
> the escrow officer what to do in order to close the deal with the buyer
> and seller.

Mistakes on the preliminary (and even on the final) escrow instructions are common, so check the math and check for accurate figures. You'll see many fees listed — understand each one. If you don't understand something, stop and question it.

- **Receive the earnest money deposit:** An *earnest money deposit,* which is also called a good-faith deposit, shows your intent to purchase the property in good faith.

- **Order a preliminary title report:** This report tells you who the actual owner of the property is as well as what loans or liens are currently on the property.

- **Order a certified survey:** This survey is ordered from a surveyor who goes to the property to verify the legal street address, its block, lot number, and subdivision.

- **Request payoffs from lenders or lien holders:** The lenders and lien holders will request payoffs so they can see how much is owed and to whom to pay off at closing.

- **Receive all reports pertaining to the closing:** The type of reports that the escrow company receives includes termite reports and deferred maintenance inspection reports.

- **Record the title to the buyer after closing:** This is the actual transfer of legal ownership from the seller to the buyer.

- **Finalize and close the escrow:** To finalize the escrow, the company pays off all loans and liens, delivers all closing documents, and pays the seller his proceeds.

Getting a preliminary title report

The title of a property is the legal evidence of rightful ownership and is given in the form of a deed. So, after you have an opened escrow, the escrow or title company officer will order you a preliminary title report. Preliminary reports are thorough evaluations of public records of the ownership chain or "chain of title" for the property. They're based on information that has been gathered by the title company over the course of many years. You can expect to receive your report within three to five days. In this report, you find the general history of the property's ownership as well as loans, liens, or encumbrances placed on the property by other parties.

If the title has problems, it can't be transferred to you at closing. In other words, each title problem must be resolved by the seller and escrow company before closing can occur. So it's important to order and review the preliminary title report early, because the owner then has time to take care of the problems while everyone works toward closing.

Here are some red flags to watch for on your preliminary title reports:

- ✔ **Improper authorization:** Make sure that the person who signed on the contract is authorized to do so and has the ability to actually sell the property to you. In other words, make sure that the person who signed the contract is the owner or can verify that he represents the owner.

- ✔ **Unsatisfied mortgages:** An unsatisfied mortgage can occur either because the seller has an outstanding mortgage on the property or because a previous mortgage wasn't recorded properly as paid and then removed.

- ✔ **Property tax liens:** If a seller is behind on paying the property real estate taxes, we suggest you arrange for the owner to pay them before closing or renegotiate the terms of the deal, especially if you end up paying for them.

- ✔ **Mechanics liens:** In the case of mechanics liens, the seller didn't pay for contractor services performed on the property, so the contractor has a lien against the property for payment.

- ✔ **Judgment liens:** If you come across a judgment lien, you know that the seller has been a party to a lawsuit and a judgment has been awarded against him and the property.

- ✔ **Leases:** Here the seller is under a lease agreement for either equipment or a service and the property is used as security for the lease.

- ✔ **Easements:** If the seller has easements, that means he's granted the right to use another person's land for a stated purpose, such as the right to travel across a property owned by another person. This becomes a red flag to new owners who thought they could use the property exclusively for themselves.

Don't get too worried about having to be an expert at reading preliminary reports. Your escrow officer and real estate attorney can pick up on the red flags. Your main task is to follow up with the seller to get these red flags addressed within the due diligence time period.

The preliminary title report then becomes the final title report, on which title insurance is based. _Title insurance_ is an insurance policy that covers the title of a property if for any reason problems appear on your title after closing.

The buyer has the right to approve or disapprove the preliminary title report and back out of the deal unless the seller can provide a clean title by eliminating certain exceptions to the title before closing. But the buyer will only have a short period of time, as stated in the purchase contract, during which to act on the preliminary title report. So it's extremely important for a buyer to carefully review a preliminary title report immediately and to take appropriate action if any red flags appear.

Keeping an eye on contingencies

A key component to your purchase contract's due diligence process and to protecting yourself while under contract is the *contingency clause*. This clause is also sometimes called a "subject to" or "escape" clause. Basically, these clauses make your purchase of the property contingent upon something happening.

For example, most purchases are contingent upon the buyer inspecting the property and approving of its condition prior to closing. Another example may be that the purchase is contingent upon the buyer getting approved for a loan for the property. In both cases, if the buyer doesn't like the condition of the property or can't get approved for a loan, she may back out of the deal.

That's the good side of contingencies — the side that protects you, the buyer. Here's the flip side, however: Purchase contracts state how much time you have to perform due diligence duties. The amount of time usually ranges between 30 to 45 days. If you fail to perform those duties or don't reply to the seller concerning those items within the time period, you automatically waive your rights to those contingencies and they're considered "removed" from the purchase contract. After the contingencies are removed, the earnest money you put into the escrow becomes nonrefundable and belongs to the seller if you back out of the deal. So be sure that you pay strict attention to every contingency clause and its time periods during due diligence. Negligence can cost you thousands of dollars and a mean headache.

Check out these commonly used contingencies:

- ✔ **Financing contingency:** This contingency makes your purchase contingent upon getting financing for the property. Usually the contract states that you have 5 to 10 days to apply for financing through a lender, and then you have a total of 30 to 45 days to get approved for a loan. If you get approved for financing within the contingency time period, you simply contact the seller in writing that you have been approved for financing and that you're hereby removing this contingency from the contract.

  After you waive this contingency, your earnest deposit becomes nonrefundable. So, if you don't get approved or can't find acceptable financing, make sure that you notify the seller within your contingency time period so you can get out of the deal and have your earnest money returned to you.

- ✔ **Inspection contingency:** Usually this contingency involves two inspections: a physical inspection of the property and a financial and business inspection of the property's books and records. For the physical inspection, you basically hire a professional inspection company to walk the property and report to you on the overall condition of the property. During the financial and business inspection you review, among other things, income/expense statements, leases, rent rolls, and service contracts. And typically you have 30 days to complete this contingency. Again, if your results tell you that you should get out of the deal, do so within the contingency time period so that you get your earnest money returned.

✔ **Title contingency:** This contingency, which usually has a due diligence time period of 7 to 14 days, allows you to make sure that the title is cleaned up before closing. For example, let's say that a seller was behind in her property tax payments and also failed to pay her contractor for some roof work that was completed. Both parties can file a lien against the property to "cloud" the title and stop the closing from happening until both parties are paid.

✔ **Appraisal contingency:** This contingency can help you get out of a bind where there are differences in appraisal and purchase price amounts. For example, if the lender says that the property is only worth or has been appraised for $750,000, but your purchase price is $1,000,000, you have a problem. You're coming up $250,000 short. You have three choices here. Take $250,000 from your own pocket for the difference. Ouch! Ask the seller to reduce the price by $250,000. Good luck there. Or, finally, you can make the deal contingent upon the property appraising for no less than the purchase price. If the lender's appraisal comes up short, this contingency allows you to get out of the deal.

Here are a few tips on managing and using your contingencies like a pro:

✔ Keeping track of contingency periods and expiration dates can be trying, so try posting a contingency log on your office wall. That way, all the dates are visible and trackable with a blink of an eye. This is especially helpful if you, like your humble authors, make several offers at once on many different properties. Also consider setting up reminders for contingency and expiration dates on your computer's desktop scheduler.

✔ If you find yourself running out of due diligence time in one of the contingencies, it's okay to ask the seller in writing for a time extension. Usually, the seller will grant you more time if you can show good intent toward removing the contingency. However, don't wait for the last day of due diligence to ask for a time extension on a contingency. Doing so leaves you in a weak and vulnerable negotiating position.

✔ Adding too many contingencies to your contract weakens your offer in the eyes of the seller. It makes you look like you want to get out before you even get in.

✔ A neat (and sneaky!) way to lengthen your due diligence time period for a contingency is to change the word "calendar days" to "business days." For example, a contingency clause may state that you have 30 calendar days to perform your duties. But if you change the wording to 30 business days, you have just bought yourself 10 extra days of due diligence (because business days don't include Saturdays and Sundays).

You Found Problems, What Now?

Okay, so you've done your due diligence and you have all the reports in front of you. Take a deep breath because this is the part where surprises always seem to come up. The first question to ask yourself is this: "If I already owned the property would this be a big problem or a minor annoyance?" The biggest challenge all of us face is that we're too close to the deal. We can't keep ourselves from thinking about the thousands or millions of dollars we're going to make on the property we haven't even bought yet.

To figure out how to proceed, as best as you can, (and it isn't going to be easy to do), answer this question: "If I first saw this deal today, and knowing everything that I know at this point, how much would the property be worth to me?"

You basically have two options here (which if you read carefully are actually three):

✔ You may have such a great deal that the problems you've uncovered really don't matter. The property is still worth buying even if you can't or don't want to renegotiate further with the seller. (We tend to renegotiate anyway. But then again we think it's fun!)

✔ If the problems are serious enough that your current price and terms with the seller no longer make sense, you can walk away from the deal or renegotiate.

If you're already going to walk away from a deal, why not take the extra step of renegotiating with the seller — just for the fun of it. The worst case is that you end up losing the deal (which you've already decided to walk away from anyway).

After reviewing the reports, you probably have a good idea of what the issues are with the property. So make a list of every issue that you need to address. Rate those items on a scale from 1 to 10. Assume that 10 is a property issue that definitely scares the living daylights out of you and affects the value of the property, that 5 is an issue that can be taken care of at a later date with minimal cost, and that 1 is an issue that you can say "oh well" to. After rating the issues, present your prioritized findings to the seller and start renegotiating.

Renegotiating with the seller

At this point, you've probably had the property under contract for 60 days or longer. During that time the seller has likely been thinking and hoping (even though he knows you can still get out of the deal) that the deal goes through. This situation tends to work in your favor as the buyer, especially if you remember that there are plenty more deals out there for you if this one doesn't work out. And hopefully the seller is thinking about the chunk of money that he's going to get or the next commercial investment property that he wants to buy.

Here's a quick script showing the best way to explain to the seller that you need a lower price:

> *Mr. Seller, any other buyer who comes in and finds out about this property problem [insert your issue here] is going to want to reduce the price at least as much as I'm asking for, and possibly more. Rather than taking all that time to find another buyer who's just going to make the same reasonable request that I am, why don't we save everyone time and money by agreeing to the same price that you'd end up with anyway?*

Because you have contingency clauses in the purchase contract that allow you to walk away from a deal that doesn't make sense, you shouldn't feel obligated to follow through with a deal unless it's a big win for you. What this really means is that the time period after you've found problems is when the real negotiating begins. In fact, some of our mentoring students don't consider a property a "real deal" until they have renegotiated after the due diligence process is completed.

Making the final decision: Stay in or run away?

When you're making the final decision as to whether you want to buy a property or not, you want to talk with your mentor or other trusted investor friend. If the deal just doesn't make sense, make one last effort to renegotiate the deal. If that doesn't work, be willing to walk away. We have a saying that keeps us positive and always wanting more: "Every deal that I walk away from is just practice for the next deal."

Make sure that you leave the door open when you walk away. Let the seller know that the deal isn't a fit right now but that the future could bring a different situation. Some of our best deals have come from working with sellers who were mad at the previous buyers for not closing on the deal.

Sometime sellers actually make poor business decisions by not selling to you. Yes, that's right! So, the next time a deal doesn't work out and you walk away, wait 20 to 30 days and then go back to the seller to see if the deal is still around. He or she may be more motivated to negotiate now, especially if no other investor has made an offer since yours. In a few of our deals, we actually were able to get *better* deals than the original one by following up in this way.

Setting the sails for the closing date

As you work through all of your due diligence tasks, it's vitally important that you keep an eye on the day that your contract says you're supposed to close. If you know that you won't be able to complete all of your due diligence tasks or you have encountered problems and need more time to resolve them, you have a few choices to make. You have the following three options:

✔ You can back out of the deal, especially if the problems you encountered make this deal a bad one.

✔ You can get an extension of time to complete your due diligence.

✔ You can strive to complete your due diligence and set the sails for the closing date.

The goal here is to get to a point in giving this deal the green light or the red light. If you're giving the green light, assume the following:

✔ The physical inspection due diligence is complete.

✔ The financial inspection due diligence is complete.

✔ The legal inspection due diligence is complete.

✔ You have satisfied every contingency clause in the contract.

✔ You have completed your renegotiating with the seller and everything agreed on is in writing.

Chapter 7

Closing Your Deal

*T*his is the day you've been waiting for: The day when you finally get to close your deal! Whether this deal is your first or your tenth, every closing day is special. All those hours spent negotiating, late evenings spent crunching the numbers, long days spent walking through and assessing the property, sleepless nights spent waiting for loan approval, not to mention all that time spent dealing with your partners and handling investors — all of it is scheduled to come to an end on closing day. This day should be one of celebration and accomplishment. Ultimately, closing your deal is the beginning of a new investment in a great property, in your bright future, and in your hardworking team.

In this chapter, we tell you where getting to the closing table actually begins, we help you decide when to pull the trigger, and we help you identify when a deal is a real deal. We also help you dodge those inevitable delays in closing. Finally, we explain what's involved in taking legal ownership and what crucial steps you need to take immediately after closing.

Residential closing versus commercial closing

Q: What's the difference between closing on a single-family residence and closing on an 80,000-square-foot shopping center?

A: Very little. If you've closed on a house, you're familiar with the nuts and bolts of closing your first commercial property. The basics of a residential closing — such as opening an escrow account, handling deposits, dealing with closing costs, obtaining title insurance, transferring titles, and moving buyer and seller monies — also take place with the closing of a commercial property.

The Anatomy of a Close

In order to really understand how a deal gets closed and how you get the keys or a big check at the end, it helps to look at what a commercial deal entails — from the signing of the contract to the closing day. The following big-picture view helps you get a handle on what takes place with the person making the offer, the escrow/title company, the lender, and the attorney:

1. **The buyer makes an offer to purchase and, if the seller likes the offer, the seller accepts and signs it.**

   Congratulations, you're officially under contract!

2. **The buyer opens escrow with an escrow/title company or attorney and sends in earnest money as a deposit to the escrow holder.**

3. **The buyer starts the financing process with his lender and sends necessary documents to the lender to qualify both the property and himself (and/or his partners).**

4. **The buyer does his due diligence (such as reviewing the property's financial statements and other property-related information as set forth in the contract) and does a physical inspection of the property.**

5. **The buyer examines the title and removes contract contingencies.**

6. **The buyer and seller satisfy any remaining obligations as set forth in the contract.**

7. **The buyer finalizes the loan with the lender by getting an official letter of commitment from the lender.**

8. **The buyer reviews the closing statement and finalizes any final closing instructions with the escrow company.**

9. **On closing day, the buyer signs the closing paperwork with the escrow company and makes a down payment.**

10. **The deed is recorded, monies are disbursed, and the buyer gets the keys.**

    Congratulations, your deal is closed!

Closing 101: The Basics of Closing a Deal

If you're brand new to buying and selling real estate, you probably have all kinds of questions regarding the critical stage of closing a deal. Not to worry: Where you have questions, we have answers. Read on.

What is an escrow and who is an escrow officer?

An *escrow* is a neutral, impartial third party that serves others (the buyer, the seller, the lender, the real estate agents, and the attorneys) in a property transfer. An escrow officer is the central point person throughout the closing process. Her duties include all the following:

- Clearing outstanding liens held against the property
- Disbursing monies to all parties
- Handling the in earnest deposit, the down payment, the loan documents, and the closing fees associated with the property transfer
- Minimizing the chance of fraud when the money and the property are transferred
- Obtaining payoff amounts of loans associated with the property
- Obtaining title insurance
- Ordering the title search and examination for the title report
- Preparing and issuing the final closing statements
- Recording the deed after all deal and legal obligations have been satisfied
- Returning signed loan documents to the lender

The escrow officer is also sometimes referred to as the *escrow holder, the title officer, the closing agent, the closer,* or the *settlement agent.* In the eastern half of the United States, attorneys are commonly used to close deals and they often act as the escrow company.

What is title insurance?

After you have legal title of the property, you're considered the owner. But what happens if the title came to you with a lien against it? What if the liens against the property total thousands of dollars? That's where title insurance comes into play.

Title insurance insures you against such things as liens, undiscovered liens, improper recording of deeds, and other things that could negatively affect the title. The protection period of the title insurance extends backward, which means that it insures you against losses from the past ownerships of the property. And the insurance is in effect as long as you own the property.

If the person you're buying the property from already has title insurance, you can't have the current owner transfer his title insurance to you, even if it's brand new. You have to buy new title insurance yourself. Who pays for the cost of title insurance, the buyer or seller, depends on what's customary for that city.

Some lenders give you a choice of whether to buy title insurance. We recommend that you buy title insurance even if you're *sure* there's nothing wrong with the title. Some title problems can be so bad that they can cause the title to be deemed "unmarketable." This kind of situation is exactly what title insurance protects you against. Some people think that if they paid cash for the property, they don't need title insurance. Just because you have a grant deed with your name on it doesn't mean that you have clear title.

Do I need an attorney for my closing?

All of our East Coast closings were completed through a real estate attorney. On the other hand, all of our West Coast closings were done by escrow/title companies. So whether you need an attorney for your closing depends on where your property is located. Look and see what's customary in your state or city by asking an experienced local real estate agent.

Attorneys commonly handle commercial real estate closings. And having the help of an attorney is advantageous, because so many things can go wrong during a closing. With all the complex language that's used in closing paperwork, an attorney can help you wade through it all.

When you hire an attorney to step into the shoes of an escrow company, the attorney will do the traditional escrow company duties, plus they'll also

- ✔ Coordinate the closing date and help keep the buyer and seller sides and the lender on track
- ✔ Help review all documents for accuracy
- ✔ Personally attend the closing
- ✔ Write up any needed contract amendments

Don't hire your family attorney to close your commercial deal; instead, hire a real estate attorney. Real estate attorneys, unlike general attorneys, are trained to understand zoning, real estate laws, bylaws, environmental restrictions, tax issues, and entity issues, among many other small legal — but important — details that can come back and bite you on the rear end.

Do closing costs differ in commercial real estate?

Folks always want to know whether closing costs are an issue in commercial real estate (just as they are in residential real estate). The quick answer is yes. And there are two main reasons for this:

- ✔ **Typically, commercial real estate deals are bigger than residential single-family deals.** The fees that are calculated based on the size of the deal, such as title insurance, are larger in scale.

- ✔ **Commercial closing involves a few more third-party costs that are larger.** For example, a new survey generated on a single-family property could cost a few hundred dollars and is only necessary if a lender requires it. For a large apartment complex, however, the survey could cost tens of thousands of dollars, and commercial lenders nearly *always* require a survey. Similarly, an appraisal report for a single-family home will cost around $500 and take one week to deliver, but for a shopping center, it may easily cost $5,000 and typically take three to four weeks to deliver.

As a general rule, you can expect commercial closing costs to be about 3 percent of the purchase price. This figure is just a quick estimate, though. If you want a more specific figure, call an escrow company and ask for the typical closing costs incurred. *Note:* You'll have to give the escrow company a purchase price, or at least an estimation of a purchase price, in order to receive an estimate.

Closing costs are *always* negotiable and never etched in stone. Some closing costs may be customary for the city you're in, but they're still negotiable. Closing costs are usually spelled out in the purchase contract; if not, they should be. Negotiate with the seller by having him pick up some or most of the costs, or have the seller credit you a certain dollar amount at the time of closing for closing costs. The only nonnegotiable closing costs pertain to the loan (such as transfer taxes and recording fees).

Is it better to close at the end or beginning of the month?

If we had to name one real estate question that starts bar fights, this is it! We don't want to start a fight, so we make the case for both and let you decide which one is most beneficial for your unique situation.

For the most part, the choice comes down to reducing your out-of-pocket costs at closing by paying less in prepaid interest on your mortgage. Or you can get credited for almost a full month's rent at closing. Your choice.

Here's an example to guide you: If you close on June 2, for example, you prepay 28 days of interest to cover June's interest. In this case, you have to bring more cash to the closing than if you had closed three days earlier, on May 31. And your first mortgage payment would be due August 1. Your August 1 payment includes the interest payment for July. On the other hand, you would also receive 28 days of rent (prorated and credited to you at closing), plus all of July's rent without having to make a mortgage payment in July.

If you close on June 29 instead, you prepay one day of interest to cover the last day in June. Your first mortgage payment would be due August 1. Your August 1 payment includes the interest payment for July. The main benefit is that you minimized out-of-pocket costs at closing. Of course, this helps investors who are coming close to running out of cash after closing. You would also receive July's rental income without having to make a mortgage payment in July.

Being able to collect one month's rent and not having to pay the month's mortgage is a big benefit to either scenario. You'll be able to start off with a sizable savings account or have the capital to do immediate improvements, if needed.

How long does it take to close a commercial deal?

We knew you were going to ask how long a closing takes. Patience is a virtue, my friend! Here's our answer: Commercial closings can take two to three times longer than residential closings. And the simple reason is this: You're buying not only a piece of real estate but, in the lender's eyes, a business as well. The lender is lending you millions of dollars to operate an income-generating entity. Therefore, the amount of time and effort everyone spends to confirm the integrity of the "business" takes an average of two months, maybe longer on more complicated deals.

Chapter 6 is dedicated to the subject of due diligence and gives you the scope of work that's required in a commercial closing. As you'll see, it takes time to get your arm around the whole deal. So give yourself a minimum of 45 to 60 days to close your deal.

The Big Picture Show: Questions to Ask Yourself Before You Pull the Trigger

Before you start ordering everyone around to finalize their duties and obligations for closing, you need to do a couple of things. Start by thinking about the big picture. Why are you purchasing this property? How will you make a profit? Is your plan doable? Do others agree with your plan? Most likely, you had big plans and dreams for this deal when it first went under contract — is that dream still alive this late in the game? Odds are, you found out some things — some good and some bad. Are you ready and willing to pull the trigger? The following sections can help you decide.

What are my exit strategies?

An *exit strategy* is your means of earning a profit on your property. You can have an exit strategy to sell, or you can have an exit strategy to refinance. Or you may just want to hold the property for a monthly income. Even though they're all different, all exit strategies get your profit out of the property. Know your exit strategies inside and out, but hold them loosely. Don't force one just to make yourself right.

Have an exit strategy designed *before* you make an offer on a property. And before you close, come up with multiple exit strategies. Why? Because market conditions may change, loan parameters may be altered at the last minute, problems with the property's title may appear at the 11th hour, or your personal life may shift in some way. If you're stuck on only one exit strategy and you aren't flexible, any change in the deal's circumstances can kill the deal, even though it may still be a good opportunity.

Are my investment goals being met?

After spending, say, three months to get your newest deal headed toward a closing, do you stand a chance of meeting your investment goals? After months of due diligence and weeding out the good, the bad, and the ugly, does this deal still make you tons of money? Those are the million dollar questions, aren't they?

Because these questions are obviously worth a lot, don't take them lightly. Here are four safety checkpoints to consider:

- ✔ **What's your time frame?** From what you know now about this deal, is the time frame for your exit strategy still valid? Will you be able to execute your exit strategy quicker or will you have to delay it? If you delay it, how much longer will it be?

- ✔ **Is your profit what you expected?** Now that you've studied this deal inside and out, is the profit that you projected still there? Do you see an even greater potential? Do you see any hurdles on the road to cashing in?

- ✔ **Does your loan work?** A big part of understanding the big picture is knowing exactly what type of loan you're getting. You should know your monthly payment, interest rate, loan term in years, prepay penalty, and amortization period at this point.

✔ **Did your tax guy or gal approve?** Have you run your exit strategy scenarios by your tax advisor for any possible tax issues? Can she validate your strategies and give you a thumbs up?

If you can nod your head "yes" confidently to these four safety checkpoints, then what are you waiting for? Pull that trigger!

Sweating the Details before Signing on the Dotted Line

As the closing nears, you want to adopt a certain type of attitude — an attitude that may save you thousands of dollars in mistakes and miscalculations. So what's the attitude we're referring to? Being pesky! Question every figure on every document. Double-check any math. Don't assume anything. Take nothing for granted. Sweat the details. Being a pest will save you not only money, but precious time and headaches as well.

The title work

A title examiner will research the property's chain of title. The *chain of title* is the history of ownership going all the way back to the original owner. It shows an exact description of the property, dates of purchases, loans put on the property, liens, and encumbrances. The title examiner's primary goal is to ensure that the seller has clear title to the property before selling it. The examiner does the following:

✔ Looks for defects in the title, such as:

- Easements

- Delinquent taxes

- Judgment liens

- Mechanics liens

- Pending lawsuits

- Restrictions

- Tax liens

✔ Confirms the current owner and the property description

✔ Determines how the title company will issue title insurance

Defects make the title "unmarketable" and stop the seller from legally selling the property. So defects must be cleared from the title before the seller can sell the property. However, in some instances, the buyer may agree to move forward with exceptions to the title.

Have your real estate attorney review the title work; if it's found to be clouded in any way, work to get it cleared within the time constraints on the purchase contract.

A good commercial purchase contract will have a title contingency clause in it. This means that the title has to be delivered "clean" within a certain number of days, or the contract is null and void. Make sure your contract has this contingency.

The closing instructions and closing statement

Closing instructions are just that: written instructions for the escrow officer, explaining how the transaction will take place. The closing instructions specify who pays for what costs, who gets what disbursement (and when), and when the recording takes place. The instructions should also list all the conditions to be met prior to the closing (such as inspection report findings and work to be completed), items to be credited or prorated (such as rents, taxes, insurance, or repair credits), and the closing costs that the seller and buyer will be paying.

The *closing statement,* which is also known as a settlement statement, is legally referred to as a HUD-1 settlement statement. If you've purchased any kind of real estate before, you've seen a closing statement. It's the official form used to show all fees, charges, and commissions. It lists the final tally of what the buyer and seller are paying for, including the following:

- ✔ Appraisal fees
- ✔ Escrow fees
- ✔ Loan origination fees
- ✔ Loan payoff amounts
- ✔ Notary fees
- ✔ Premiums for hazard insurance and title insurance
- ✔ Prepaid interest
- ✔ Recording fees
- ✔ The principal of the new loan

> ✔ Transfer fees
>
> ✔ Various taxes

We fill you in on the closing statement in greater detail in the later section "What's on a closing statement?"

Ask to see and review the closing statement at least 48 hours before the closing. There is a 50/50 chance that the closing statement includes a mistake. The mistake could be a charge or credit not in your favor, something missed from the closing instructions, or just a plain old typo. That's why you want to see it early, rather than an hour before closing: You then have time to request that the mistake be fixed. And the more people who review the closing statement, the more mistakes you'll find. So have your attorney, your real estate agent, and your escrow officer study it. And don't forget to study it yourself.

The lender

The lender often is the bottleneck in getting to the closing table. After all, the lender has a lot of paperwork to go over and confirm. So it's your job to call the lender *every day* (we're not kidding!) a week before closing to keep him on track. You can also ask the lender if there's anything you can do or your attorney can do to help him stay on schedule.

Part of the lending process involves an underwriter who scrutinizes the property, the borrower, and the loan. Before the underwriter can give the thumbs up, he'll ask at least a thousand questions (a slight exaggeration) beyond the information that you provided weeks ago. When the underwriter has a good understanding of everything, he issues "conditions under which a loan can be made" on the property. The conditions to be satisfied may be further cause for delay. Some typical conditions to close may be having certain repairs completed on the property or for the property to be at least 85 percent occupied for at least three months. Make sure your lender jumps on meeting the conditions and that you make every effort to get them completed as well.

Closing Day: What to Expect

The first thing to expect on closing day is for the sun to rise and for it to be a beautiful day! If you've prepared properly, the day of closing should be another wonderful day in the life of a commercial real estate investor (even if it happens to be raining).

If you follow the safety checkpoints in this section, you'll be in pretty good shape on closing day. But as luck always has it, at least one or two things are bound to fall through the cracks. If you count on these minor glitches to happen, you won't be stressed when they do.

On closing day, expect to sign a stack of documents, and expect small mistakes and miscalculations to take place. Expect that some of the documents will need to be reprinted. And expect to spend at least an hour signing and reverifying all the paperwork.

What's on a closing statement?

The document at the center of the transaction of closing is the final closing statement, which is also called the HUD-1 settlement statement. The closing statement is important, so in this section we explain what's on it.

The closing statement for commercial real estate is the same form that's used in closing residential single-family home transactions. It lays out the charges in getting the transaction closed (see the earlier section "The closing instructions and closing statement" for a list of charges you might see on a closing statement). The amounts shown on the HUD-1 statement are final when agreed on and signed by the buyer and seller.

Sections A through I: General Information

Sections A through I show basic information, such as the loan type, the borrower information, the lender information, the location of the property, the closing office information, and the close date.

Section J: Summary of Borrower's Transaction

Section J shows the borrower's specific settlement charges. Here's how the section is broken up:

- ✔ **Line 100: Gross Amount Due from Borrower:** Line 120 totals the cumulative total of the purchase price plus total closing fees.

- ✔ **Line 200: Amounts Paid By or on Behalf of Borrower:** Line 220 totals the amount needed to satisfy the transaction, such as the new loan, the earnest deposit, the down payment, taxes, and any amounts the seller owes the buyer (such as for repairs and so on).

- ✔ **Line 300: Cash at Settlement from/to Borrower:** Line 303 totals the amount of cash the buyer needs to bring to the closing.

Section K: Summary of Seller's Transaction

This section shows the total amount due to the seller. Here's what the one line number in this section looks like:

Line 400: Gross Amount Due to Seller: Line 420 totals the purchase price plus any adjustments for prepaid taxes or unpaid taxes.

Section L: Settlement Charges

Section L basically breaks down all the fees and amounts, referred to as "settlement charges," that the buyer and seller are responsible for. Here's how the section is broken up:

- ✔ **Line 700: Total Sales/Broker's Commission Based on Price:** The commission charged by the real estate broker for services

- ✔ **Line 800: Items Payable in Connection with Loan:** The loan origination fee, any discount points paid to reduce the mortgage rate, the appraisal fee, the credit report fee, and the application fee for mortgage insurance

- ✔ **Line 900: Items Required by Lender to Be Paid in Advance:** The interest on the loan for the period before the first monthly payment, and the initial mortgage insurance and hazard insurance premiums for 12 months

- ✔ **Line 1000: Reserves Deposited with Lender:** Escrow items that the lender holds to cover future expenses, such as property taxes and annual assessments

- ✔ **Line 1100: Title Charges:** Costs of changing ownership of the property, such as the settlement or closing fee, title examination fee, and attorney's fee

- ✔ **Line 1200: Government Recording and Transfer Charges:** City, county, and state taxes or stamps needed to transfer ownership

- ✔ **Line 1300: Additional Settlement Charges:** Surveys and inspections (for pests and lead-based paint, for example)

- ✔ **Line 1400: Total Settlement Charges:** Sum total of all the previously listed fees

The amount listed in the buyer's (or borrower's) column should be identical to the amount listed as "settlement charges to borrower" (line 103), while the amount in the seller's column should be the same as the "settlement charges to seller" (line 502).

What exactly will I be signing?

The exact documents you have to sign depend on the state in which you're purchasing the property and the type of loan that you're getting. But here's a list of typical documents you can expect to sign:

- ✔ **HUD-1 settlement statement:** This is the document we explain in detail in the preceding section. It's basically your final tally on what's transferring dollarwise between the buyer and the seller and what each side is responsible for in fees, charges, and taxes.

- ✔ **Mortgage and deed of trust:** You'll be signing the originals. Many other loan documents are included in this package as well.

- **Escrow instruction from lender:** This form states that you acknowledge meeting the conditions for the loan before the deed of trust can be recorded. These instructions also explain to the escrow officer the sequence and timing of the recording.

- **Truth-in-lending disclosure statement:** This is a federal disclosure statement that gives the buyer information about the costs of the credit so that the buyer may compare those costs with those of other loan programs or lenders.

- **Various affidavits:** The lender may have the seller sign an affidavit stating that she has completed certain property repairs and improvements prior to closing.

- **Fire insurance coverage:** The lender may require the buyer to sign an acknowledgment form stating that she'll maintain fire insurance on the property and that, if she doesn't, the lender will enforce its own insurance coverage and bill the buyer for it.

- **Bill of sale:** This is a receipt for the personal property items that the seller is leaving behind for the buyer to take possession of.

- **Grant deed:** Only the seller's signature is needed here.

What if you can't be at the signing on closing day? No problem at all. Life happens, right? All you have to do is get a power of attorney signed for the person who can step into your place. That person can be your attorney, a family member, a partner, or someone else you trust. A power of attorney is simple to get from an attorney, or you can ask the escrow officer to set one up for the signee.

Don't be worried if a few documents have to be redrawn while you're signing. Small errors can and do happen at this stage of the closing. It will only take a few minutes to recompute and reprint.

What should I do before signing?

Whether you're the buyer or the seller, you can ask yourself some key questions before the signing, just to make sure that you haven't overlooked anything critical. Before you sign your name on all those documents, be sure to run through the checklist in the following sections — the first section is for buyers, and the second is for sellers.

Buyer safety checkpoints before signing

As you walk into the closer's office, ask questions, get answers, and confirm for yourself the following:

✔ Is the loan amount correct? Are the terms equal to what the lender promised in writing? Check the interest rate, the amortization period, the loan term, the monthly payment amount, the prepay penalty structure, and the due date.

✔ Did the lender set up an impound account for taxes and insurance payments, if necessary? Or are you responsible for paying them directly?

✔ Did the lender set up a maintenance reserves account for the property?

✔ Were there any additional credits assigned to you, such as credit repairs or closing costs credits?

✔ If the seller has promised to perform any physical repairs on the property, are those completed?

✔ Are the rent prorations and tenant security deposit credit amounts correct?

✔ Did you agree to have any personal property be assigned to you? Is there a bill of sale?

✔ Are the purchase price, names, and dates on the deed correct?

✔ Are the fee amounts the same that you agreed to?

✔ Is the title clear? Have all title defects been cured? Ask for proof.

✔ Are your down payment and closing costs ready to be wire transferred to the escrow company? Do you have the bank wiring information? Give yourself a full 24 hours or more for the wire to take place from sender to receiver.

If you're using a 1031 tax-deferred exchange (see Chapter 16) and you plan to close on the last day allowed (the 180th day), watch out for delayed wire transfers. Wire transfers have been known to hang up closings for two to three days. If you go beyond the 180th day on your 1031 exchange, you're out of luck and haven't met the strict exchange rules, and that means you'll pay capital gains taxes. Ouch! Plan ahead.

✔ At the bottom of the settlement statement is an amount that you have to bring to the table to close the deal — do you agree with this amount?

✔ Have you decided how you're going to hold title as a form of ownership? Limited liability company (LLC)? Limited partnership (LP)? If so, bring this to the attention of the escrow officer as soon as possible for processing.

Seller safety checkpoints before signing

As you walk into the closer's office, ask questions, get answers, and confirm for yourself the following:

✔ Is the purchase price correct?

✔ If you're giving credits, are the amounts what you agreed on?

✔ Are the loan payoff amounts correct?

✔ If you're assigning any personal property to the buyer, is the bill of sale filled out correctly?

✔ Are the security deposits, credit amounts, and rent prorations correct?

✔ At the bottom of the settlement statement is the amount of profit — does it match your expectations? If not, why?

When am I officially closed?

After the closing escrow officer has the signed loan documents, after the buyer has paid all monies due, after the buyer and seller have signed off on the final escrow closing instructions, and after choosing a specific date to record the deeds, then a closing may happen — or, escrow may close (as it's said in the industry).

Next, the escrow officer will get a check from the buyer's lender to pay off the seller's loan. From there, the escrow officer will send the lender the closing loan documents. When the lender receives and approves of the completeness of the loan documents, the lender will give the go-ahead to release the buyer's payment to pay off the seller's loan and give the okay for the deed to be recorded. Ownership is hereby transferred to you! You're now officially closed!

To top off the deal, we like to send the closing escrow officer a bouquet of flowers or a small gift, whichever is appropriate. And we send thank-you cards to the lender's staff, our attorney, and anyone else who has played a part in making the closing happen. These small gestures display class and appreciation on your part and acknowledge their hard work and dedication.

Taking Legal Ownership

Well before the closing, you're going to have to make a decision on how to hold title of your property. In other words, what form of ownership are you going to use? The decision you make has huge legal, tax, asset protection, and exit-strategy consequences. Talk to your attorney, as well as your tax advisor, before making such a decision.

When we first started investing, we had both of our advisors talk with each other to provide us with the soundest advice because there was so much to consider the first time. If we held title in our personal names, we'd be exposing ourselves to potential liability and privacy concerns. If we held title as a corporation, we could face double taxation. How would we take title if we had two investment partners?

So what do you do? Look at holding title the same way you would look at buying a new car:

✔ You buy a car that fits your lifestyle. So, choose a form of ownership that fits the goals and nature of the investment.

✔ You buy a car that makes sense financially. So, choose a form of ownership that your tax advisor says gives you the best tax advantages.

✔ You buy a car based on your research in terms of safety and costs to maintain. So, choose a form of ownership that provides you the greatest privacy and most efficient asset protection.

Legal forms of ownership, called *entities,* are typically held in the following entity types:

✔ Sole proprietorship

✔ Corporation

✔ Limited liability company (LLC)

✔ Partnerships (such as limited partnership or general partnership)

✔ Trust

✔ Individual retirement account (IRA)

We cover this topic in much more detail in Chapter 12.

You're the Boss Now: What Next?

Okay, you own the property now, you have a handful of keys, and you've actually pinched yourself to make sure you aren't dreaming. You're actually the owner! So what do you do next?

Start by taking a deep breath, because this is when the real work begins. You're going to have to take steps to ensure a smooth takeover of the property. Getting off to a fast and well-organized start makes all the difference in the world in the first few months of ownership.

We divide this process into four stages. In Stage 1, you get basic property information from the previous owner and previous/current property management company. Stage 2 entails getting the takeover teams prepared for landing. Stage 3 involves securing the property on the takeover date. And Stage 4 is the debriefing stage, where you report on the findings from Stage 3.

Stage 1: Assess the situation

When in this stage, you're on an information and fact-gathering mission. Your goal is to get any and all relevant property information that you can from the previous owner, manager, and/or property management company. After you've gathered all this information, you're going to set up all the various business systems for the property. Here are some guidelines to follow:

✔ Before takeover, contact the previous owner/manager to get:

- Contact information regarding the onsite manager

- The number of units or spaces

- A detailed rent roll that includes rent/lease amounts and square footage of the units or space

✔ Get the name of the new owner and a signed management agreement with the agreed-on compensation.

✔ List the current employees on the payroll with duties, salaries, part-time/full-time status, and tenure.

✔ Obtain copies of the year-end and current month's income and expense statement.

✔ Get a copy of the operating budget, if there is one.

✔ Find out whether the bank account is set up.

✔ Determine whether there are any legal actions pending against the property.

✔ Make sure you and your new management agree on the type of financial reporting that's expected.

✔ Get copies of the property's service contracts, list of vendors, and existing warranties.

✔ Get insurance information. Is it paid from impounds or will it be paid directly when due?

✔ Get property tax information. Is it paid from impounds or will it be paid directly when due?

Stage 2: Assemble the team

At this stage of the game, you have to decide who's on your team. Here's what to do:

✔ "Shop the property" by visiting it with a "secret shopper." What you're doing here is sending in one person to act as if they're interested in renting. That person will then report to management on these things:

- How they were greeted?
- Was the sales pitch good or weak?
- Was the property being shown in impeccable condition?
- How was the visit tracked?

✔ Assemble the takeover team and assign duties to the onsite manager, the leasing agent, the assistant manager, and the maintenance staff.

Stage 3: Secure the site

This stage is similar to sending in the Navy Seal team to secure the beach for the ensuing takeover. Your management team will be in place implementing their staff and operations on the property. Here are some specific steps you need to take:

✔ Secure the cash at the property, secure the office, change the locks on property, and reset passwords of any type.

✔ Secure all master keys from any existing personnel.

✔ Have the senior-level manager introduce all new staff to the existing staff and conduct individual meetings with all staff to discuss duties, salaries, and so on.

✔ Set up management and maintenance staff work schedules.

✔ Start advertising for leasing and hiring, if necessary.

✔ Input rent roll and tenant profiles in your computer.

✔ Prepare the delinquent tenant rents report.

✔ Set up the operating budget.

✔ Do a complete personal property inventory.

✔ Change over the utilities — electric, water, trash, gas, phone, cable — to the new ownership.

Stage 4: Use the info that you discovered

After the storm has calmed, at this stage you're in a position to debrief and set goals moving forward. Make sure that you take care of these duties:

✔ Have the senior-level manager prepare a status report of the takeover of the project by the new ownership.

✔ List any major work needed on the property — whether those improvements are regarding physical property or personnel.

Part III

Funding Your Deals: Financing and Lending

The 5th Wave   By Rich Tennant

"Let's see if we can determine your capacity for assuming risk. Now, how familiar are you with snake handling?"

In this part . . .

In Chapter 8 of this part, you find out how to get approved for conventional financing. Or, if you like the idea of getting creative and buying commercial real estate without using any of your own cash or credit, check out Chapter 9, which presents some ideas for more creative financing. We close this part by helping you discover the secrets of raising private capital and putting together profitable partnerships.

Chapter 8

Conventional Financing Options

. . . .

. . . .

*O*kay, so here's a riddle for you: Out of all the tasks when buying commercial property, which takes the longest? And what requires you to file enough paper documents to kill a forest full of trees? Give up? Here's the answer: getting a loan for your deal!

Well, it isn't really that bad, but sometimes it can sure feel like it. Getting your property financed involves jumping through quite a few hoops. For example, you have to figure out how much income the property brings in, what the quality is of the people or companies that make up the income, how well the property supports the mortgage, what condition the property is in, whether the property appraises for the price that you're buying it for, and, how financially strong the buyer or buyers are.

Deciding on the type of financing you need or want depends on many factors as well. One of the most important deciding factors is your exit strategy. Simply put, your exit strategy is why you're buying the property in the first place. For example, if you plan to buy and keep a retail center for a long time, you might consider a long-term permanent loan with a fixed interest rate. Or if you want to buy an apartment building for a short period of time, you may want to consider a loan that has a low upfront cost and low interest rate.

We show you what lenders like and don't like in a deal, what makes interest rates tick, and last, what the lending process looks like — from A to Z. At this rate, you may know more than Mr. Lender wants you to know! Read on my friends.

The Commercial Lending Process in a Nutshell

There's a lot to wade through in the world of commercial lending, but developing an understanding of the processes and jargon definitely pays off as you begin making decisions in what could possibly be your biggest financial investment ever.

Personally, we like to look at the whole lending process as we would look at making online travel reservations. For example, you start off by researching what's out there. Then you dig deeper and narrow your wants and needs. From there, you start making decisions and booking hotels and flights. And at last, it's time to reap the rewards of your efforts. There's a process to everything we humans do — even when it comes to lending.

The more you understand and go through a process, the easier it becomes because the steps start to become much more predictable. This goes for the lending process, too. So, in this section, we give you the information that you need put the pieces of the lender puzzle together. The first puzzle piece is an inside look at what the lender goes through in getting you to the closing table, and the second is the power of momentum.

Seeing the process through your lender's eyes

There's one question that I (coauthor Peter Harris) always had early on in my career: How does the lending process work? What does it look like from A to Z? After I understood the process, I was in a much better position to understand what goes on at every step of the way. For instance, being familiar with the process helped me help my lender get to the closing table quicker, and sometimes it helped alleviate some of the frustrations I had with my lender or with the whole process in general. I'm sure it'll help you as well.

The following is an overview on what your typical lender goes through to get you to the closing table. As you read through these steps, make two assumptions: that you're under contract to purchase the property and that your due diligence period has started:

- ✔ **Preapproval begins:** At this stage, you send your lender three years of income and expense property statements, a current rent roll, and exterior and interior pictures of the property. Do this as quickly as possible so that the lender can preapprove the property before you get too deep into it.

✔ **Borrower investigation:** The lender sends you a loan application to qualify you financially, including your creditworthiness.

✔ **Lender-ordered reports:** After the property is preapproved and you're deemed creditworthy, the lender orders an *appraisal report* to be conducted for the property. This report ensures that your purchase price matches with the lender's value of the property. In most cases, the borrower pays for the appraisal upfront and not at closing.

The lender also orders a *termite report*. The termite report is performed on the property to inspect for pest infestation. If the inspector does find an infestation, this issue must be addressed before closing by either party.

✔ **Miscellaneous lender duties:** At this point, many things jump into action on the lender's side, including a review of property tax returns, proof of funds to close, a survey review, a title review, a borrower entity review, a proposed property management review, and so on.

✔ **Underwriting:** The entire file is reviewed by a loan assistant or document checker (these folks review the file for accuracy, missing signatures, or missing or incomplete documents), and then it goes into the underwriting phase. *Underwriting* is when the lender thoroughly examines the debt coverage ratio and the loan-to-value ratio. During underwriting, the lender also performs a market and operational analysis of the property. (Debt coverage ratio, loan-to-value ratio, and simple analysis are covered in the later section called "How Lenders Evaluate Properties.")

✔ **Loan approval:** After underwriting is complete, the file goes up against a loan approval committee. The committee can either approve or disapprove your loan. If it approves the loan, you move into the closing phase, but if you aren't approved, you can find out why, meet their conditions, and reapply. Or you can try a different lender.

✔ **The closing:** The lender, the borrower, and the closing/escrow company all work together to finalize a closing of the transaction. Final loan documents are drawn and sent to the closing/escrow company. After you review and sign the final loan documents, the transfer of the property takes place.

Keeping things moving without incident

The biggest deal-killer we had early on in our career was a lack of momentum. We lost many good deals because we failed to keep the deal's momentum going strong. We were under the assumption that the lender and our real estate agent would follow up on our deal and make sure that everyone was doing what he or she should be doing. Boy, were we wrong! Following up was our responsibility. And guess what? That's your responsibility as the investor, too. Here's some sage advice: If you don't keep your deal's momentum going by staying on top of your lender, your deal will probably fizzle out because of the lack of follow-through, either by you or your lender.

Here are some ways of keeping your deal momentum going strong:

- **Pay close attention to the financing contingency period in the purchase contract.** The *financing contingency period* is a period of days written in the contract in which you have to get your loan approved. For instance, if you have 45 days to get an approval for financing or to back out, make sure that your lender is well aware of this limitation and that by day 45 the lender can give you a letter stating that he will provide a loan for the property. If you wait until after the contingency period, your chances of getting a loan have dropped significantly because it probably means the lender is having trouble with the property itself — either financially, or because of its poor physical condition, or maybe it's a creditworthiness issue.

- **Call your lender every day.** That's right, call every day. Be nice. Be polite. But hold him accountable to his promises and actions. The good lenders are busy — and they expect to be busy. So, tell him upfront that you plan to call frequently and that you expect timely updates as well.

- **Don't stand for seller delays.** Make it known to the seller that you'll back out of the deal if deliverable items (for example, documents for pre-qualifying property) are delayed. Or, tell the seller that you expect to be reimbursed with additional days of time equal to the number of days that the seller delayed.

- **Don't procrastinate.** If your lender or closing/escrow company asks you for a document, give it to him right away. Every day you procrastinate is one less day you have to deal with reaching your closing. And, believe us, you need all the days you can get. Plus, if you refuse to accept seller delays, you can't very well be late yourself!

- **Remember that no one cares more about closing your deal than you do.** All the lender has at stake is his pay. Similarly, the agent's commission is the only thing at stake for him. However, you have a lot more at stake if you don't close. For instance, you risk losing your earnest deposit money, hundreds of hours of time, and thousands of dollars spent on inspections and reports. And, to top it all off, your investment goals could be shattered. So keep on top of everything involved with the lending process. Remember: This is YOUR deal.

Differences between Commercial and Residential Lending

When it comes to real estate, sales are broken up into the two following categories:

- ✔ **Residential property:** From a lender's point of view, residential property is your personal residence, which is more than likely a single-family home. A property that contains two to four family dwelling units — duplexes, triplexes, or fourplexes — is also treated as residential.

- ✔ **Commercial property:** A commercial property, from a lender's point of view, is a property that contains five or more family dwelling units. Under this category, you can have a 5-unit apartment building or a 100-unit apartment building (or anything in between!).

  These are all considered commercial as well: office buildings, strip malls, warehouses, industrial buildings, mobile home parks, and raw land. A property that contains a mix of any number of residential units and commercial spaces is also considered commercial.

Obtaining a loan for a commercial property is similar to obtaining a loan for a residential property. For example, with both types of loans you have to apply for the loan and show that you have the capability of repaying the loan, you must be creditworthy, and you must provide a down payment of some sort. But, that's basically where the similarities end.

There are two main differences between commercial and residential lending. The first involves the property's merits and the second involves the down payment. We explain both in the following sections.

The property's merits matter more than the borrower's qualifications

Commercial lenders look at property in terms of its ability to produce income to support its expenses and mortgage. So, the lender qualifies the property in this way first. The borrower's qualifications are second on the totem pole.

This approach is quite the opposite when qualifying to purchase a residential property. In residential lending, the lender looks at the borrower first, and then the property second.

What this all means for you is that you can have horrible or no credit, but if you have a great income-producing commercial property under contract, you still have a superb chance of getting approved for a loan. Doesn't this make you smile?

The down payment requirement is higher

For a commercial property, the down payment requirement is typically 20 percent to 25 percent or more of the purchase price. It is rare for a commercial lender to finance a commercial property with a zero-down payment (as you might see in residential real estate). Because loans made on commercial properties are much larger than on residential properties, commercial lenders have stricter lending guidelines. So, because of the greater risks involved, commercial lenders want the borrower to invest money or equity in the property. This way, they share in some of the risks, or have some "skin in the game" as it is sometimes called.

When purchasing a single-family home, on the other hand, the down payments can fluctuate. It may be 20 percent or more of the purchase price or it may be as low as 0 percent. When the residential lender doesn't require a down payment, it means that the buyer has no equity in the property.

How Lenders Evaluate Properties

Commercial lenders are people of a different breed. (Think about it: They live and die making decisions based on Excel spreadsheets.) They look at properties from a different point of view than the rest of us investors. So, it's wise for you to understand where they're coming from when they reject your deal. In this section, we help you to understand them, and we show you how to put your best foot forward in getting your deal approved for the best loan.

In order to understand how lenders evaluate properties, you need to examine their three main deal prequalifiers — the property's income, the quality of the property, and the strength of the borrower.

Determining the property's income

Income is a vital ingredient to the lender's approval process. Not only must there be income, but there must also be enough income to satisfy paying the mortgage and property operating expenses. Lenders measure this in two ways as described in detail in the following sections: *debt coverage ratio* and *loan-to-value ratio*.

Debt coverage ratio

A lender's first checkpoint when determining a property's income is the *debt coverage ratio,* which is the ratio of net operating income to debt payments. This ratio basically answers these questions: Does the property bring in enough money to cover its mortgage or its debt? After paying all typical operating expenses, can the monthly income of the property adequately service the monthly debt payment on the property? Here's how the debt coverage ratio is calculated:

Debt coverage ratio = net operating income ÷ annual debt service

ANECDOTE

You never know until you try

What if you find a deal but don't have great credit or lots of capital to invest? Relax. Most of our Commercial Mentoring Program students felt the same way when they started. Consider Kim and Jose, who owned two single-family rental homes and were struggling to make ends meet because their rentals barely broke even. They decided to sell one of their rental homes and use the profits to purchase a well-built 61-unit apartment complex.

The challenge was that Jose is retired and Kim is your typical soccer mom who has been out of work for a couple of years. How in the world would they qualify to purchase a $2.2 million apartment complex? If it was a $2.2 million house there wouldn't have been a chance for

them to qualify for a loan in their current financial situation. But because it was a commercial property, getting the loan was possible. Jose and Kim had two positive things going for them:

- The apartment complex was well-run and cash flowed excellently.

- The current owner took excellent care of the property and it looked great inside and out.

These two key items caused the bank providing the loan to overlook Jose and Kim's weakness in personal finances. As we're writing this book, Jose and Kim are still retired, and the couple happily reports a cash flow of $96,000 per year from their apartment complex.

REMEMBER

Net operating income is the yearly gross income minus operating expenses. However, don't include any mortgage expenses in this number. *Annual debt service* is the annual mortgage payments or monthly mortgage payments multiplied by 12. So, for example, if you have a monthly payment of $6,000, the annual debt service is $6,000 × 12, which is $72,000.

Commercial lenders figure the debt coverage ratio because they require a minimum ratio to approve a property for a loan. Many lenders have debt coverage requirements that range from 1.1 to 1.35, but typically the minimum is 1.2. From the lender's perspective, the higher the debt coverage ratio, the more income that's available to cover the debt payments, which means less risk for her.

On the other hand, if the debt coverage ratio is less than 1, typically this means that there isn't enough net income to cover the debt payment. In this case, you have negative cash flow, meaning that someone will be responsible for digging deep in her pockets every month to cover the shortage in cash flow.

Here's an example showing how to calculate the debt coverage ratio: Say that a property generates a net operating income of $60,000 and the annual debt service is $50,000. If you divide the net operating income by the annual debt service, this gives you a debt coverage ratio of 1.2, which meets most lender criteria.

Loan-to-value ratio

The *loan-to-value ratio,* commonly referred to as LTV, is an important factor in the income of a property. A lender figures the loan-to-value ratio by comparing the appraised value of the property to the size of the loan that you're requesting. This ratio is a percentage:

Loan to value ratio = mortgage amount ÷ appraised value of property

Commercial properties are valued for the most part by their net operating incomes. The person who officially values the worth of the property for the lender is called an *appraiser.* Your goal is to have the appraiser value your property at least for the purchase price. Here's a quick example of how to figure the loan-to-value ratio:

75% = 600,000 ÷ 800,000

So, from this example, if the purchase price equaled the appraised value of $800,000, the down payment or equity in the property would be $200,000, or 25 percent of the purchase price. In other words, the lender will provide a loan for up to 75 percent of the appraised value of the property.

Typical loan-to-value ratios for the lenders are based on the income strength of the property and the financial strength of the buyer. For example, if the property has strong income and the buyers are strong financially, the loan-to-value ratio requirement would be higher, thus requiring a lower down payment from the lender. Similarly, if the property has weak income and the buyers aren't that strong financially, the loan-to-value ratio would be lower and would require a larger down payment from the lender.

A property that has a strong stream of income can help overcome a weak buyer or buyers. And vice versa; financially strong buyers can help overcome a weak property.

Revealing the quality of the property

Lenders take risks on properties they don't manage themselves, so how they deal with this is to lend on properties that are in reasonable physical and financial condition. They also look at the type of tenant in the building. Are they reliable payers, for example? Lenders go back in time and look at how the property has been performing because that's a good indication of how risky lending money is going to be. This all has to do with the quality of the property, and in this section, we touch on all the quality issues.

A lender looks at the following six specific areas when trying to determine the quality of a property:

✔ **Physical quality of the property:** The lender rates the property according to its present physical condition. For example, have you ever walked onto a property that you wanted to purchase and realized immediately that on a scale from 1 to 10, it was a negative 2? Your reaction was probably something like, "This property is not worth the amount that you want, Mrs. Seller. It's worth much less because of all the repairs and maintenance that are needed." Your lender rates property in much the same way.

✔ **Quality of the lease agreements:** Lenders determine the quality of the lease by looking at things such as lease renewal options, lease termination, the number of years that are on the lease, whether rent increases are possible, and whether the lease payments include property tax, insurance, and maintenance.

Some would say that when you purchase a commercial property what you're *really* purchasing are the leases and the property comes for free. Of course this is an exaggeration, but the point here is that if the leases are weak, the property is weak — at least in the lender's eyes.

✔ **Quality of the tenants:** Lenders rate the tenants of a property based on things such as the tenants' financial strength and how long they have been in business, just to name a few. If you were a lender, would you rather lend on a building whose tenant is Wal-Mart or would you rather lend on the building whose tenant is BJ's Used Discount Mattresses? As a lender, you have to decide which would be a high risk and which would be a sure bet. If your choice of a sure bet is Wal-Mart, you get a gold star!

✔ **Historical performance of the property:** We all have ups and downs in our personal finances, and properties are no different. So, lenders rate the quality of a property by how well it has been operating in the past. Usually a lender favors a property that has at least 12 months of stable operation. As you may have imagined, a rocky financial history can hurt a property's ability to get a loan. For instance, if an apartment building had income collection problems and now isn't operating to its potential, because the income is lowered, the value placed on the property would be lowered as well.

✔ **Property occupancy:** Do you recall the saying, "Build it and they will come?" Well, in the commercial real estate business, the saying is, "Build it, and then give them a reason to come." If your property isn't desirable for any reason, you probably have a history of vacant space. Lenders frown on vacancies. They look at the occupancy of a building as a desirability factor. In fact, typically lenders want to see a property at least 90 percent occupied. Lenders have this type of mind-set: "If the property stays full, it must be desirable, and if it's desirable the income will be consistent. I like the risk, so I'll make a loan on it."

✔ **Market occupancy:** Market occupancy is just as important as property occupancy. Say, for example, that you want a loan on an apartment building. In the neighborhood in which the property is located, every apartment building is currently 95 percent occupied, but the apartment building you want a loan on is 75 percent occupied. We don't suggest you try this, but if you do, the lender may require you to put up a higher down payment to make this a less risky deal for her. On the other hand, if the neighborhood occupancy has always been 75 percent, the lender may consider not loaning on the property due to a weak market for tenants to rent the available apartments.

✔ **Rental concessions:** This factor has to do with the quality of the market just like market occupancy. *Concessions* are incentives to the tenants to move in. These incentives rear their heads when the market is soft, and they're usually in the form of rental discounts. And if the lender sees that concessions are ongoing, she'll annualize the discounts and subtract them from the gross income, which will affect the loan amount approval. And you thought move-in specials were a good thing!

Assessing the strength of the borrower

Just like when you apply for a loan for a home, you have to apply in a similar way for a commercial loan. The commercial lender uses this application process to check out your financial strength.

While your financial strength as a borrower does come into play, remember that it is priority number three. Here are the financial items that your lender will check out:

✔ **Liquid assets:** The lender wants to determine your available cash, stocks, securities, 401(k), and individual retirement accounts (IRAs). What they're looking for is your ability to come up with cash in emergencies.

✔ **Credit score:** A credit score of 680 or higher puts you in the *A paper* class of loans available. The A paper category provides the best options and best loan terms. A score of less than 680 puts you in a lower class where the loans are a lot less attractive, including being more expensive to get into. Moral of this story: Pay your bills on time!

If you have poor credit, there's still hope for you to invest in commercial real estate. One way is to have a limited liability company (LLC) purchase the property. That way you can just own a part of the LLC. For example, you can start an LLC with a bunch of partners (with good credit) to invest with. Your poor credit will be overshadowed by the combined credit of the partners. For more information on LLCs, see Chapter 10.

✔ **Net worth:** Lenders like it when your net worth equals the size of your loan. The reason? Risk. Lenders feel it's a good risk when what you are worth equals what they themselves are putting at risk.

✔ **Real estate investing experience:** The number one cause of commercial loan default is investor inexperience. So, if you have no experience, get a partner who has some. Doing so will make you stronger and make you seem like less of a risk. To help you in your cause, you can also hire an experienced professional property management company to manage the property.

✔ **Money reserves:** Lenders want you to have a minimum of three months of loan payments in your savings account at the time of closing. They require this backup cash just to make sure that you didn't spend your last dime on purchasing the property.

If you have shortcomings in any of the previous areas, find a person with high net worth to be on your team. Lenders love it when a person who's worth a lot of money signs on the loan with you, just in case the property runs into trouble and needs cash to fix the problem. As an exchange, that high net worth person may want a percentage ownership, a fixed return, and/or a slice of the profits.

Getting Your Lender to Say "You're Approved!"

Some of our long-time investment buddies really believe that getting your commercial loan approved is like flipping a coin. They believe that getting their lender to say "you're approved" depends solely on what side the coin lands on. Even though we understand their concern a bit (it certainly does feel as if loan approval is a haphazard ordeal sometimes), we have to disagree. And here's why: We believe that, for the most part, you can control the loan approval process.

Throughout the years that we've been investing in commercial real estate, two things have consistently brought us success when working with commercial lenders. Here they are:

✔ We bring the lender a good property, and if it isn't a good property, we include a plan of action to get the property to the "good" level. (For more on getting a property in good shape, see Chapter 14.)

✔ We prepare ourselves and our team by compiling all the documentation that we need for the approval process. For example, when you choose a lender to work with, he'll request a list of specific items from you. The quicker you can get these items to him, the faster he can get started on qualifying your property's loan.

Because these tactics worked for us, we're assuming that they'll work for you too. So, focus on putting yourself and your team in the best light for the lender. Get the lender excited about you and your team and about guiding you on the road to loan approval. And don't forget to give him the appropriate information at the appropriate times. We explain all of this in the upcoming sections.

What's needed from you

To get started on your loan approval process, your lender will ask for some information concerning you (the borrower) and your finances. These documents need to be given to your lender as soon as you have a signed purchase contract in hand. These items from you set everything else into action and headed toward approval. Here's a list of things that the lender needs from you:

- ✔ **A completed commercial loan application:** You can get this document from your chosen lender.

- ✔ **Personal tax returns:** Your lender will likely want two previous years of your personal tax returns, including any schedules.

- ✔ **Schedule of real estate owned:** This schedule lists every piece of real estate that you own. You can generate this list on your own or have your CPA prepare it. On it, include the type of property, the address, when it was acquired, what you paid for it and what you guess it's worth today, loan information, gross income, and total expenses.

- ✔ **Escrow information:** Send your lender the contact information of the escrow/title company that will close the transaction. An attorney's office may handle the closing as well.

- ✔ **Type of ownership entity:** You need to provide your lender with the type of ownership method or entity that you plan on closing with: LLC, corporation, or LP. You can find information on how to choose the right entity for your deal in Chapter 12.

What's needed regarding the property

Besides needing info regarding you and your finances, your lender also needs certain items concerning the property itself. She uses these documents to start building a case of why this property is a good risk for the multimillion dollar loan that you're seeking. You need to get these items to her within five days after the purchase contract is signed. Here's a list of things that your lender will request from you:

- ✔ **Purchase contract:** A copy of the purchase contract (rather than the original) will do.

- ✔ **Operating statements:** Send statements for at least the two previous years as well as the current year-to-date operating financial statements for the property. There are two other names you might find these under: income and expense statements and profit and loss statements. If the property is brand new, you obviously won't have any historical data. In this case, you'll have to make up your own statements much like you would when building a budget of any sort.

- ✔ **Property rent roll:** A *property rent roll* is an "attendance list" of tenant info, such as name, rent amount, square footage, and start and end dates of the lease. You get this document from the seller.

- ✔ **All property leases and rental agreements:** Your lender needs copies of every current lease or rental agreement.

- ✔ **Preliminary title report of the property:** You can order this report from your escrow/title company or your closing attorney's office.

- ✔ **Six to 12 color photos of the property:** You can give your lender more pictures, but do make sure to include photos from the west, east, north, and south and from the street.

What lenders like in a deal

Lenders are people too, don't forget. They have feelings, and they have things that they like and get excited about just as the rest of us do. So, when lenders evaluate your deals, give them things that they can be excited about. Keep in mind that the good-deal points can actually sometimes overshadow some of the bad-deal points. Here are a few of those good-deal points that lenders really like to see:

- ✔ **Cash flow:** Properties that have positive cash flow are a lender's delight. Lenders like these properties because they have the extra oomph to overcome problems, such as your low credit score, being in a below-average neighborhood, or having overdue repair needs on the property. Remember the saying, "Cash is king," because it surely applies here!

- ✔ **A good purchase price:** Lenders like it when you buy low. When you buy low, your debt will be low, so your debt coverage ratio will be higher. The higher the debt coverage ratio, the wider the smile on your lender's face (we discuss debt coverage ratio earlier in this chapter).

- ✔ **Strong operating history:** Remember the feeling of bringing home a date that your parents actually liked? Well, if you bring a property to your lender that has been operating really well for the past two or three years (it has experienced stable or increasing income and low vacancy and has been maintained well), you can expect your lender to greet you with open arms — and an open wallet.

Commercial real estate is a business that's based on relationships. More deals and loan approvals are settled because of relationships than anything else. You need to approach the lender with integrity, respect, and honesty. Get the lender to like you by building a solid and friendly rapport as best you can.

What lenders don't like in a deal

Most lenders that we know work diligently to get loans approved as quickly as possible, but sometimes they're faced with roadblocks that can cause your loan to be declined. Many times, these roadblocks are especially frustrating for lenders because they're controllable problems. Here are the most common problems that lenders hate to face:

- ✔ **Insufficient financial records:** This problem usually occurs when the seller is unable to provide sufficient financial records of the property due to disorganization or unwillingness.

- ✔ **Discrepancies in the financial records:** For example, say that a seller provides an income/expense statement that shows that the property produced $250,000 in income for the year, but the property tax returns list the income as $200,000. Which document does the lender believe? And if the actual income is $50,000 less than what he thought it brought in, he'll probably wonder whether it's worth what he has already offered. Findings like this definitely aren't the way to get on your lender's good side.

- ✔ **Hidden deferred maintenance:** Lenders don't like to play hide-and-seek with the property's maintenance and repairs. If they sense that either party is playing this game, they'll begin suspecting every part of the process. And distrust isn't a characteristic that you want in a person who's responsible for lending you hundreds of thousands or millions of dollars — it can kill your deal very quickly.

So, in a nutshell, to keep yourself and your deal on the good side of the lender, make sure the documents that are asked for by the lender and sent by you are complete, accurate, and truthful.

Choosing the Best Loan for You

When choosing the best loan for your deal, it's a lot like going out to buy a new car. For instance, you probably go from dealership to dealership and brand to brand to narrow your choices as best you can. You may even do your shopping and comparisons on the Internet — that's okay, too. But sooner or later, you have to make a decision; you have to select which new car to buy.

Choosing the best loan for your deal involves the same types of actions and thoughts as buying that new car. First, you do your research on the different lenders that are out there. Then you determine the types of loans that may possibly suit your deal. Finally you decide on the type of loan that's best for the property based on why you're buying the property. And along the way, you need to get some understanding on how much the loan will cost you to get into, how much it costs to get out, and what determines the interest rates on your loan. We discuss all this and more in the following section.

Getting to know conventional lenders

First of all, what's a conventional lender? A *conventional lender* is a source of financing for your deal that's usually from a commercial bank, a savings and loan bank, an insurance company, a pension fund, a real estate investment trust, or a mortgage broker. The following list breaks down these conventional lenders and shows you what makes them tick:

- ✔ **Commercial banks:** These lenders like to lend locally. In their eyes, the closer to their front door, the better. You can often find these lenders acting as the financial backers of major neighborhood projects.

  Commercial banks are pretty conservative in their lending. They won't hesitate to ask for higher down payments and they have overall strict guidelines, including shorter loan terms. Believe it or not, it actually helps you if you have a checking account at the bank in which you apply.

- ✔ **Savings and loan banks:** Even though they may have branches across the nation or state, these banks like to lend locally. Their source of money used to lend out comes from customer deposits and this is what enables them to provide better rates than commercial banks. They have the capability to do everything in-house (for example, processing, appraisal, and closing), which can keep your out-of-pocket loan cost lower in comparison to a commercial bank. We've also found that these lenders allow you to leverage yourself a bit more. What we mean by this is that they're a little more flexible on down payment requirements and on making other exceptions to get the deal done, especially when it's a property that they have confidence in.

- ✔ **Mortgage brokers:** These guys take your file of information and, acting as middlemen, they shop it to their financing sources, such as other banks, mortgage bankers, insurance companies, real estate investment trusts, and maybe even pension funds. Like using any other type of broker, mortgage brokers can save you time and effort.

  Mortgage brokers and most mortgage bankers work strictly on commissions. So, if they don't close your loan, they don't get paid. On the other hand, an employee of a bank gets paid whether your loan closes or not. As you can see, it just makes sense to work with someone who's motivated to close your loan.

  Mortgage brokers and mortgage bankers are the most flexible, so you'll find interest-only payment programs, programs that require very little documentation, loans based on the market rents, and loans using a lower debt coverage ratio — all under one roof. It's one-stop shopping!

✔ **Mortgage bankers:** These lenders lend nationally and are know for favorable interest rates and sell "wholesale" to mortgage brokers. Most often they operate from a large financial institution's line of credit. They also quickly sell their loans after the close so they can lend out the same money again.

✔ **Insurance companies and pension funds:** These lenders like to lend only big money for long-term projects at very low rates. If you're a big player, shop here.

Besides only liking to lend out big dollars, the only other drawback to these lenders is that they move like snails in getting your loan approved and to closing.

✔ **Real estate investment trusts (REITs):** These lenders, which are known as REIT funds, are a cross between a savings and loan bank and the institutional lenders, such as an insurance company or pension fund. Because they often invest by using pension and retirement funds, they are extra cautious.

Understanding the available conventional loans

Many different types of conventional loans are available for the different types of commercial real estate. Here's a list of the most commonly used loan options and types:

✔ **Long-term loans:** These loans can go up to ten years in length at a fixed interest rate. If you don't plan on selling the property for a while, consider a long-term loan. These loans are typically amortized for 30 years.

Long-term loans have an early payoff penalty, which is called a *prepayment penalty* or *defeasance payment.* So, if you commit to a seven-year loan, but want to sell the property in two years, you'll be socked with a substantial penalty for doing so. (See the later section, "Knowing the costs of getting out of a loan," for more details on this early payoff penalty.)

✔ **Short-term loans:** These types of loans are usually up to three years in length and typically have lower interest rates than long-term loans. If your investing strategy calls for you to sell the property in three years or less, this may be the loan for you. These loans are amortized for less than 30 years in most cases.

✔ **Conduit loans:** These loans are good for properties that are stable and well established with solid tenants. Interest rates are usually low and fixed with long amortization periods. And remember that these loans can be nonrecourse. *Nonrecourse* means that the borrower isn't personally guaranteeing the loan. And not being liable for the loan just in case something goes wrong is good for investors.

✔ **U.S. government agency loans:** Believe it or not, about 20 percent of all commercial loans given in the United States are somehow tied to the government. For example, the Federal Housing Administration (FHA), Fannie Mae, and the Department of Housing and Development (HUD) are just a few types of government loans available. But keep in mind that these agencies aren't lenders, they're insurers. You must find a government-approved lender who's willing to grant this type of loan. These loans have some of the most favorable terms, such as lower down payments, longer loan terms, up to 40 years of amortization, and lower interest rates.

✔ **Construction loans:** These loans tell a story. They tell the story of how you plan to construct a property. If the story isn't a good one, the lender won't lend you the money. It's that simple. These loans are taken out to fund the building of a property to completion or until certain leasing percentages are met. With these loans you usually have a timed payout or a scheduled draw where funds are released for construction as you build. Interest-only payments and loan terms of only one to three years in length are normal.

✔ **Take-out loans:** A *takeout loan* is the loan that comes after your construction financing. It's a permanent loan that goes onto the property. It can be a long-term, short-term, conduit, or government loan.

✔ **Mezzanine loans:** These loans combine themselves with permanent or construction loans. Most banks won't exceed 80 percent loan-to-value, and so that's where these loans come in. They stack themselves, hence "mezzanine" on top to achieve loan-to-values as high as 90 percent financing. Large projects, such as skyscrapers and large shopping centers, which cost tens to hundreds of millions of dollars, use mezzanine financing.

One important characteristic of this type of loan is that it's secured not by a mortgage or deed of trust, but by holding a security agreement against the owner's stock in the LLC. If the owner defaults on the loan, the lender takes the stock that owns the building.

✔ **Bridge loans:** These loans are sometimes referred to as *gap financing* or *opportunity loans.* Short-term financing is used to bridge the gap between finding a permanent loan and actually closing on a permanent loan. These loans are useful in funding deals quickly, but they can be costly due to their effectiveness in allowing you to capitalize on a deal that you otherwise wouldn't have been able to.

✔ **Small Business Administration (SBA) loans:** If you plan to occupy at least 51 percent of the property yourself, check out an SBA loan. With these loans, a down payment that's as little as 10 percent is possible if you have a stable property. Another benefit is that the interest rates will be lower than a conventional loan. You can also use this type of loan as a construction loan if you plan to occupy at least 60 percent of the property. But remember that SBA loans aren't made by the Small Business Administration — it merely insures the loans. So, you have to go to an SBA-approved lender to actually receive the loan.

✔ **Stated income/no documentation loans:** If you have no job, but you have a home with equity and good credit, getting a loan for your commercial property is still possible. Stated income and no documentation loans (also called *no doc loans*) don't require borrowers to show proof of monthly income or income tax returns. However, the property must have a high cash flow and be in excellent condition. In the right conditions, 85 percent loan-to-value is possible.

✔ **Hard money loans:** If you have bad credit, had a recent bankruptcy, or the property needs to close in a few weeks, you can use a *hard money loan*. These lenders usually require a hefty down payment (35 percent or more), and have exceptionally high interest rates (12 percent to 18 percent), and three to ten points. However if you find a deal of a lifetime, have no time left on the clock, and need money yesterday, this may be the way to go.

Selecting a lender for your deal

Remember buying your first house? You had to choose a Realtor or broker to work with who could show you homes and educate you on the marketplace. You called a few and interviewed a few. Some called you back, some didn't. Some were really nice, but they just didn't have the experience you desired. Some had the experience, but your relationship didn't click. Choosing a lender is exactly the same. But don't worry. We have a few tips to get you started in selecting qualified lenders. Here they are, in no particular order:

✔ **Find out how much experience your lender has.** We prefer not to use a lender who's new to the business of commercial lending no matter what institution she works out of. Also, consider working with a lender outfit that focuses on commercial lending only. The lenders in these types of outfits have more focused experience than those who work in both residential and commercial lending.

✔ **Do your homework.** Although we appreciate the first lender that returns our phone call, we tend to avoid going with the very first one. We prefer to get several bids for our project. So, do some homework on each, making sure that they've been in the business for several years and are familiar with the type of property that you're buying. Ask for references as well.

✔ **Find out if he or she is your type.** No, this tip has nothing to do with dating. Instead, we mean that you should make sure that your lender has relevant experience in putting together loans and closing loans of your product type. If you're purchasing an apartment building, for example, it makes much more sense to use a lender who specializes in apartments rather than one who specializes in construction financing.

✔ **Determine what your prospective lender can and can't do.** Some lenders only lend locally and some lend in all 50 states. Some lend on apartments and retail properties, but don't lend on office buildings or warehouses. So, get a good idea of what you need and then ask questions to find out if your prospective lender has what it takes.

✔ **Remember that actions speak louder than words.** If a particular lender has the best rates and terms in town but is slow in returning your phone calls, doesn't answer your questions well, or is rude on occasion, she's telling you who she really is. Believe her! Just because she comes recommended or has a good product, her behavior is telling you how she'll treat you when you get farther along in the process. If she treats you not so great now, can you imagine what behavior will emerge when there's a bump in the road?

Deciding what you want out of your property

You can actually turn a good deal into a stinky deal by choosing the wrong type of loan for your property (see the earlier section, "Understanding the available conventional loans," for more on the different types of loans available). Taking the time to create a game plan for your property is critical because it allows you to determine what you want out of the property. And when you know what you want out of your property, you can decide what type of loan is appropriate. What you want out of your property or the reason you're buying the property is called your *exit strategy*.

We recommend that you ask yourself the following exit strategy questions before you begin searching for your loan. Asking yourself these questions and answering them thoughtfully and thoroughly will allow you to determine what types of loans you should consider and research further:

✔ Is this loan for a construction project or for a property that's already standing?

✔ What's my long-term or short-term investment strategy?

✔ Am I going to refinance at some point?

✔ How important is the interest rate to my strategy?

Share your answers with the lenders that you plan to interview so they can help you decide which type of loan is the best for your situation.

Determining how much the loan will cost you

Commercial real estate investing has fees everywhere you turn. If it were possible to charge a fee for breathing air in an office building, believe us, someone would do it. Fees on loans are no different. Lenders charge what they call *points* on the loan. For example, a one-point fee charge means that the fee will be one percentage point of the loan amount. The higher the risk and complication for the lender, the higher the points charged to the borrower. We've seen lenders charge up to six points in conventional loans.

Here's a quick example. Say you're borrowing $1 million to purchase a corner strip shopping center. The lender will typically charge you an origination fee of one point or 1 percent of $1 million. The fee would be $10,000.

Don't think you're out of the woods yet. You're sure to run into many other types of loan fees or out-of-pocket costs in order to close your deal successfully. Here are the most common ones:

- **Appraisal report fees:** Lenders often order appraisals to be performed on properties. These appraisals can cost from $1,500 to $5,000 or more, depending on the size and type of the property. If it's a land deal where construction is involved, fees can be thousands of dollars more because appraisers must make sure that the land can accommodate your building needs.

- **Environmental surveys and reports:** Lenders want to protect themselves if your property has any type of potential hazardous wastes in its immediate surroundings — for example, gas stations come to mind. So, to protect themselves, they order environmental inspections. A Phase I environmental inspection costs $1,500 to $4,000. If the building requires Phase II inspection, which is a higher level of testing, expect to pay $3,500 to $10,000.

- **Property inspection:** You can expect your lender to send out field inspectors to inspect your property's physical condition. During this inspection, the inspector will check roofs, the parking lot, the structure, and the interior. He'll also check for any pest infestations. Expect to pay around $500 for this inspection.

- **Due diligence:** Lenders often run credit and background checks to gauge your credit worthiness. This can cost several hundred to a few thousand dollars depending on how many signers are on the loan. This is just a part of the lender's due diligence on you.

- **Legal review:** To protect themselves, lenders often have their attorneys review in-depth items, such as loan documentation, entity formation, and exceptions and waivers, and title and survey reviews (just to name a few). The cost of this legal review ranges from $500 to $1,000 depending on the size and complexity of the deal.

✔ **Document preparation:** As you probably know, commercial real estate lenders get buried in paper on daily basis. So, they have staff members that review your deal from A to Z and prepare all of your documents for closing. This document preparation can take several days and costs range from $300 to $1,000.

✔ **Application and processing:** Don't forget the application fee! Lenders charge you for applying for the loan as well as for their time spent processing the loan. You can expect to pay from $50 to $2,000 in application and processing fees.

Don't be shocked at the closing table! As early in the process as possible, bug your lender for an estimate of your costs to close. Ask your commercial lender to give you a preapproval letter that lists and estimates the interest rate and all the loan expenses. If you don't, you may be shocked to find out that the cost to close your loan may be up to 2–3 percent of the loan amount. So be prepared to inquire about your closing costs and then budget appropriately.

You can negotiate lender fees. The stronger the borrower you are, the more leverage you have in negotiating the lender fees. Don't be afraid to bargain. And, if necessary, take your business elsewhere if you feel that the lender is bombarding you with junk fees.

Knowing the costs of getting out of a loan

You may expect the usual upfront costs to close a loan, but what about the costs to get out of the loan by either selling the property or refinancing it? Just because you don't think about these costs doesn't mean that they aren't there! Don't overlook these costs because if you do, it can cost you very big dollars.

Nearly all commercial lenders charge borrowers a penalty if they decide to pay off a loan before the loan term ends, especially in the first one to three years. This penalty is commonly called a *prepayment penalty* for us normal investors, but the more sophisticated ones like to use the term *defeasance structure*.

Here's how it works on a typical loan: Let's say that your loan amount is $500,000. If you sell or refinance your property in the first year, your typically your prepayment penalty would be up to 5 percent of the loan amount, or in this case, $25,000. In the second year, it would be 4 percent, or $20,000. In the third and following years, the penalty would go down 1 percent each year until you reach year five, which would be 0 percent.

As you can see, you can lose out on some serious cash if you decide to pay off your loan early. So pay attention to the prepayment penalties when you're selecting a loan.

A way to sidestep the prepayment penalty and still be able to sell your property is to make sure that your loan can be assumed by the next buyer (see the later section, "Assuming the Seller's Preexisting Mortgage," for more on these types of takeovers). In this case, the next buyer would also be assuming the existing loan terms. In fact, this buyer would essentially be stepping into your shoes! You get to move on, the buyer gets the property, and the lender gets to keep the loan intact. Everybody's happy.

Controlling the interest rate (to some extent)

I (coauthor Peter Harris) have always found it intriguing to discover what makes interest rates change from property to property, from deal to deal, or from investor to investor. I finally realized that I had more control over interest rates than I knew I had. Of course, I have no control over the Federal Reserve Board, the bond market, the economy, or the lender's portfolio, but I've figured out how to maneuver interest rates to work in and around my deals.

These are the items that you (the borrower) can control, which in turn affect the interest rate of your loan:

- **Property type and risk:** If you were a bank, which is the riskier loan: A loan for an apartment building that's 100 percent occupied or a loan for a gas station in the middle of desert country? You guessed it. If the gas station closed down and the bank foreclosed on it, how difficult would it be to sell or rent it? We're guessing pretty difficult. But, with an apartment that's 100 percent full, you shouldn't have a problem.

   What this all boils down to for you is that the gas station (or any other risky investment) is likely to have a higher interest rate. So, in other words, unless you have a good reason for going with a high-risk property, stick with those that are more conservative.

- **Loan amount:** Lenders like to lend big bucks. Believe it or not, the amount of paperwork for a $10 million loan is the same as a $300,000 loan. But guess what? The interest rate could be over 3 percent higher on the smaller loan. The bigger the loan, the lower the interest rate. Think big.

- **Creditworthiness:** Just like with residential loans, the stronger the borrowers are, the lower the interest rate is. Strong borrowers are lower risks. So, pay your bills on time if you're looking for a good interest rate!

- **Age of property:** Again, it comes down to risk. Lenders make a direct connect between newer properties and low risk. The newer the property, the lower the interest rate.

✔ **Prepayment penalty option:** If you want to secure the option of paying your loan off early without being socked with the normal prepayment penalty, you'll have to pay a higher interest rate.

✔ **Loan-to-value:** The more equity you have in your property, the lower the risk is for your lender — the lower the risk, the lower the interest rate. So, to gain that much-needed equity, put a larger down payment down.

✔ **Terms factor:** When it comes to loan terms, you have two things to consider. First, the shorter in years your terms are, say three years as opposed to ten years, the lower the interest rate. As for years of amortization, here's the general guideline: The shorter the duration, the lower the interest rate.

✔ **Lender/broker points:** You can pay down your interest rate considerably by paying more points on the loan at closing. In other words, if you agree to pay the lender more points, she'll lower your interest rate. (See the earlier section, "Determining how much the loan will cost you," for more on the point system.)

Interest rates are negotiable between you and the lender. Otherwise, why would they vary from lender to lender on the same property with the same borrowers? It's because one lender is cutting you a better deal, that's why. Get out there and start negotiating!

Assuming the Seller's Preexisting Mortgage

Let's say that you're selling your property. The purchase price is $1 million and you have an $800,000 mortgage balance. The loan has a term of seven years and was originated only last year. Because the loan is a new one, the prepayment penalty is 5 percent of the mortgage balance, or $40,000. If you sell the property and the buyer gets a new loan on it, you'll have to pay a $40,000 penalty just to sell the property. Ouch.

How do you sell your property and avoid paying the prepayment penalty? The solution is this: Have the buyer *assume* your loan (this is called a *loan assumption*). What we mean is have the buyer assume all of your loan obligations, including the balance, interest rate, years remaining on the loan, prepayment penalty structure, and monthly payments. Basically, the buyer will be walking into your loan and taking it over. The cost for the buyer to assume your loan is a down payment, which is the difference between the purchase price and loan balance ($200,000 in this case), and a 1 to 2 percent loan balance assumption fee. Your cost would be nothing more than the traditional transaction costs. Cool, eh?

The following two lists are the general guidelines that you can follow when deciding whether you should assume a loan.

Advantages to assuming a loan:

- ✔ The loan exists already, so you save time and money by not having to apply for a new loan.
- ✔ The existing loan terms may be much better than today's loan terms.
- ✔ Possibility of leveraging yourself into the property by having a down payment of only the difference between the purchase price and what the seller owes.

Reasons you may not want to assume a loan:

- ✔ Existing loan terms aren't better than what a new loan would have.
- ✔ A large down payment is required or the loan is due soon.

When you're considering assuming a loan with supposedly favorable terms, pay close attention to the loan's amortization period. We almost assumed a loan with no assumption fee, but upon a deeper check, we found that the loan amortized over 15 years. When we calculated what our monthly payments would be on a 30-year amortization period, our payments would be 25 percent lower than on a 15-year amortization period. We're glad we did our homework!

Chapter 9

Getting Creative with Financing

- -

In This Chapter

▶ Surveying creative financing techniques

▶ Using the Master Lease technique

▶ Getting the owner to carry the financing

▶ Finding secondary financing

▶ Investing with your own equity

- -

*W*ould you like to buy a commercial property and get the owner to help you out with most of the financing? How about buying a property without using any of your own cash or credit? Sound too much like a late-night infomercial? Well, it's not. Creative financing is just what you've been waiting for. You can use these ideas or not, but you only need to do one or two big deals like this to retire fast.

You may have read our book *Making Big Money Investing in Foreclosures Without Cash or Credit*. If so, then you know how to buy houses without using your own money. Similarly, this chapter talks about how to buy a big commercial property without using any of your hard-earned dollars.

You won't put one of these creative deals together every single day. They take plenty of hard work, a willingness to learn from others, and plenty of desire that keeps you after it until you succeed. Is it worth the hard work and dedication? We think so.

This chapter covers the "creative" ways of funding your commercial deals without having to go to a bank or fill out big piles of paperwork to get a conventional loan. Commercial properties are bought and sold every day using the seven different ways we cover here to invest without using your own cash or having to talk to a commercial lender.

Creative Financing Techniques

Creative financing is any method of funding other than making a down payment and getting a new loan for the balance of your purchase price. Because you can often structure creative financing so that you get in using little or none of your money, you'll come to love these techniques just like we do!

One of the risks of discovering creative financing is that it can cause you to want to creatively fund every single deal that you do. While this is a worthy goal, many of the deals that we're finding right now are great deals even without creative terms. Don't bypass a deal just because it may require conventional financing.

Here are the most common creative financing techniques:

- **Master Lease technique:** This method is often used with an owner who doesn't want to pay taxes on the gain from the official sale of his property, yet he's tired of being an owner. The investor agrees to pay the owner a set lease payment every month. Typically the investor is going to run the property, including collecting all the income and paying all the expenses associated with the property over a three to five year period. The reason you'd want to do this is that you also get an option to purchase the property, usually at about its current value. Your goal is then to increase the value and the cash flow as much as possible.

- **Owner carry firsts:** Why go to a lender for your loan when the seller might be willing to be the "Banker" for you. We purchased one property in California where the seller carried back $560,000 at 5 percent interest for five years. This was better financing than we could get anywhere else, and the low interest rate allowed the property to have an excellent cash flow.

- **Owner carry seconds:** Whether you're taking over an existing first mortgage or getting new financing, having the seller carry back all or a good portion of the balance of the purchase price can sometimes make or break the deal for you. We love to get sellers to agree to "investor-friendly" terms like low or no interest for the first few years. Some of our Mentorship students have persuaded sellers to carry back seconds with no payments at all for the first two years.

- **Other sources of secondary financing:** What if you can't get the seller to carry back a second mortgage? Then you might look to either a conventional lender (which doesn't fit our definition of "creative") or find a private lender who will provide the funds for your second mortgage.

- **Wraparound mortgages:** *Wraps* are instances where the seller gets one big payment from the investor every month to cover both a second mortgage due to the seller and the amount due on the existing first mortgage. This allows the seller to make certain that payments are made on all loans and if payments aren't made, the seller has the right to foreclose to get the property back. Sometimes the seller gets a little extra interest if the first mortgage has a lower rate than the wraparound mortgage.

- ✔ **Options:** Options are one of our favorite methods to buy properties. An *option* is simply an agreement with a property owner that gives you the right to buy at a set price for a certain time period. Sellers will give you an option in exchange for an upfront payment, ongoing payments such as covering the property taxes for them, or as an extra something that was perhaps thrown in along with another property that you bought from them.

- ✔ **Blanket mortgages:** A *blanket mortgage* is a mortgage where you offer a seller or traditional lender the added security of the equity in other properties you own as collateral for the loan he or she gives you. This is important to creative financing because sometimes when you're financing 100 percent of your purchase price, the seller or lender that you're dealing with will be smart enough to insist on having additional properties to secure his or her interest just in case you don't make the payments.

- ✔ **Investing using IRAs:** Did you know that you can invest in real estate using your IRA money? Most people don't know this. While there are some rules to follow that restrict what you can and can't do, using your retirement funds and encouraging your friends to do the same can be profitable and much more fun than investing in boring mutual funds.

Creative financing isn't just about talking sellers into doing something that's good for you. The secret is to discover how your creative terms can get the seller exactly what she wants out of the deal. You see, many owners of commercial property have this little problem: They don't want to pay tax on the gains that they have in their property. Using creative financing is one of the quickest, easiest ways to solve the seller's problem, and get a great deal for yourself.

The Master Lease Technique

With a *Master Lease,* you pay the owner a set amount as a lease payment each month, and then you run the property just like you own it. You lease out the space, collect the rents, and oversee and pay for the maintenance and repairs. Your option price is typically set at an amount equal to the value of the property at the beginning of your Master Lease.

Using the Master Lease technique, we were able to come in and buy a commercial property from a seller who was scared to death to sell because he didn't want to pay the capital gains tax on all the money he had made in his property over the years. So, instead of buying the property, we leased the property from the owner, and negotiated an option to purchase the property within the next ten years. We closed the deal on the 1st of October and our first payment wasn't due to the seller until the 15th of that month. Because of this payment schedule, we were able to collect enough money from tenants who were already in the property to make the first payment to the seller. Over the next three or four years, we never put any of our own money into the property. We used the cash flow from the property to take care of all the costs of running the building and fixing it up over time.

Four years later when we determined what the property was worth, our option price was $600,000 less than the value of the commercial property. So, we decided to go ahead and exercise our option at that point. We simply called up a lender from our network and got a new loan to pay off the seller. Because we rolled the new loan fees into the loan, we still don't have a dime of our money invested into this deal.

When using the Master Lease technique, make sure that you record a *performance mortgage* against the property. This document allows you to enforce your right to purchase at your option price, even if the seller changes his mind. It cost us hundreds of thousands of dollars in lost profits until we discovered how to use this important document. (Find samples of this and other commercial agreements at www.investingforms.com.)

Cleve is a coach in our Commercial Mentoring Program who has been a commercial broker for the past 27 years. His advice is to listen hard to find out what the seller really needs. For example, he found a seller several years ago who wanted to sell for $700,000 so he could move his equity into another property. Cleve realized the seller had not found the new property yet. Cleve offered to lease the property for $3,500 per month, and got an option to purchase for five years at $640,000. This arrangement gave the owner more time to look for a replacement property because the owner wanted to exchange into another property rather than an outright sale. Cleve also shrewdly negotiated to get half of the lease payment every month applied towards the purchase price for the first two years. After Cleve was able to fix up the property a bit and increase the rents, the cash flow was $60,000 per year. Last month Cleve had an offer to purchase the property for $1.8 million.

Getting Someone to Carry Secondary Financing

Some of the sellers that you come across won't want to get their money out upfront because they want to get completely out of real estate investing. When you structure a deal where the owner carries back a first mortgage for all or most of the financing, you'll make monthly payments at whatever interest rate(s) you're able to negotiate with the seller.

The seller is able to get a return by charging the investor interest, and she also only pays taxes on her capital gain based on the principal amount received each year. If you're a good negotiator, you can often get great terms, such as starting out at a lower interest rate for the first two to six years. You get the cash flow you need in the first few years and the seller gets her property sold. Everybody wins.

Any time that you're making payments to the seller of a property, make sure that the promissory note includes a "first right of refusal" clause that allows you to buy the note in case the seller (or the seller's heirs) ever want to cash out of the note. We like to use the special wording used on the promissory note from www.investingforms.com so that any other investor is hesitant to offer very much to buy the note. This one idea has made us tens of thousands in extra profits.

Getting the Owner to Carry Seconds and Other Secondary Financing

Most commercial real estate purchases require getting a new first mortgage to buy the commercial property or leaving the existing first mortgage in place. Then you have the seller carry back part of the purchase price as a second mortgage. That's called *secondary financing*. You can also get secondary financing from outside lenders or one of the private lenders in your network.

Why secondary financing works

One of our favorite methods of buying properties is to buy them subject to the existing first mortgage. That way, you don't have to go out and find a new loan. And then you can have the seller to carry back secondary financing on top of the existing first mortgage.

The fastest way to increase the cash flow from a property is to refinance it with financing that has a lower interest rate. You already have lenders with good rates, you say? Guess what? The right sellers will give you even lower interest rates! This fact applies to properties where the seller carries back all the financing or properties that the seller provides secondary financing for.

The key is being able to negotiate what we call "soft terms" with the seller of the property. Your goal is to see if you can get the seller to carry back secondary financing with below-market interest rates, no payments for the first year or two, or maybe graduated payments. The end result is that your payments are lower, and you end up with more cash flow. That's what it's all about, right?

One of the really cool things about commercial properties is that you can often find sellers who don't want all cash when they sell their property. Why? If you give the seller cash for the property, he suddenly has two big problems:

- ✔ The seller will have to pay tax on the gains made.
- ✔ The seller has to find something else to invest his money in.

You can solve both of these problems for the seller by using creative financing. After all, when you have a seller carry back secondary financing, you can structure the payment stream in any fashion that both you and the seller agree to. Think of the options: no payments, pure principal payments, interest-only payments . . . the sky is the limit.

Pay attention when talking with owners of commercial property to notice what their "needs" are versus what their "wants" are. After you discover what the seller really needs what he's going to do with the cash (or what immediate problem they hope to solve with the cash), you're much closer to putting your creatively financed deal together. A good question to ask when negotiating secondary financing is: "Help me out here, Mr. Seller. What can we do to make sure that the property generates the income that I need to turn the property around while still meeting your needs?"

Finding sources of secondary financing

Deciding on getting a new first mortgage, taking over or assuming payments on an existing first mortgage, and picking any secondary financing is often a matter of where can you get the best terms. You're going to compare the interest rates, length of the loan, upfront costs, and so on that you can negotiate with the various sources here to make your decision.

Secondary financing, other than owner carry, is going to usually have a higher interest rate than the first mortgage on the property. The reason for this is that there is obviously higher risk for someone who's secured in second position as opposed to being secured by the first mortgage.

We've found that when we can get the seller to carry back secondary financing, the terms are always better than anywhere else. The reason for this is that the seller is a part of the transaction and is emotionally motivated to make the sale. If the seller doesn't have immediate need for the money, she can get a nice return so that it's a good investment for her as well.

Commercial seconds

If you're buying a nice property, a number of lenders are out there that are willing to lend you money to be used as secondary financing. With money that you get from a commercial lender for secondary financing, you can expect to pay points, fees, and generally a higher interest rate than you would when you get the financing someplace else.

Owner carry seconds

Okay, we admit it. Getting sellers to carry back financing is one of our all-time favorite financing sources. That's why we keep talking it up so much for you. We've even put together deals where sellers have provided secondary financing and the property was 100 percent financed.

Private lenders

If you can't get the seller to carry back secondary financing, your next best source may be private lenders. Private lenders are comfortable with real estate and are looking for safe returns on their investments. Obviously they're in second position, which isn't as safe as having a first mortgage, so you can expect to pay private lenders a higher interest rate than you would on first mortgage money.

The advantage of working with private lenders is that they will come in and quickly finance a deal for you. This allows you to close quickly, and "steal" a property that other investors may not be able to get their funding in place to buy right away.

The key here is to make sure that you're working with people that know you and trust you. Don't waste your time trying to work with strangers who don't know what you're about, don't understand that you have integrity, and don't know you as a person.

Understanding common pitfalls of secondary financing

One of the biggest pitfalls of secondary financing that you find is that if you have the property highly financed, you may end up having negative cash flow. This might be okay for a short period of time, such as when you do a turn-around, but in the long term, you need to have an upside. There's nothing like a property taking longer to turn than expected, or having an unexpected shift in the marketplace, that puts you in a position where you're becoming a motivated seller because you have to cover negative cash flow.

Depending on where you get your secondary financing, you may end up paying higher interest rates than you will on your first mortgage. If you get the seller to carry back the financing, oftentimes you can structure terms where you get great interest rates.

Sellers want price, you want your terms

We're amazed at the number of property owners who are stuck on price when they're selling their properties. We think it boils down to this: At some point, every property owner starts to think "Wow! This property that I bought for $2 million 15 years ago now has a value that's close to $4 million." The truth of the matter is that the property may be worth only about $3.6 or $3.7 million.

The secret is to put together offers that give the seller his price but that have great terms — like no interest for the first two years. Look for a way to make cash flow, not get stuck on price.

For one shopping center that we bought several months ago, we were able to get the seller to carry back over $900,000 of secondary financing with an interest rate that was just over 3 percent. Oftentimes the interest rate on the secondary financing can be what makes or breaks a deal.

Getting the owner to help you out by financing all or part of the purchase

When you're trying to get an owner to help you out with creative financing, remember this: Many owners of commercial real estate, especially those who are getting older, often want monthly cash flow rather than just a big chunk of money from the sale. We have found that if you can connect with the owner, and get him to relate to you as if you're a younger version of himself, he will often get an emotional thrill out of giving you an opportunity to purchase his property. It harkens him back to the days when he was seeking and receiving his own financing breaks.

If you agree to cash out the seller when you resell the property, and you give him some kind of a timeline, you'll give the seller an optimistic projection. Doing so will also indicate that you're going to want to make your money as

You can also agree to cash out the seller after a certain number of years (whether you're selling or not). You can do that by using an all-inclusive trust deed (AITD) with a balloon note. This AITD says that you're going to cash out the existing loan balances within five or seven years.

When you're trying to convince a seller to take the bait on cashing out after a certain number of years, say something like this:

Because I'm a conservative investor Mr. Seller, and I'm not a real risk-taker, I want to make sure that I have enough time to get the property value up and do the improvements and things that I talked about doing. Here's the

worse case scenario: Let's say that the market really flattens out. I'd want to make sure that I've got at least another couple of years beyond the time that we've already talked about to make sure that I can get you your money.

Dealing with seller objections

When negotiating, sellers are more than likely going to raise some objections to some of your creative financing options. But don't worry: This section shows you how to respond and change their minds.

Objection 1: "I don't want to master lease it; I just want to sell it"

When this objection comes up (using the Master Lease technique), the sellers are usually thinking about their families. They want their families to be able to keep the money that they leave when they die. This way, they don't have the hassle of dealing with any of the investments.

You can either switch gears and buy the property subject to the existing financing, or point out how much the Master Lease will save the seller's family in taxes. By delaying the sale beyond when the seller dies, the family usually saves tens if not hundreds of thousands in taxes.

Objection 2: "I want a larger down payment"

When this objection comes up, it's important for the seller to understand that you can put a larger down payment into the property, but the more money you put down, the lower the price is going to be. You may want to ask the seller to step into your shoes. Here's how:

> **Investor:** This property here is a million-dollar property and you're asking me for 20 percent down. That's $200,000. If you were me — a young investor just getting started — and you could go out and buy four or five other properties with that same money, isn't that what you would do?

> **Seller:** Yeah, I guess you're right. I would probably do the same thing.

> **Investor:** I thought so. That's the real reason it doesn't make sense for me to use that large of a down payment. Because one of your concerns is security and making sure I'm going to take good care of the property perhaps we should talk about some ways that we can help you to feel more secure about the transaction.

To help a seller feel secure, try this: "If we don't make the payments on this property, we will not only allow you to come in and take back the property that we're buying, but we'll also allow you to take this other nice property that we have lined up." This is called a *blanket mortgage*. Sometimes it's a great way for you to get in a property with a smaller down payment.

Objection 3: "I need a higher purchase price"

When you hear this objection, you need to remember one thing: The neat thing with real estate is that there are so many different ways to structure your profit in a transaction that you can often give the seller exactly what she wants and still make a healthy and significant profit for yourself.

For example, one of the things that you can do is give the seller her price but make sure that you get terms that are good for you. Those terms will help you make a good profit on the property. Use these language patterns to create a context for them to give you a great price on the property. Here's what it would sound like:

> **Investor:** Well, you're asking for $974,000 for this property Mrs. Seller. What did you *realistically* expect to get out of the property?
>
> **Seller:** $974,000 — that's my asking price.
>
> **Investor:** What did you *really* expect to get out of the property?
>
> **Seller:** $900,000.
>
> **Investor:** That makes sense. If a broker brought you a buyer who was willing to pay that full asking price of $900,000, you would probably say no, correct? You would probably turn it down?
>
> **Seller:** No, I'd sell it anyway — if he would want to buy it or sell it with an agent. I'll sell it to anyone who wants to buy it. (This allows you to then discount the price further by subtracting the amount the seller would be willing to pay to a real estate agent.)

Operating the Wraparound Mortgage Like a Surgeon

When you're buying a property subject to the existing financing, one of the seller's biggest concerns is that if you don't make the payments on the first mortgage, the seller is going to be liable for the default on the existing loan. When you're selling a property, you'll have the same concern if you're leaving the existing financing in place and carrying back a second mortgage.

To protect the seller's interests and give him the comfort level that allows him to move ahead with the deal, you can use something known as a *wraparound mortgage*. In some places, this is known as an "AITD," which stands for "all-inclusive trust deed." To keep things simple here, we refer to these as wraparound mortgages.

To understand how this mortgage works, here's an example: Say that you've negotiated with the owners of a small strip center to purchase their property subject to the existing financing and the owners are willing to carry back secondary financing to help you get the deal closed. Here's what the numbers look like:

Purchase price: $2 million

Down payment: $200,000

Owner carry second: $300,000

Existing first mortgage: $1.5 million

The owner carry second in this example is going to be written up as a wraparound mortgage. The reason it's called a wraparound mortgage in this case is that this mortgage is going to "wrap around" both the owner carry second and the existing first mortgage of $1.5 million. The way this works is simple: The paperwork is set up so that you send an amount equal to your payment on the owner carry second and your payment on the existing first mortgage directly to the owner.

Here's where it all starts to make sense: The owner then takes the amount necessary to make the payment on the first mortgage out of the money that you sent and forwards it to the first mortgage holder. In this case, the owner is protected because he's able to make sure that the payments are made on the existing first mortgage before they're made on the owner carry. In addition, if you don't make the payments to cover both the first and second mortgages (which are really wrapped together in one mortgage now), the owner has the right to foreclose against the property. This way he protects his interest in his owner carry second and any liabilities he may have from the first mortgage.

Using an Option to Buy

Options are simply an agreement with a property owner that gives you the right to buy at a set price for a certain time period. Sellers will give you an option in exchange for an upfront payment, ongoing payments such as covering the property taxes for them, or as an extra something that was perhaps thrown in along with another property that you bought from them.

Thomas, who is one of our Commercial Mentoring Program students, was doing a small land development project. He had found a piece of land that was an "infill" project in the town that he lived in. Instead of buying the property outright, he arranged to control the property using options.

Thomas found a friend of his who had a self-directed IRA and was willing to provide the money the seller wanted in exchange for giving Thomas an option to buy based on the current value of the land. This purchase price for the property was close to $500,000. But instead of coming up with a down payment and having to make mortgage payments, Thomas set up a series of option payments over time. The first payment of $5,000 was due after his 90 day free look period. This bought him another 60 days to work on getting the approval to build on the property. Every 60 days from that point forward Thomas owed another payment. He was able to negotiate so that each option payment went toward his purchase price.

By the time Thomas got the final approval to build on the property, the total amount invested from his friend's IRA was just $80,000. He was able to provide a high rate of return to his friend. This was way more than he would have made with his money sitting in a traditional IRA account. With the approvals in place to build, the value of this land had jumped up to almost $1 million. After all of his costs, Thomas will clear several hundred thousand dollars on this one deal. Are you starting to see the power of using options?

Leveraging the Equity in Your Portfolio

Another creative financing technique that you can use is to tap into the existing equity that you have in commercial or residential properties that are already in your portfolio.

Employing blanket mortgages

One of the very first "no money down" deals that coauthor Peter Conti did was put together with a blanket mortgage. The owner of the property ran a small construction company, and he simply wanted to get rid of the apartment building he owned. All Peter had to do was come in and assume the existing mortgage and take over the payments. Now understand that at this point, Peter was no Donald Trump. He didn't have a huge track record or lots of money in the bank to convince a lender that it was okay for him to go ahead and assume alone.

However, Peter did have some other properties he owned. He was able to put these up as additional security to convince a lender to go ahead and allow him to assume the loan. The key in using blanket mortgages is knowing when it's absolutely necessary. You never want to cross-collateralize properties unless you need to.

One of our Commercial Mentoring Program students named Mike came across a small classified ad for a 20 unit apartment building. After calling the owner and getting the details Mike ran through a quick analysis of the property. He could see where even if he ended up paying the price the seller was asking the building would make money from day one. Mike sat down with the owner and got to know him while creating a good connection. Mike found out that the seller was upset because all the other investors were contacting him with low offers. The seller had worked hard for many years to build up his property and was disturbed by all the people who wanted to beat him down on his price. Mike decided to offer a blanket mortgage to get the seller to carry back 100 percent of the financing for his purchase. At this point, Mike has over $600,000 of equity in this property that he bought without using any of his own money.

Be careful when you're dealing with blanket mortgages, because you really are pledging your equity and those other properties. If something should happen on the property that you purchased using a blanket mortgage, the seller or other lender will be able to foreclose not just on the property that you purchased, but on the other properties as well.

Drawing on 401(k)s or IRAs

One of the best sources of secondary financing is money from other people's IRAs. This concept may seem strange, but stick with us on this one. In order to provide loans for you to buy real estate, the only thing a person needs to do is move her IRA from a traditional account to something known as a *self-directed IRA account.* The only difference is that with a traditional account, the institution decides how to invest your money — usually in stocks or bonds.

With a self-directed IRA, your new friend can decide where that money is going to be invested. To get started with this technique, ask everyone you know this question: "Do you know of anyone who would like to make higher rates of return on their retirement funds?"

When someone answers that she would, simply give her an application to transfer her funds to a self-directed IRA company. Then keep in touch with her to let her know about potential investment opportunities. Typically, with funds from an IRA, you want to make sure that they're secured with a mortgage against the property. Companies that allow you to self direct an IRA are listed at www.realstateinvestinglinks.com.

Chapter 10

Raising Capital and Forming Partnerships

*F*or most people, if they're going to do big deals, they need to raise the funds to make it happen. In this chapter, we explain how to fund your deals without using your own capital. Our favorite method of raising the money needed to fund a deal involves finding other investors who can provide the private funds that you need. When funding a deal with private funds, you need to have the following:

✔ A great deal that you're excited about and that is under contract

✔ A Rolodex full of people who know you and your character

✔ A system that allows you to get the word out about your pending deal

The good news: After you master raising the money that you need to fund your deals, you'll be unstoppable! The bad news: Getting to this point doesn't happen overnight. You need to get good at meeting people and finding a way to stay connected with them. Everything you need is right here in this chapter.

Identifying the Keys to Raising Private Funds

The first key to raising private funds to support your real estate deal is simple: You must believe with all your heart and soul that this is a great deal. In fact, you must believe so strongly in your deal that you would put your parents' retirement funds into the deal. You should also be willing to put your *own* funds into the deal (if you have them). After all, when you're getting started, putting your own money on the line is a good way to prove to your investors that you're willing to put your money where your mouth is. This is exactly what we did when we started raising the capital.

When funding a deal with some personal funds along with funds raised from private parties, many commercial investors choose to arrange the deal so that the private funds are paid back first — before they themselves get any of their money back. This preferential repayment helps your deal funders know that in order to get *your* money back out, you have to make sure the deal works for *them,* too.

If you try to convince someone who doesn't know you that you have a great deal, you may succeed in getting him to accept that the *deal* is good. But that brings us to the second key to raising private funds: Unless the investors you're approaching are comfortable with who *you* are as a person, the chances of getting funding from him or her are slim to none (even if the deal is a winner).

If you take the time to get to know that person and earn his trust, you'll find that most investors will also want to know about the deal — but the real reason they're willing to fund the deal is because they believe in you.

Building Your Rolodex of Potential Investors

People who will invest in your deals are going to do so because they know you and trust you. So how do you get to know more people beyond just your immediate circle of friends?

Start by finding a way to keep in touch with the people in your Rolodex over time. If all you ever do is add a name, phone number, and address to your Rolodex, and you don't find a way to create a relationship, the person probably won't even remember meeting you.

Set a goal for the number of potential investors you want to add to your Rolodex every month. Instead of simply focusing on the people who you think have money, open up to the idea that everyone is a potential private deal funder for you. When you're talking to someone at the store, the library, the gym, the beauty shop, or at your church, use this script:

> *Right now I'm looking at investing in a big _____ [office building, land devel-opment, whatever you may be looking at that particular week]. It's a _____-square-foot project in _____ [the name of the state, city, or area]. This one is*

probably already funded, but if I come across something in the future that would create a healthy rate of return for the investors I work with, would you want me to at least let you know about it?

The next step is simple. Make sure you get the person's name, address, phone number, and e-mail address. Then make sure that you develop an easy way to stay in touch with the potential investors on your list. Because people need to get to know you and trust you before they feel comfortable funding your projects, you want to create as many *touch points,* or chances for them to get to know you, as possible.

Raising money from private parties involves some strict guidelines. If you do it wrong, you can easily get into hot water by violating the securities laws. One of the special training sessions we did with our mentoring students was called "Funding Deals without Violating the Law." To see a Web video of this training session, go to www.commercialquickstart.com. We recommend that you speak with a real estate attorney before you raise one penny. Have that person explain to you what you can and can't say or do in capital raising. The laws are not only strict, but they're also very complex.

Creating relationships with potential investors

Do you want your Rolodex full of investors who are eager to fund your deals? Well then, you're going to have to put in the effort to create a relationship with these folks first. It takes time, but if you do it in a systematic fashion, it'll get easier over time.

Looking to your existing relationships

Among your best resources are the people you already know. You may be a bit uncomfortable getting out there and letting them know that you're going after investing in commercial real estate. But the biggest mistake that many new investors make is failing to tap into the group of people they already know.

If you need help approaching people you know, you can use this script:

As you may have heard, I'm moving into investing in commercial real estate — things like apartments, office buildings, and maybe even some land development. Because it can be challenging at times, I'd like to ask you for some emotional support if that's okay with you.

If I'm working on a big deal like a $5 million property and I need a little encouragement, is it okay if I call you from time to time?

See how easy it is to start the process?

Funding from an unexpected source

Emanuel is a Commercial Mentoring student who has been a chiropractor for the past 12 years. He needed to create $10,000 per month or more in income to retire. Like most of our students, Emanuel was in a hurry to change his life. He decided to focus only on big deals right from the start, knowing that he would have to raise funding once he found the right property. It took him ten months to finally get a winning deal under contract. He purchased a 300-unit apartment for $17,000 per unit for a total of $5.1 million.

The funding ended up coming from someone close to Emanuel. He was visiting his in-laws on the way to inspect the property and happened to mention it. To Emanuel's surprise, it turns out they had several million dollars that was just sitting there earning 2 or 3 percent interest. When the property sold in 12 months for $30,000 per unit, it will provide a great return for Emanuel's relatives and pay off a cool $1 million to Emanuel. The lesson is that you never know who may end up funding your next commercial deal.

People like to help other people. Many of your friends will be willing to support you. If you're feeling confident, take it to the next step by saying:

> *Thanks for your support. So if I came across something in the future that would create a healthy rate of return for the investors that I work with, would you want me to at least let you know about it?*

Make sure that no matter who you're using to fund your deal you get the proper paperwork done by using your attorney. This rule doesn't change if you're working with family or friends. Treat every investor the same, right from the start — whether they're family or not.

Make sure that your family members have the same expectations as you do from the investment. You may need to spend some extra time with them to make sure that they really understand what they're getting into. Avoid the relative who says, "Oh skip the details — I trust you." He may be thinking that he can get his funds back out at a moment's notice. If he needs that money in six months because his kid has to go to college, well, don't spend the kid's college fund on your deals. Let this be surplus money that your relative won't be upset about if he loses it.

Don't rule anyone out as a potential investor. Sam Walton, the founder of Wal-Mart, was one of the wealthiest people around, but he drove a pickup truck and appeared to be a "normal" person. If you don't tell someone about the investing opportunities that you run across, you're doing a big disservice to him and his family.

Knowing where to meet potential investors

When you're trying to beef up that Rolodex, you have to search out people and groups in many different places — not just at work. Here are a few individuals and groups that you can tap into to begin building your relationships and adding names in your Rolodex:

- **Folks you do business with:** You probably work with real estate brokers and lenders on a daily basis. And most of them are so busy that they don't invest themselves. So, convince them that they can increase their credibility with their clients if they were to invest in the same type of property they're selling. And of course, they'd be investing with you.

- **People you work with:** You may be friends with your co-workers. If so, make sure that they know what you're doing if you want them to be potential investors for your next project.

- **Church or other spiritual groups:** If you have friends at your place of worship, make sure those folks know that you invest in commercial real estate. You want them to know what you're doing so that they're more likely to be potential investors for your next deal.

- **Athletic events and clubs:** We love to bicycle. And what a great conversation piece it makes to talk about what you're doing during a ride with your buddies. After your ride (or whatever activity you choose), exchange contact information. This works with all sorts of activities, from sports to hobbies.

- **Mastermind groups:** These groups are focus groups, usually business related, that are terrific ways to promote your efforts to serious and like-minded people.

- **Networking groups:** These groups can help you and the other members to refer leads to one another. For instance, we once belonged to a local networking club, called BNI (www.bni.com), that met once per week for breakfast. Everyone got a chance to share what they did and the whole purpose was to refer business leads to one another.

- **Real estate investor associations:** A great place to start "real estate clubbing" would be with the National Real Estate Investor Association (NREAI). This group has established club meetings year-round and nationwide. Check out www.nationalreia.com for a club near you.

If you're talking to someone from one of the previous groups (or just an individual you know), you may want to use a script like this:

With the great weather, I've been having a blast with _____ [something you love to do] lately. It's been crazy, because I'm also looking at a couple of big commercial real estate deals right now, a good-sized apartment building, and an office building that's downtown. The rates of return are amazing. Say, if I came across something in the future that would create a healthy rate of return for the investors I work with, would you want me to tell you about it?

Now that you have the person's name, address, phone number, and e-mail address, it's time to kick your connection campaign in gear. Find ways to spend time with the people in your network. Taking them out to dinner, playing golf or tennis, or simply hanging out with each other's families can be a great way to really get to know someone and allow her to get comfortable with you.

Using executive summaries to nab potential investors

After you've built some trust with the folks in your Rolodex as prospective private investors for your deal, you need to create a plan to get them interested in your deals. And after they're interested, you need a way to get them to step up and write you a check. This is where most investors fall down. If you don't have the ability to get the check, your deal won't be funded and you'll be in tears.

Remember during your job search when you had a résumé and cover letter? The cover letter's purpose was to capture your future employer's attention in the first few sentences. If it caught his attention, he read your résumé. If not, it went straight into the circular file (also known as the trash can). Well, when we're putting together written information to prospective investors, our cover letter is referred to as an *executive summary*. It's a short one-half to one-page document that is a compelling and condensed version of your investment opportunity.

Your executive summary is going to be competing to get the attention of the busy people you have in your Rolodex. This means you need to be short, sweet, and to the point.

Here's an example of an executive summary sent out via e-mail:

> **Subject:** You'll Kick Yourself if You Miss This
>
> Hey Brett,
>
> You are about the busiest person I know — and the rates of return on this deal are going to make you stop and salivate. . . .
>
> **The Property:** 80,000-square-foot strip shopping center in El Paso, Texas
>
> Rents are 75 percent of market in an area that is booming, and 30,000 more troops are on the way!
>
> Under contract for $4.2 million — worth $5.1 million or more after raising rents
>
> **Opportunity:** Invest $270,000 and get a great base rate *plus* equity sweetener!

Next steps: E-mail, call, or wagon-train it right now 'cause we're looking to work with just one investor on this one. Call or e-mail ASAP for details — 303-233-2233.

You probably know that I've sent this out to a number of other VIPs just like you. . . .

Don't wait. . . . First come, first served on this, baby.

Yours for Passive Income,

Peter Harris

This quick executive summary is followed up with a longer document with all the details. The trick is in getting someone to slow down long enough to realize what a great deal you have.

Connecting with your investors

When you've started growing your Rolodex or database of potential investors, you need to stay in touch with them, keep them excited about the possibility of investing, and maintain the accuracy of your database. We have discovered that a great way to do this is by giving away helpful information to our prospective investors. It's free for them, and each time they say "Yes, please send it to me," we're getting their latest e-mail address and adding it to our database.

The secret is in the title of the information you provide. Think of the special reports that you offer as if they were books in a bookstore. You can write the most incredible book in the world, but if it doesn't catch the browsers' attention and make them want it, using just the words of the title, then no one is going to buy your book. And that means no one is going to read it.

Here are some of the titles we've used over the years:

- ✔ "How to Create Multiple Streams of Income Buying Homes in Nice Areas with Nothing Down"
- ✔ "Making Big Money Investing in Real Estate without Tenants, Banks, or Rehab Projects"
- ✔ "Making Big Money Investing in Foreclosures without Cash or Credit"

Compare these to some of the losing titles that we didn't use:

- ✔ "Nothing But Money"
- ✔ "Big Changes with Commercial Real Estate"
- ✔ "How to Find, Buy, and Manage Shopping Centers"

To find out whether your titles are winners or losers, you need to get feedback from the people who really count. The way to do this is to create three slightly different special reports along with the three titles that you want to test out. Then you can send an e-mail out to your database offering "Your choice of any *one* of these three reports." Track which report is the most requested to determine which of your titles is the strongest.

The special reports that we offer to our prospective investors all have pretty hot titles. Check them out:

- ✔ "How to Use the Velocity of Money to Retire Fast"
- ✔ "The Five Warning Signs of Bad Commercial Deals"
- ✔ "The Ten-Minute-a-Day Guide to Making Millions in Commercial Properties"
- ✔ "How to Get Healthy Rates of Return by Investing in Commercial Real Estate"
- ✔ "How to Retire Fast Investing in Commercial Real Estate"

We send an e-mail to our prospective investors that gives them a choice of any two of the previous reports. It's all automated, so our investors get a response within minutes, which means that we've created another touch point. If you'd like to look at our reports to use as models for your own, or if you simply want to see how this part of our investing system works, send an e-mail to investorreports@mentorfinancialgroup.com with the word "Reports" in the subject line.

Deciding Whether to Go It Alone or Use a Partner or Two

If you can do it by yourself, by all means go for it. However, we've found that with most really big deals in the range of $5 million or more, having a team helps to keep you motivated and also makes sure that everything gets done on time.

One of the things we do in our commercial training is to have everyone complete their profile/test at www.kolbe.com. It helps you understand what you're really good at, and what you're better off letting someone else take care of. It also shows what you or your partner's tendencies are under stress. The Commercial Mentoring students who have done this have really begun to get to know each other and some of them have partnered up into teams where three or four of them are working on one deal together. They've found that this is a way they can do the things they love to do while leaving the other pieces available for someone else who loves to do their part.

When you're picking someone to partner with, remember these two critical keys to long-term partnerships:

- ✔ **Character means more than anything else.** The best agreement in the world can't fix someone who doesn't have the integrity that you're looking for.

- ✔ **Someone who's just like you doesn't add anything to the mix.** While it's fun to hang out with others who process the world just like you do, you're going to want to find people who are different from you. For example, if you're a big-picture person, you're going to need someone who's great at details.

Here's an example of one of the teams that has been put together in our commercial program. The following students, who are all different, make up this group:

- ✔ **Emila:** She's a great project manager. She can break things down into steps and follow through.

- ✔ **Calli:** She's able to make anything happen. For her, the bigger, the better.

- ✔ **Rodriguez:** He has money and wisdom from his experience.

- ✔ **Bob:** He's great at coming up with the vision and the really big ideas.

- ✔ **Stan:** He's all about details and numbers, and he loves to play with spreadsheets.

Creating the Right Teams and Partnerships

When Eric and Sara first got started, it was just the two of them. Eric was unclogging toilets and doing maintenance, and Sara was doing the books. They were filling the buildings and their cash flow was increasing. Then we challenged Eric to start growing their business. He suggested bringing a bookkeeper in and getting maintenance people on staff, because Eric doesn't make much money doing maintenance.

The value of the right type of partnership is that each person brings a very unique skill set. For instance, Eric isn't the type of person who wants to sit down and create an Excel spreadsheet that shows whether the project is going to be profitable. But Sara loves doing that. Eric and Sara have a partner on their team who actually loves getting in his car and driving for two weeks across the state looking for deals. He enjoys talking to agents and driving to small towns and looking for 20-unit apartment buildings or strip centers. They have another person on their team who's excellent at marketing.

The value of the team is in finding people who are passionate about an area of the business that you understand is important but you don't naturally gravitate toward yourself.

Structuring your partnership

If you're raising more than a few thousand dollars and you're anticipating working with multiple investors, you'll probably want to form something called a *private placement memorandum* (PPM). This is just a fancy phrase that means "Large pile of paper that costs a good chunk of lawyer's fees so that you don't violate any securities laws." Here are a couple of tips if you're considering a PPM:

- ✔ Find another investor who's already formed a PPM and ask him who he has used. Doing so could save you thousands of dollars.
- ✔ Don't get intimidated by the paperwork. If you have the right team behind you, you can do anything!

For a smaller deal, you'll probably want to create a simple limited liability company. Make sure that your operating agreement spells out everything that can happen both in good times and bad. For example, make sure you have a buyout clause in case you decide at some point to part ways. Either way, we suggest having a real estate attorney draw up any of the agreements needed.

Knowing how much to pay your investors

If you want to know how much to pay your investors, here's the correct answer: "As much as it takes to get the deal done." You want to keep enough to make it worth your while, though. The good news with commercial deals is that there's usually enough profit to go around.

Typically, you would offer your investors a double-digit return. A 10 percent return on their investment is a good starting point. In some cases, you could offer the investors a fixed return plus part of the profits when you sell or refinance.

One of our Commercial Mentoring clients named Rob wanted to create enough passive income so that both he and his wife could retire from the police force. Because they felt that they needed a track record, they bought a large apartment complex and gave almost all the profits to their investors! Before you feel bad for them, understand that it was a nothing-down deal for them and that now they have the experience to offer a much smaller piece of the pie to their investors than they did when they were first starting out.

Writing up the agreements to use with your investors

Writing up agreements is simple. Make sure that you consult your own legal counsel, however. You want to explore using a private placement memorandum, a limited liability company, or perhaps a partnership agreement. Take the time to stay involved so that you get something that you understand and that meets your needs.

How much does it cost to raise funds and do all the paperwork? Actually, the way our Commercial Mentoring Program clients do it, nothing. After you have the property under contract, you can start looking for investors. Several of our students have offered a crazy rate of return for an investor who offers the upfront money needed to create the other funding documents. This investor knows that if the deal doesn't fly for some reason, the investment is worthless. You'd be surprised how many people are willing to roll the dice on your behalf. Just make sure you let them know what they're getting into and put it in writing.

Considering how long you want to partner with someone

Take the time to find out what your partner's intent is. Some people may want to partner for ten years; others may only want to partner for a year or two as they get started. One of the reasons that our Commercial Mentoring Program has taken off is that we split the profits, with 75 percent going to the student and the other 25 percent going to our company. We commit to doing this together and agree that we'll all continue to work together until the student makes at least $300,000. Some people don't like this level of intense support, but we've found that it separates the wannabes from those who are willing to do whatever it takes.

Interviewing a potential partner

Choosing the right partners starts with asking the right questions. It's important that you interview your potential partners so that you can get to know that person and how they do business. And you need to be the very best listener possible during the interview because other questions will evolve from her one answer. It's okay to keep asking deeper and deeper questions. After all, this person could possibly be working with you every single day for years whether you like it or not.

Here are some important questions you should ask:

- ✔ **What's your ideal exit strategy for a project?** What are you good at on making profits in commercial real estate? Are you skilled at doing rehab projects? Do you have a knack for buying and operating cash-flowing properties?

- ✔ **Are you looking for long-term growth or short-term cash flow?** Are you a "buy and hold" type of investor? If you are, how long do you typically hold a property and under what conditions would you consider selling? If not, discuss some of your short-term goals.

- ✔ **What are your other long-term goals?** Describe your "big picture" investment objectives.

- ✔ **Do you have enough capital set aside to survive during a 24- to 36-month project?** How much cash or liquidity do you bring to the table? If it takes us longer than expected to make a profit, will you be okay with that?

- ✔ **How much of a time commitment can you make to the team?** Are you a full-time investor or do you have a daytime job? How about family commitments? Do you have time to travel, if needed?

Check the credit score of all potential partners before you admit them to your group. Each person's credit score affects the group as a whole when it comes time to apply for loans.

Part IV
Day-to-Day Ownership and Operations

The 5th Wave   By Rich Tennant

"Of course I could never afford a shoe this size if I weren't collecting rents from a tennis shoe across town and two espadrilles in Florida."

In this part . . .

In this part, we show you how to keep tabs on your important investments by revealing our simple "manage the manger" process. In addition, we offer plenty of advice on protecting your assets. The part ends with something you won't find in most investing books: the reasons why some properties fail and how you can avoid making the same mistakes.

Chapter 11

Property Management: Who's Minding Your Ship?

In This Chapter

▶ Being the boss of your commercial property

▶ Hiring a professional property management company

▶ Putting your best foot forward as an absentee owner

Commercial properties are similar to cruise ships in some ways. If you have a successful, well-informed captain steering the ship to your destination, you'll get there and have lots of fun doing it. You may even relax a little. However, if your captain takes you off course and into choppy waters, you could get seasick and end up on a deserted island. Well, the same applies to your commercial property investment: You have to make sure that your "captain" is a good one or else your investment may receive a burial at sea.

In this chapter, you get down to the business of discovering the essential skills of navigating and managing your property. We give you tips on how to do it yourself and how to hire and manage a property manager. We give you an inside look into the day-to-day responsibilities of a property manager. We also help you discover the world of absentee owners. Knowing how to successfully manage a property from afar is a critical navigational skill to possess. It allows you to put the pieces together in owning and operating a commercial property successfully and profitably.

I'm the Boss: Managing Your Commercial Property Yourself

You want to manage your own commercial properties do you? Well, here's a little secret about making nice profits, growing your real estate business, and making smart investment decisions: It's not about the property. That's right, being successful in managing your own property has little to do with the property. So, if it isn't about the property, who or what is it really about? The answer is you! It's about you, the investor; you, the property owner; and you, the property manager. In the following sections, we give you all that you need to know in order to successfully manage your real estate.

Your property's success will *never* go beyond your own personal business development. So, go forth and spend money and time educating yourself on how to successfully manage a property and improve your overall business skills. Your future depends on it!

Improving your management skills with a few basic tips

We've already spent the time and money educating ourselves regarding all things real estate, so we're happy to provide you with some time-tested advice. When managing the property yourself, keep the following general tips in mind:

- ✔ **Never be friends with your tenants.** Instead, make sure your relationship is a business-friendly one. The last thing you want to do is take your friend to court for an eviction (which means that you probably won't and you'll be the one to lose out).

- ✔ **Know that people (not properties) cause problems.** Properties don't pay late, cause damage, or cause high vacancy. People cause these problems. So, make it a point to lease to good tenants and good companies. Having no tenant is better than having a bad one, we say.

- ✔ **Record everything in writing.** As manager of any real estate, words *spoken* are like sticks and stones — not worth very much. So make sure that you write everything down, including rent increases, promises to pay, renewals, or improvements or repairs that the tenant has agreed to do.

- ✔ **Know your market like the back of your hand.** Always know what your competitors down the block are doing with their properties. Know what they're offering to their tenants, know what sells, and know what the tenant-landlord laws are in your area. To find out how to best become familiar with your market, check out Chapter 3.

- ✔ **Have nothing in your name.** Protect yourself and your personal assets from lawsuits by having your properties and businesses legally detached from you personally. First of all, the property should be in an LLC (a limited liability company) or in another type of legal entity that you and your real estate attorney and tax advisor agree on. That way if a tenant files a lawsuit, he can only go after what's in the LLC or entity, not after your home and personal belongings. Also, don't commingle the finances between the property and your personal expenses in any way because, in most cases, that will negate the protection an LLC or entity provides you. For more information on LLCs and other legal entities, see Chapter 12.

The success and profitability of your commercial real estate investing business also depends a lot on your management techniques and how you implement them. Here are a few tips to help you get the ball rolling:

- **Work on your people-handling skills.** When managing commercial real estate, you're responsible for managing people of many different types: your tenants, employees, contractors, vendors, government employees, and the list goes on. The key to success is patience and tact (and it doesn't hurt to be nice either).

- **Know your lease agreements inside and out before they're signed by either side.** It's often said that when you buy a commercial property, you're buying the lease and the building comes for free. In other words, if your lease is legally "weak," then your investment is financially weak in the eyes of other investors, lenders, and appraisers.

- **No matter how busy you get, write a business plan for the property.** Remember, commercial properties are businesses. Treating them that way allows you to sleep at night because you know exactly what needs to be done and when. A good and well-thought-out business plan has a property summary, a market analysis, a sales and marketing plan, a management summary, and a financial plan.

- **Know your strengths and weaknesses in managing the property.** After you assess your strengths and weaknesses, be sure to build on your strengths. Take on those tasks that you do well and that give you joy. Hire out those that you don't do well or that you don't like to do.

- **Do it right the first time.** Pay for good help. The lowest bid may not be the best choice. Focus on quality, thoroughness, and attention to detail in everything you do concerning the property. After all, it's your property (and it's what pays the bills!).

Set a benchmark for your own personal cash flow. When you get right down to it, you're in this business to make money, right? After setting up a budget that takes into account the income and expenses of the property, set an amount that you'll collect as a payment for yourself as the owner and operator. Treat that amount as you would any other expense on the property.

Developing basic business systems

When you're about to purchase a commercial property remember that what you're really about to own is a full-blown business. You're making a huge financial commitment, no matter how much of a down payment you make.

Just as with any other business, you have *customers* — the tenants that you lease to — and you have *inventory* — the spaces or apartments that you're renting. There's also a sizable exchange of money between you and the tenants. Having said that, remember that every well-operated business develops basic systems to help it run efficiently. Commercial properties are no different.

For instance, you need to develop the following basic business systems in order to successfully manage your own property:

- ✔ **An accounting system:** This type of system will help you handle the cash flowing in and the cash flowing out.

    Because the lifeblood of a business is cash, you always need to be conscientious of your accounts. Take every measure to ensure that all the cash is accounted for every day — not just once per month.

- ✔ **A sales and marketing system:** Whether you know it or not, you're a sales person when managing your own property. You're selling units of space, apartments, or entire floors to a customer, your tenant. So smile and close that sale. Your sales and marketing system may include various means of advertising, ways of tracking the effectiveness of your advertising, training of staff to show prospective tenants the property, and market studies about competition.

- ✔ **An operations system:** When managing your own property, you have to keep track of all the legal requirements of operating a property, such as enforcement of leases, building codes, local ordinances, building security, and hiring and managing contractors and vendors. And don't forget to track lease renewals.

- ✔ **A maintenance system:** Let's say that a tenant notices water streaming down into her workspace. Do you simply get her a cup or bucket? No, of course not. You need to have a system for tenants to report such things, and then you fix them quickly. Also, you need to implement a preventive maintenance plan for every moving part on your property, such as air conditioners, furnaces, fans, elevators, escalators, and whatever else has moving parts.

A do-it-yourselfer's checklist

Especially when first starting out in managing your own property, you may end up doing everything yourself (if you want to). You'll take care of advertising, showings, leasing, credit checks, some of the maintenance, hiring help, keeping the books, and the rehab, if required. Look at it as a way to learn the business from the inside out, earning your stripes, while at the same time cutting costs by doing those things yourself. If you're going it alone, all the many details can be pretty overwhelming. But if you follow our lead, you'll be just fine. Here are a few helpful questions to sort through as you get started:

✓ **Is the commercial space ready to be leased?** Is it clean and presentable, does it meet building codes, and is it approved for its intended use?

✓ **Who are you intending to lease to?** Decide who your ideal tenants would be and market to them specifically. Focus on your target market.

Don't try to be a "be-all" to everyone because it's impossible to make everyone happy.

✓ **How much are you leasing the unit or space for?** Pick up the phone and do a market survey and find out what your competitor down the street is charging for its similar space. Commercial spaces that are kept full are priced just right.

✓ **Do you have a solid lease agreement?** Make sure your lease agreement is from a reputable source and is lawyer approved. We often hear in this line of work that "Your property is only worth the strength of the lease." So, if this lease is your first ever, definitely get some help from a local real estate attorney. Remember: There's no such thing as a standard lease agreement. Office building, retail center, and apartment leases are way different from each other.

✓ **Do you have the means to do a background and credit check on the prospective tenant?** Again, whether you're leasing to a person or company, both need to be creditworthy and qualified with solid financial strength. In order to perform credit and background checks on individuals, there are many online sources available. They charge a fee each time, but these costs are passed on to the applicant. In order to have a quick check of a business's credit, obtain a Dunn and Bradstreet report from www.dnb.com.

✓ **Is your support team in place?** Your support team, which includes a contractor, an electrician, a plumber, a janitor, a landscaper, a bookkeeper, and an attorney, needs to be on hand at all times in case you need them. And, believe us, you *will* need them.

✓ **What's your CPA's name?** That's right, you need a CPA and you need to know his name. You need a CPA to do your tax planning and tax strategy. Come on, you can't do *everything* yourself.

Training your tenants to respect you and the property

When you think about it, tenants are sort of like kids (but please don't tell them we said so). For instance, if you raise and train kids properly, they'll behave most times. When they misbehave, however, you have to show them who's boss or else your house will be a mess. The same theory applies for your tenants: If you don't train them consistently and according to the rules you've established, your property will be a mess. Guaranteed.

Training tenants and expecting them to conform goes both ways. Don't expect the tenants to pick up trash if your maintenance staff doesn't do this well. Also, don't expect them to pay on time 100 percent of the time if you allow them to sometimes pay late without being penalized.

The following list provides some training ideas for your tenants. However, due to the different natures of tenants in each property type, you'll have to make them fit into your own plan of management. Here are some of the things you can do to run a tidy and successful ship:

- **Allow peaceful enjoyment of the premises.** Allowing loud noises, loud parties, and rowdy gatherings is a surefire way for things to get out of hand in a jiffy. Put yourself in the shoes of a tenant who just wants to come to work (or come home) and get things done, but he's disturbed by loud noises down the hall every day. Is he going to renew his lease when it's up for renewal? We doubt it. To avoid an exodus of tenants, give everyone a strict guideline on what noises aren't permitted, when certain noises can take place, and where those noises can take place.

- **Implement a system to report maintenance issues.** To avoid cranky tenants, make sure that everyone is well informed on how to report any maintenance or repair issue with their particular unit or with any safety issues they notice on the property. Give the tenants a very simple and convenient method of reporting such things. For instance, we have all of our tenants call a central number to report a maintenance issue. In addition, we have an emergency service available 24/7 for late at night, weekends, and holidays.

- **Conduct routine physical inspections.** As a preventive measure that's sure to create happy tenants, perform routine physical inspections of the units or space on a regular basis such as every 6 to 12 months. This gives you the opportunity to see if any property abuses are occurring. If there are, you can address them right away with the tenant. The proper way to make these inspections is to give the tenants advance notice that you'll be conducting an inspection of their units or space on a certain day and time.

- **Provide a feeling of order within the property.** Believe it or not, no matter how free spirited tenants may think they are, they all desire order and consistency in their place of stay or business. To create a feeling of order, make sure signs are well cared for and clean. Make sure any posted notices are in good shape and are up-to-date. Make sure gates are closed when and where they should be. Make sure the landscape is regularly maintained. Even make sure that your company stationery is professional and consistent. There's nothing like professionalism to set the tone.

- **Present written tenant policies and procedures.** Providing a list of policies and procedures is important because it provides a road map as to how you will operate the property. We have each tenant read, acknowledge, and sign our policy and procedures form as part of their lease package. In this form, we include our operational policies and procedures on how we expect tenants to perform their part of the lease agreement. For instance, we include expectations regarding payment, parking, environmental disturbances, maintenance, pets (if allowed), and so on.

✔ **Don't accept late payments.** Cash-flow problems start with tenants not paying on time. Properties with a lot of delinquent payments and outstanding balances usually fell into that trap by allowing only one tenant to pay late. Then the word spread like wildfire to the rest of the tenants because your "iron fist" wasn't laid down. Properties with a history of late payments are absolutely a property management problem. As we've mentioned before, cash is the lifeblood of your operation, and so the life of your property will be drastically affected if you don't take ownership of the cash owed to you by the tenants.

Your tenants' profiles will reflect the way you run your property. If you have a run-down property, you'll attract run-down tenants. On the other hand, if you own a property that shows pride of ownership, you'll attract tenants that are in tiptop shape themselves.

Operating successfully day-to-day with the proper people and tools

Managing your own property requires you to have certain things right within your reach. So, what tools do you need to get the job done as a property manager? What skilled people do you need to hire? What type of data or research do you always need to have on hand? Here's a list of things you need to have or know to manage your property:

✔ **Property management software:** A couple of years into his real estate investing career, coauthor Peter Harris found himself pushing the envelope in keeping track of all the properties he owned. Soon, he was forced to start using property management software that allowed him to keep track of tenant information, tenant payments, vacancies, delinquencies, lease rates and renewals, maintenance records, and vendor information. This type of software is a wise investment and will likely enable you to expand your business. Some of the popular software packages are available from Yardi Systems, Rent Manager, Intuit, and Rent-Right, just to name a few.

✔ **Advertising:** You must have a means of advertising your property's vacant spaces or units. To do so, use one or more of the many methods available:

- The tried and true "For Rent" or "For Lease" signs are amazingly effective and inexpensive. Banners and lawn signs are also popular.

- Referrals by tenants are quite helpful. They're cheap — the only money you have to pay is the amount that you offer a tenant for a referral. Also, it's always a compliment to your property when a tenant feels obliged to recruit for you.

- Online Internet advertising is probably the most-used method of getting the word out these days. You can sign up with numerous Web sites, some of which are free; others require you to pay a fee to use their services.

- The most-expensive, but not necessarily the most-effective method, in our opinion, is running an ad in the local newspaper.

- You can hire someone to do the advertising for you. We suggest hiring a *leasing specialist,* a person who specializes in finding tenants for your property.

✔ **Accounting software:** There's a wide range of accounting software programs that you can use to keep track of your property's finances, including Quickbooks by Intuit. When coauthor Peter Harris first started, he managed his property's finances with the spreadsheet software that came with his computer. He soon outgrew it and upgraded to a more professional program. It was worth its weight in gold. You can take this task to the next level by combining your accounting software with property management software.

✔ **Vendors:** If you're like us, any repair that requires more than a hammer and a screwdriver, you hire it out. You're going to need to contract with skilled people to do such things as electrical, plumbing, carpentry, landscaping, or anything that you're unable to do yourself due to your lack of skill or time. The best way to find these types of vendors is by word of mouth. Ask for a referral from a fellow investor or from one of your other vendors. Always check references and ask to see a sample of their work, if available.

✔ **On-site maintenance:** Handymen are invaluable in the commercial real estate business. These are the guys that are the operation behind the operation. We use them to do routine and preventive maintenance and small repairs around or on the property. In the apartment business, we figure we'll need one maintenance person for every 50 apartment units. For shopping centers and offices, property needs vary too greatly to estimate.

✔ **A maintenance reporting system:** If a window is broken in an entryway, who tells who to fix it? How does the new window get purchased? Who makes sure it's fixed quickly? How does the property manager know when the work is done? All these questions are answered when you have an internal system of maintenance reporting. When a tenant reports a problem, it needs to be taken care of swiftly, cost-effectively, and correctly, and the boss must be notified when it's done. Maintenance should focus on curb appeal, daily and routine maintenance, and last, capital improvements.

✔ **An attorney:** Evictions and tenant disputes are bound to occur at some time. It's just part of the business we're in. Unless you stay up-to-date and familiar with the local laws involving tenant-landlord matters, we suggest hiring a real estate attorney to handle these types of things. You can go ahead and handle some of the more routine evictions, but consult a real estate attorney for the more complex matters. We say this because forms and notices that are improperly drawn up can be thrown out of court and can send you back to square one with the problem tenant.

✔ **A market survey:** One sure way of increasing the value of your property is to raise the rents or lease rates. In commercial real estate, we don't rely on appreciation. We focus on the bottom line: the net operating income. So, one way of knowing if you can increase your rents is if your property consistently stays 100 percent occupied. When your space is constantly full, it usually means that your rates are low for the area.

How do you know for sure if your rents are low? The answer is to perform a rent- and lease-rate survey or a competitive analysis of neighboring properties. You do this by researching and asking those property managers what their rates are. It's that simple. Compare their rates to yours. If your rates are lower than theirs and your property is 100 percent occupied, this indicates that there's room for you to increase your rates to at least the competitor's level. Another way of getting this important information is to call a local real estate broker.

Letting Go: Using Professional Property Management Companies

After several years of purchasing properties locally, coauthor Peter Harris came across a time in his career where he had to make the decision to step away from the captain's seat to allow a professional property management company to manage his properties. As his area matured in pricing and his returns on investment started to decrease with each new purchase, he decided to look outside of his area. As he analyzed deals outside of his area, they looked quite attractive and he began to invest more there.

He had definitely begun reaping the benefits of higher returns, when something started to happen: Because he owned and operated more properties, locally and out of the area, his whole business life became managing the properties. He had virtually no time to search for, analyze, and invest in new and exciting projects because nearly all of his time was spent on operating the properties. It even began to weigh in on his personal and family life as well. In essence, his management duties had taken over his life. And, luckily, he knew there was more to life than just real estate.

So, he had to make a decision: Keep on trucking at a mile a minute or let go? He decided to let go and hire professional property management companies to oversee his properties. He soon got his life back. We don't want you to get sucked in like Peter did, so in this section, we discuss how to successfully hire and manage property management companies.

Understanding the ins and outs of professional property management

Professional property managers are a special breed. They have to be extremely effective organizers, and they must be masters of the day planner. Frankly, we don't know how they can keep track of thousands of apartment units and millions of square feet of space at any one time. But the successful ones do this quite well. And thankfully so. Here's a typical list of the day-to-day responsibilities of a professional property manager. She must do the following:

- Collect and deposit rents
- Oversee maintenance of the property
- Handle day-to-day operations
- Contract in the name of the owner for utilities
- Enforce leases
- Hire and supervise all employees and independent contractors
- Keep accounting books and records
- Pay all bills in a timely fashion
- Furnish the owner with financial reports
- Prepare and execute annual operating budget and capital expenditures
- Write a sales and marketing plan
- Monitor effectiveness of the sales and marketing plan
- Handle legal matters, such as evictions
- Handle emergencies
- Work with local officials, such as police and code enforcement

What the previous list does is help you define the role of the professional property manager or property management company. It's always helpful to know what to expect out of a person or company that you hire. Be clear and concise upfront and have everything in writing before signing on the dotted line.

Deciding to hire a professional property management company

Think of your million-dollar investment as a suitcase full of money. Now imagine that due to your busy schedule, you need to find someone to look after your suitcase when you can't be around. You can imagine how scrutinizing you would be of the person or company you chose to guard your suitcase full of money. You'd check that person's or company's background, credibility and capability, and integrity to the utmost with tough questions.

So, what we're trying to say is this: Treat hiring and managing of a property management company for your property with the same care. After all, your investment is worth a lot of money!

Determining whether you want to hire a property management company to look after your investment can be a difficult and frustrating decision. However, there are some instances where you're almost sure to hire someone. Here are those four instances:

- **The property isn't local or it's too far away.** For instance, performing the following duties can be difficult if you're operating properties that aren't in your area:
  - Picking up and depositing rents
  - Overseeing maintenance and repairs
  - Taking care of evictions
  - Handling emergencies

- **The property is too large.** Here are two questions to ask yourself if you aren't sure whether your property is too large:
  - How will I manage 100 apartment units myself and still have a day-time job?
  - Can my current self-managed apartment business handle double or triple the amount of units efficiently?

- **You want to have a life or get your life back.** Let's face it, managing property profitably takes time — your time. How is your time best used? Are you spending too much time on your apartments and not enough on the other parts of your life? If so, hiring a property management company may be the right decision for you.

- **You aren't good at managing property.** You know you're leaving money on the table each month due to your lack of skills. If that's the case, hire someone who has these skills and has a system and passion for managing property. This way, you get to do what you do (and enjoy!) best.

Searching for property management candidates

When you're trying to round up property manager candidates, start by asking for referrals. For instance, use commercial real estate brokers as a resource for referrals. Hopefully, they have done enough deals where their clients are using management companies that they can speak on their experiences. We would also ask fellow investors who own properties like yours. Inquire about their experiences with certain companies that you're looking into. If one of your referrals doesn't pan out, ask *that referral* for a referral. Because property management selection is such a hit-or-miss process, it's best to start off interviewing someone who has already used that particular management company.

Here are some search-related tips to keep in mind:

- ✔ It's helpful to drive around the neighborhood looking for "For Rent" or "Now Leasing" signs. Most times, the phone numbers listed are from property managers. Call those companies and start "feeling them out" as possible interview candidates. We suggest just being honest and straightforward and telling them the reason for the call is to find property management for yourself.

- ✔ It's best to gather a minimum of three property managers to interview. Obviously, the more you interview, the better your chances are of hiring the best suitor for the property.

- ✔ If you're unable to find a reputable property management company, don't purchase the property — no matter how good of a deal it is. Remember the suitcase of money?

Interviewing your prospective managers

Okay, so now it's time to pick up the phone and start the initial interview process. Remember, this is just a "feeling out" process, where you're looking for professionalism, prompt return of your phone call, and good rapport. There's no way you can judge the quality of the candidates' management skills just yet. In fact, we've found that you can go through all the interview situations and assessments and still not have a full grasp on a candidate's skills. You don't find out who your new manager really is until he's hired and put into action.

This interview isn't for telling every candidate everything you expect. It's merely to gather information in order to make a decision regarding who you want to conduct a full interview with.

Here are a few questions to ask during your initial phone calls:

- ✔ What is the general vacancy rate in your area? "Your area" could be a city, town, neighborhood, district, or street. This information is crucial when studying the feasibility of owning property in this area.

- ✔ How many units and/or square feet of space do you currently have under management? What type? Make sure that the company has experience with your type of property. After all, a property management company that manages 400 single-family homes isn't the same as one that manages 400 units of apartment buildings.

- ✔ How long have you been in business? If a candidate has less than a year of experience, don't use him. A candidate really needs to complete at least one cycle (spring, summer, fall, winter) to know what's going on. We personally wouldn't use anyone with less than three years of actual experience.

- ✔ What are your percentage management fees? Plug these fees into your property cash-flow analysis. Compare fees and services with other companies.

- ✔ Do you have your own maintenance staff or do you use independent contractors?

- ✔ What is the cost for an eviction process from start to finish? Have the candidates review with the whole process with you.

- ✔ What are the costs of new leases to the new owner?

- ✔ How do you advertise your vacancies? Who pays for advertising?

- ✔ What are your business hours?

- ✔ How are tenant emergencies and weekend calls handled?

- ✔ What monthly reports do you typically send owners?

 After hanging up from a phone interview, it helps to sit back and ask yourself this important question: "What does my gut feeling tell me about this person and his company?" Gut feeling and instinct are an important part of this process, so honor your perception. If you feel that there wasn't a connection between the two of you, move on to the next candidate. Whatever you do, don't continue with a candidate just because he was really nice. Nice doesn't cut it in property management.

Checking credibility and capability

After conducting your initial phone interviews, you have to narrow your choices. To do so, ask those companies that you're interested in whether they're interested in managing your property. If the answer is yes, the next step is to invite them to the property for a face-to-face meeting and walk-through. During this meeting, you have to gauge their credibility and capability. Asking yourself the following three questions can help:

✔ **Is this company a "Mom and Pop" operation?** Smaller-sized operations don't have the manpower to get the job done. They're just too small to consistently deliver what they promise. You may want to steer clear, because you'll likely need to hire a medium-sized property management company. Medium-sized companies have more structure, more employees, and have a "company feel" to them. On the other hand, hiring a very large property management company that manages 5,000 units and millions of square feet may be a bit too expensive for you at this point.

✔ **Does the company's management style match yours?** Is your preference to work with a very aggressive "in your face" manager or one that's more diplomatic. Both styles can be effective in their own ways. Choose a type that settles with what you've been exposed to in your own life. It's only natural to gravitate toward what you feel would be more effective.

✔ **Is the company local?** Find out if the company operates in the same city as your property. If it doesn't, how far away is it and does it currently manage property in the vicinity? If the company is not local, and has no presence, you'll have to question how well they know the area, the market, and potential tenants.

A big chunk of hiring an excellent property management company and being successful is being in agreement with one another. What we mean is that you need to make sure that you and the manager have a complete understanding of each side's expectations. So, be sure to express, in detail, as much about your expectations as you can to the property manager. In general, and from an owner's point of view, here are your likely expectations plainly put:

✔ Maximize potential rental income and reduce operating costs

✔ Strengthen tenant retention and relations

✔ Enhance visual appeal of property and increase property value

These are ultimate goals for a property when you get right down to it.

Inquire whether any of the property management companies you're considering hiring owns and manages properties they personally own. We consider this a huge potential conflict of interest. The property they manage for you may be in direct competition with yours. Whose property gets the best tenants and whose property gets occupied first are two questions we would constantly ponder.

Drafting the property management agreement

After you've selected a property management company, you need to create a legally binding agreement, called a *property management agreement,* between the both of you. This agreement should describe the duties and responsibilities of both the owner and the manager. Before you sign one of these agreements, make sure that you have certain clauses in the contract. In our experiences, property managers want to get away with as little as possible on the agreement. The following are basic "must-have" clauses of a property management agreement:

- **Leasing clause:** This clause says that the manager must use her best efforts to keep the property rented and leased by procuring tenants for the property and negotiating and executing on behalf of the owner.

- **Rents clause:** Under this clause, the manager is required to collect and deposit the rents and any revenues from the property and serve all notices for the collection of rent and other charges. The manager is also required to initiate actions for evictions and when necessary, to settle, compromise, or release actions or suits and reinstate tenancy.

- **Service contracts clause:** A service contract clause requires the manager to execute in the owner's name for utilities and services for the operation and maintenance of the property.

- **Accounting clause:** This clause says that the manager must keep proper books of account for the property and that these books need to be open for inspection by the owner. Also, the property manager must give the owner a monthly statement of financial status and operations on a specified date of each month.

- **Owner approval dollar amount clause:** This clause states that the property management shall seek the written approval of the owner before spending an amount of money that exceeds a previously established amount.

- **Reserve account clause:** Under this clause, the owner must maintain a specific amount of money in her account as a reserve amount. If the balance falls below this amount, the owner shall replenish it within 30 days.

- **Compensation to property manager clause:** Under this clause, the owner agrees to pay the property manager on a monthly basis for the services that the manager provides. Compensation can be a percentage of collected revenues or a fixed fee. The percentage typically ranges from 4 percent to 10 percent of collected income.

Before signing your contract, find out if there's a *per new lease fee*. A per new lease fee is a dollar amount charged to the owner every time a new lease is signed. In some cases, this fee can be as much as one month's rent. Find out who keeps the late fees, and determine whether there's an extra charge at any time during the eviction process. Will the property manager charge you every time they go to court? All these fees can quickly add up and erase your cash flow.

✔ **Obligations of owner clause:** This clause states that the owner's requirements include providing direction, specifications, and plans to the property management, reimbursing the property management for expenses occurred, and maintaining proper insurance levels.

✔ **Terms of agreement clause:** This clause obviously provides information on the terms of the agreement. Initial terms are usually for 12 months. Never sign on for more than 12 months at any time because the property manager may not be a good fit for you after all. Either party may terminate the agreement by giving a 30-day written notice to the other party.

✔ **Default clause:** This clause states that if either party fails to perform his obligations per the agreement, the performing party may terminate the agreement. Legal action on either side is discussed in this clause as well.

✔ **Terminations clause:** According to this clause, immediately upon termination, the property manager must provide the owner with all originals or copies of leases and all agreements and related documents. All property financial records in possession of the property manager must be delivered to the owner. A 30-day notice is required for termination.

✔ **Fiduciary responsibility/statutory of compliance clause:** This is the code of ethics clause. It states that the property manager will perform all duties in the agreement. It also states the following:

- That the property manager's main obligation is to obey and abide by the law

- That the property manager will notify the owner of professional opinion matters

- That the property manager shall keep the owner's information strictly confidential and shall not share it with the public

Be wary of fine print embedded in the agreement. For instance, if you ever see a "hold harmless" clause, have it removed from the agreement. This type of clause grants the property management company immunity from any harm and liability it causes on your property whether it's the company's fault or not. If it's a professional company and you're taking a risk on hiring them, they must take some of the responsibility. That's only fair, right? Also, be sure to delete any clauses stating that the property manager will act as real estate agent or broker or will receive commission if and when the owner sells the property. Hire a real estate agent to market and sell your property and let the property managers do what they do best, and that is, manage.

When working with property management companies on either capital improvement projects (such as replacing a roof or repaving the parking lot) or on rehabilitation projects, never pay for the whole project upfront and never put all the money into an account that the property management has access to. It's human nature to spend, rather than save, when money is readily available — especially if the money being used isn't theirs. Instead, have the money available on an "as-needed" or "draw" basis.

Getting your reports: Monthly and weekly accountability

Remember getting report cards from school? They showed how well you were doing in each subject and what you needed help with. Your property receives a similar report from the property management company. Property management will likely send you status reports on different parts of the property. For example, it will send you reports regarding the income, the delinquent income or late payments, the expenses in detail, how many vacant apartments or spaces you have, and what maintenance was performed on the property during the month, just to name a few. In the following sections, we explain the two different types of reports that you're likely to receive: monthly and weekly reports. Weekly reports are rarely used, but they are just as important as monthly reports. To get the most out of reporting, make sure you incorporate weekly reporting. Later in this chapter, we go into detail about what weekly reports are composed of and more important, why we do it.

Typical monthly reports

Certain property management reports are sent to you once a month. These reports are sent monthly to give you the "big picture" of how the property is performing both financially and operationally. See Table 11-1 for a list of the typical reports that you're likely to receive each month.

Table 11-1	Typical Monthly Reports
Monthly Report	*Details within the Report*
Accounts receivable report	Detailed rent rolls of tenants with gross potential rent included Vacancy report showing empty units or space Vacancy report showing if empty units or space are preleased
Accounts payable report	Check register showing who each check was paid to Expense distribution breaking down the expenses into sections

(continued)

Table 11-1 *(continued)*

Monthly Report	Details within the Report
General ledger report	Balance sheet Profit/loss (operating statement) — monthly Profit/loss (operating statement) — year-to-date
Maintenance and work order activity report	Requests for maintenance (by tenants) and status of the repairs
Budget and capital improvements report	A list of work that's scheduled, in progress, and completed

Don't stand for late reporting. If you were promised a set of reports on the first of every month and the reports are late, contact your property manager. Ask why the reports are late and be adamant about getting them immediately. If you don't hold the property manager accountable for this now, other important duties may start slipping as well. After all, it's human nature for folks to procrastinate when they can.

Weekly reports

We've come up with a weekly accountability system that's simple and easy to follow and understand, but most important, that's very effective. First of all, this system is designed to be easy for the property manager to follow, fill out, and report on. Because there's nothing complex about it, your property manager can't come up with any excuses why she can't turn it in on time. You should ask to receive this report every Monday morning.

The idea of accountability is to focus weekly on key items such as occupancy, marketing, rent collection, rent delinquencies, and maintenance items. Why ask for a weekly rather than a monthly report? Well, think of it this way: Normally, owners speak with their property managers once per month (or once every 30 days) on the status of their properties. So, what happens if a vacancy issue occurs on the fifth of the month? You probably wouldn't find out until the first of next month, right? So, almost a month goes by before you can even address this vacancy issue. However, if you get a weekly accountability report, you would know about this issue and could promptly set forth on resolving it on the same day that it's reported. In this case, you have the ability to be *proactive* rather than *reactive*.

We like to describe this accountability system with a sports metaphor. For example, when you're playing a game and you want to look at the score quickly, what do you do? You look at the scoreboard, of course! The scoreboard lets you know how you're doing — how many points you're ahead or behind, who has the ball, who's up next, how much time is on the clock, and so on. Figure 11-1 shows an example of a one-page property scoreboard.

The _____ Apartments (Your Property)
To: _____ (Property Owner -- You)
From: _____ (Management Company)

Date: 10/21/05

Re: weekly report as of 10/21/05

Pages: 1

Property: _____ Apartments   Total Units: 94

Occupancy Status:

Type	# of units	Rate	Sq. Ft.	Vacants	Leased	Notices to move out
1 beds	26	$499	650	4	2	1
2 beds	60	$599	850	2	2	
3 beds	8	$699	1050	0	0	
		Total Available		6		

Current move-in bonus: one month free stopped as of 10/1

Vacants: 6   **Leased:** 4   **Move Ins:** 2   **Total Made Ready Units:** 5

Traffic Generated From: resident referral, drive by, local paper

Potential Income (if 100% rented): $54,506

Collected Income: $48,730 as of 10/10

Delinquent Amount: $2582

Maintenance Calls:

Appliance	AC	Plumbing	Electrical	Key	Other
2	6	1		3	3

Figure 11-1:
A weekly property report.

This report is an exact copy of what we get on a weekly basis. Show this to your current or to-be-hired property manager as an example of what you require. The key to making it not overbearing to your property manager is to keep it to a single page in length. From this report we can see critical information that gives you a "scoreboard" view of how your property is performing from week to week. You'll be able to see upward or downward trends in income, vacancies, and maintenance issues — all important accountability items.

Part IV: Day-to-Day Ownership and Operations

Knowing How to Be an Effective Absentee Owner

An *absentee owner* is an owner of a property that doesn't personally manage or reside on the property owned. An out-of-state owner could fall into that category. These types of owners often get a bad rap. Why? Because absentee owners have been known to ruin properties and cause decay in the neighborhoods where the properties are located. This weakening happens not only because the owner is physically absent from the property, but because they're emotionally absent as well. Their lack of involvement in the care and operation of the property causes the property to head in a downward spiral. This in turn affects the quality of the tenants that the property attracts as well as the overall neighborhood feel.

Here are signs and symptoms that you may be turning into an absentee owner:

- ✔ You never visit the property.
- ✔ You're in denial that the property is in financial trouble.
- ✔ The city officials don't like you.
- ✔ Your property has become or is located in what people refer to as a "war zone."
- ✔ Nobody, except criminals, wants to live on the property.
- ✔ You don't spend money on preventive maintenance and capital improvements.
- ✔ Your maintenance solution for everything is to place temporary bandages on much-needed fixes.

However, don't worry; it is possible to be a positive, well-respected, and successful absentee owner. The first step is to turn the previous list of negative symptoms into positives. For instance, simply visit your property more often and see what's going on and what needs fixed. Second, give thoughtful attention to the way the property looks. Also, be sure to get (positively) involved with the city officials — they can help you out more than you'd think. And don't allow criminals on the property.

Here are some other ways that you can put your best foot forward:

- ✔ **Have a precise management plan.** Before you buy the property, know who the property management will be. Hire a well-known and battle-proven property management company that knows exactly what it's going to take to successfully run the property. As one of our mentors once said, "If you fail to plan, plan to fail." A good and well-thought-out business plan has a property summary, a market analysis, a sales and marketing plan, a management summary, and a financial plan.

✔ **Understand the infrastructure.** A successful property infrastructure means having an accounting system, a sales and marketing system, an operations system, and a maintenance system. When considering a property, make sure that it has an infrastructure and determine how well it's working. If it isn't working, can it be fixed without breaking the bank? Know exactly what you're buying.

✔ **Know the market.** Before you buy a property, understand the market conditions and know what's going on. Be sure to consider lease rates, rental rates, move-in bonuses, vacancy rates, job growth, population growth, and any upcoming economic development in the city.

✔ **Have an exit strategy in place.** Know upfront, before you even make any offers, why you're purchasing the property. Are you buying it for cash flow, to refinance later, as a tax shelter, or for long-term growth? In fact, knowing your reasoning upfront may even cause you to pass on the deal altogether. It may even stop you from purchasing a property that's hundreds or thousands of miles from your area.

✔ **Be ready to commit.** Be ready to commit time, money, and management to the property to ensure its success. And remember that not all properties — even those of the same type — are the same. Some properties may take years to stabilize the income and occupancy, while others may take months. So, always plan for longer than you expect.

✔ **Buy a large enough property.** Purchase a property that allows you to afford a staff for operation. The smaller the property, the smaller the income. And the smaller the income, the less hired help you can afford. In your analysis of the property, make sure that you can afford a property management company and its staff.

✔ **Plan for a rainy day.** Rainy days are bound to happen in the commercial real estate business. Roof failure, water damage, and broken boilers are all common problems that you may come across. Have money saved up for these issues, and be sure to have reputable vendors lined up for when the problems strike.

✔ **Visit the property routinely.** No matter how far away you are from the property, plan on paying a visit to the property at a minimum of once per year although twice or three times is recommended. However, during the first year of ownership, quarterly visits are recommended. Throw in a surprise visit every now and then too.

Chapter 12

Protecting Your Assets

. . . .

In This Chapter

▶ Understanding why you need protection

▶ Determining how to protect your assets

▶ Using common-sense strategies

. . . .

*W*ant to hear some things that may keep you up at night? More than 90 million lawsuits are filed in the United States each year. And in this country there are more attorneys per capita than in any other civilized country in the world. Right now the United States has over 700,000 attorneys with another 100,000 in law schools. To stay in business and support their families, many of these attorneys have to file or defend lawsuits instead of preventing the lawsuits from happening.

That's where asset protection comes in. You may be thinking "I don't want to have so many assets that someone is going to try to come after me." The sad truth is that you can be sued for anything. With attorneys willing to take cases on a contingency basis, you may very well become a target whether you think you are or not.

Asset protection can be quite confusing to the newbie investor. And because every real estate investor needs to have it, you need to get a handle on it. We've got you covered in this chapter. We provide tips on some of the best things you can do right now to help protect yourself against any legal attacks that may come your way.

Always take the time to properly set up your business, including getting any operating or partnership agreements in writing and signed by all parties. If you're already in business and don't have any operating or partnership agreements in place, make it a top priority to complete these as soon as possible. If you purchased an investment with buddies and you have no operating or partnership agreements in place, you're setting yourself up for a potential headache. Countless times we have seen "once-in-a-lifetime" deals for sale, and when we inquired why the owner was selling, we often found that it was because the partnership was dissolving due to "business differences." In other words, the partners are fighting and the property is paying the price. And by not having the correct agreements in place, each side's attorneys get involved, and we all know what happens when attorneys get involved, don't we?

Taking Asset Protection Seriously

Most investors never get around to setting up any type of asset protection for themselves. Why? Because of the following two reasons:

- ✔ They think they don't have enough assets right now to worry or do anything about protecting them.

- ✔ They have assets and are steadily building their net worth but are either too busy or too confused about the process to do anything about it.

People face so many financial disasters today stemming from events like divorces and deaths of family members to lawsuits. The IRS can also be a major threat to your financial success these days.

 Preventing all these financial woes rolls into what is called *asset protection*. It's a combination of legal protection, tax planning, and estate planning. All these areas act together to form a foundation so that if you get sued, you don't necessarily lose everything you own.

 Understanding asset protection can be quite difficult at first because every "expert" seems to recommend something different. Our advice is to read *Guaranteed Millionaire* by Lee Phillips, Esq (www.guaranteedmillionaire book.com). Unlike any other book we've read, this one spells out what to do to create the asset protection that you need without having to set up complicated offshore trusts. However, because the book is self-published, you may not be able to get it from your local bookstore.

Create a plan to avoid lawsuits

Part of running a successful business includes having a plan to help create a consistent, predictable outcome for your customers. It's amazing how many property owners don't follow an asset protection plan that's designed to keep the financial dragons away. You can avoid lawsuits by doing the following:

- ✔ **Conducting your business in a professional manner:** This covers everything from hiring, leasing, and negotiating. Keep it professional and you'll avoid the hot water that others may fall into.

- ✔ **Keeping your properties in good operating condition:** Owners who allow their properties to deteriorate into unsafe or unlivable conditions are just asking for a lawsuit. So step up to the plate and create the systems to take care of your properties.

- ✔ **Staying mum about your money and equity (especially if you have a lot):** If you flash a lot of cash, you may attract the attention of someone who may be looking to start a frivolous lawsuit. Frivolous or not, a lawsuit is still going to cost you in time, frustration, and attorney fees.

The fact of the matter is that law schools are graduating so many lawyers these days that in order to eat, they have to fill in a gap by conjuring up lawsuits. So, if you're investing in real estate and conditions are ideal for a lawsuit, then that lawsuit will likely rear its ugly head.

Plan for the worst and be happy if it doesn't happen

One of the challenges you may have with proper asset protection is that you may never need it. You may hope that you never have anyone challenging you for the wealth that you've built up, but unfortunately in today's society it's crazy *not* to have proper asset protection in place. In fact, if you never have a situation come along in your life where someone goes after the wealth you have protected, you're fortunate indeed.

After a disaster occurs, it's too late to set up your asset protection. You have to do it now. The question we often hear is "Who needs it?" Our resounding answer: Everybody needs it! We're talking about the tools of wealth here. And we've never met a wealthy person who doesn't use these tools. You can't build a house from the roof down. You have to have a foundation first. The same goes for your financial fortune. Check out the upcoming section to find out how to set up your protection.

 We operate today in a society that relies on the written word. So, to protect yourself, your agreements need to be in writing; otherwise, all bets are off. Remember that old saying, "The pen is mightier than the sword?" We've seen situations in which people thought they had agreements, but then they read what they actually had in writing. The language turned out to be different than they thought, leading them to lose out on big bucks in addition to possibly taking on more liability than originally thought.

Building a Legal Fortress for Personal Assets

The right time to prepare for an attack is before it ever comes. You wouldn't want to start building a castle when an enemy is marching over the hill. A little preparation ahead of time goes a long way toward giving you the peace of mind you deserve.

Proper asset protection can save you an extra $10,000 to $20,000 a year in taxes. For example, with it in place, if someone in the family dies, there usually is little to no economic tax loss and very little legal loss to the family members. These are important things to think about today.

So, it's time to ask, "How do I legally protect my assets from those who want to put their hands in my pockets?" And to find out how, simply read on.

Making use of entities

If you aren't into paperwork and details, putting together business entities such as corporations and limited liability companies can seem pretty intimidating. What do we mean by *entity?* An entity is considered to be a separate "legal person." The advantage of entities is that by keeping all of your investing business in the legal name of your business entity, any liabilities from the business may harm the business itself but not you personally because you're a different "legal person."

You can create multiple entities so that if you do have a loss, you only risk losing a part of your business rather than losing everything. The advantage of this strategy is that your personal assets, such as your house, your car, and your bank accounts, are kept separate from your business. That way if something goes wrong with your business or someone sues you, your personal assets aren't lost also.

Make sure that whenever you sign anything for your business, you add both your title and the name of your business entity after your name. To make it easy for someone to get in touch with you, include your phone number and e-mail address.

Corporations

A *corporation* exists entirely apart from its owner. It has unique and beneficial legal and tax advantages when compared to owning and operating real estate as an individual. Corporations must have at least one owner, but there's no maximum. The owners are called *shareholders* or *stockholders.* The legal benefits include liability protection of your personal assets. Incorporating your real estate business safeguards your personal assets against creditors and lawsuits. Stockholders usually aren't liable for their company's debts and obligations. They're usually limited in liability to the amount they have invested in the corporation. For example, if a stockholder purchased $1,000 in stock, he can't lose more than $1,000 of his personal assets.

It isn't a good idea to hold real estate in a corporation. It will most likely cost you an arm and a leg in taxes. Why? You'll be taxed twice. The way corporations are set up, you'll pay taxes on the income reported. Then the left over income is distributed to shareholders as dividends and it's taxed again. So you're doubly taxed and defeat one of the great perks of real estate investing: tax sheltering.

A great use of corporations in real estate investing is to use them to manage properties. Here's how: You hold your real estate in limited liability companies (LLCs), which are explained in the following section, and the LLCs report to the corporation that you set up. This way, you completely remove yourself individually from liability because you have two layers of protection.

Limited liability companies

The most popular choice these days for holding real estate is the limited liability company (LLC). It isn't a corporation or partnership, but it has the liability protection of a corporation and the tax benefits of a partnership. The main benefit of a limited liability company is that the income, expenses, and profits flow through to the members of the LLC, and then they're taxed individually and only once. Also, members can't be held personally liable for company debts and liabilities unless they signed as personal guarantors, hence the term "limited liability." Whereas in corporations, you're required to hold meetings and keep minutes, LLCs require no meetings or minutes. Even though LLCs have been around since 1977, their overall flexibility makes them the most popular form of ownership used today. A great resource for getting up to speed on using LLCs is *Limited Liabilities Companies For Dummies* (Wiley).

The beauty of an LLC lies in its "check one box" taxation, meaning that you can literally choose how you want to be taxed — as a sole proprietor, a partnership, or a corporation.

LLCs do have certain disadvantages, however. They're dissolved when a member dies or goes bankrupt. A corporation, on the other hand, can go on forever, even as shareholders die.

Don't put too many properties into one LLC. If you have six properties being held in one LLC, and you get sued from one of the properties, the other five properties become a target as well. The rule of thumb that we use is this: If one property has 10 percent or more equity in it, give it its own LLC.

Don't throw your entities under the bus

Entities are a great way to protect your personal assets when business deals go sour. But if you make the mistakes we mention in the following sections, you can lose the protection that the entities give you. For example, if you fail to follow the guidelines and rules of your entity, the protection it provides may be removed, opening yourself up to personal liability (lawsuits) and loss of tax advantages.

Mixing personal and business funds

Your business account should have its own checking account that isn't ever used to pay for personal expenses. We've found that having a separate credit card that's used just for business expenses helps to keep things separate as well. So, when you're paying for something for your commercial real estate business, use the business checking account, and when you're out having dinner with your friends or family, use your personal funds.

The risk is that if you're mixing personal and business funds, then you really aren't running your corporation or LLC like a real business. In other words, if you take a trip to the Bahamas on your business's credit card, someone may be able to "pierce the corporate veil." This means that a business creditor can claim that because you aren't running your business like it should be run she may be able to come after your personal stuff.

Ignoring your state's laws or corporate formalities

Some states have guidelines that may be required for you to get the asset protection that you're expecting. For example, some states require your limited liability company to have at least two members in order to receive liability protection. Or if you fail to meet certain annual state requirements like filing an annual report, paying franchise taxes, or maintaining a Registered Agent, the Secretary of State may dissolve the company.

You also need to make sure that you follow the formalities of running your entity. For example, be sure to keep minutes of your meetings and to document the major decisions that your entity has made.

Signing personally on real estate or business loans

When your investing business, say, ACME Investing, LLC, for instance, needs to borrow money to purchase a commercial property, you may be asked to sign personally to guarantee the loan. What this means is that if your LLC can't make the payments, you're responsible for making the payments out of your pocket. If you don't or can't make the payments, the lender then has the right to go after your personal assets as further collateral after foreclosing on the property. This situation is obviously one you want to avoid. So what are your options?

The best type of loan to get is a *nonrecourse loan,* which is secured solely by the commercial property itself. And in the event of a default on the payments, the lender's only collateral is the property itself, meaning that you, personally, have not signed on or are guaranteeing the loan.

However, one of the interesting parts of commercial real estate is that the larger properties are much more likely to get nonrecourse loans. In most cases, loans in the range of $2 million qualify for nonrecourse consideration. The reason for this is that if your entity, ACME Investing, LLC, owns a shopping center that's worth $30 million dollars, your personal assets probably won't be able to cover the payments. So, with larger properties, the lenders are usually very cautious and lend only on commercial property that can easily make the payments. Unfortunately, smaller commercial properties (less than $2 million loan amount) aren't eligible for nonrecourse loans. Here the investors must personally guarantee the loan.

Gathering essential fail-safe documentation

When you're ready to put your asset protection in place, spend some time with your attorney and tax planner to make sure that all the appropriate documents are properly prepared. Have these documents handy when you're meeting with your attorney and tax planner. Here's a checklist of those documents that you need to have prepared:

- A will
- A living will or living trust
- A list of assets (to make it easier for your family when you die)
- An operating agreement (if you own an LLC)
- Articles of incorporation (if you own a corporation)
- A family trust
- Partnership agreements
- Purchase agreements
- Residential leases
- Commercial leases

When people get into trouble, the attorneys or mediators refer to what's in writing to see if the language will settle any differences. What you write down is huge, so you have to direct the lawyers to write down what you want. Simply getting a piece of legal paper from the lawyer won't do it for you. You have to at least be actively involved enough in your real estate investing to know if what's being written is what you want. You can't blindly walk in off the street and trust the lawyers and other professionals to take care of you if you haven't taken the time to at least master the basics.

Common-Sense Protection Tips

We've been in business for a combined total of more than 27 years, and in those years we've had — knock on wood — hardly any legal issues come up. The reason for this boils down to some common-sense formulas. It's amazing to see people mistreating their clients and colleagues and then wondering why everyone seems to be suing them.

The very best way to protect your commercial properties, the equity that you've built up from them, and all of your other assets is to follow these guidelines:

- ✔ Treat others as you would like to be treated.
- ✔ Meet any potential problems head-on.
- ✔ Always have proper insurance coverage.

Treat others as you would like to be treated

Life is uncertain. Part of this uncertainty is that although you can't eliminate potential legal challenges, you can do business in a way that will help you avoid most of the problems that are caused by things as simple as basic greed and disrespect. An example of greed and disrespect would be taking unfair advantage of a situation where the seller is powerless, for your own gain. Or it could be when a seller decides to do everything in his or her power to cancel your purchase contract because someone after the fact has offered a higher price for his or her property. In both instances, lawsuits are possible.

If you don't believe us that mere respect and congeniality can make you successful, consider our experiences. We have found that in our millions of dollars of real estate deals we've had almost no problems from a legal standpoint. The reason for this is that we tend to do deals that work for everyone, and we try our best to avoid making decisions based on *just* the money or profits.

Meet any potential problems head-on

As soon as you know that someone is unhappy with you, instead of waiting for a lawsuit to come along when you least expect it, go sit down and meet with him. Sometimes just taking the time to really hear someone out will work wonders for both of you.

Most books can tell you how to listen to someone when that person wants to talk to you. Sometimes, however, it's important to be able to listen to someone when he wants to yell at you. Here's our secret formula, which we call the Empathy Unwind Process:

- ✔ **Connect with the angry person.** Get in touch as soon as you can with the unhappy person. Thank him for getting in touch with you or for bringing his concerns to your attention.

For example, say something like "I know that this is difficult for you. It would have been easier to simply keep quiet, so I want to thank you for taking the time to bring this to my attention."

✓ **Clarify the process.** Let the person know that your goal is simply to listen. Then get his agreement by saying something like this: "I'm not going to promise to come up with a solution today. I just wanted to take some time to really understand things from your perspective. Is that okay with you?"

✓ **Draw out the feelings.** Draw out all the feelings that the person has so that he can start to unwind a bit and, more important, understand that you've taken the time to really listen.

✓ **Check for empathy.** Ask the person if he feels that you've taken the time to really understand how he feels. Point out that you have your own side to the story as well, but tell him that isn't what you're focusing on today.

✓ **Explain the next steps.** Let the person know that you're going to process what you've heard from him today, thank him for taking the time to share, and give him a time frame (at least three or four days away) when you personally will get back in touch with him. Tell him again that you understand that there are two sides to every story, but that today all you wanted to do was to simply listen. Then ask the client if he thinks it's fair for him to perhaps listen to your side of the story at some point.

Always have proper insurance coverage

Having proper insurance in place to cover your business and assets is essential to avoiding lawsuits and protecting your assets. To find a good insurance agent, ask other commercial investors whom they have used in the past. The right agent will be willing to take the time to both listen to your needs and also explain which type of coverage is best for you. Here are some tips for when you're buying insurance:

✓ **Get new bids every two years.** If you get new bids every two years, you can potentially save yourself thousands of dollars. And as an extra bonus, the building will be more valuable because you've increased the net operating income.

By looking at our options, we recently were able to lower our insurance payment 20 percent by switching to a new insurer for one of our large apartment buildings. With a large complex, this percentage could amount to tens of thousands of dollars that we save each year.

✓ **Read the entire policy along with any updates that are sent to you.** Look at the coverage amounts and make sure you're covered sufficiently, neither over- nor under-insured. And pay close attention to the exceptions. In other words, make sure you determine the things that aren't covered and the things that have limited coverage or higher deductibles.

✔ **Ask your agent about getting an umbrella policy as an add-on to your homeowner's insurance.** You may be able to get additional coverage of $2 to $5 million for a small increase in your premium. Your goal is to have another line of defense if someone were to sue you personally or if they were able to somehow break through the other steps you've taken to protect your assets.

✔ **Get help managing your risks.** Your insurance company can help you manage your risks by inspecting your commercial properties for you. Many insurance companies are glad to pay a visit to your property once or twice a year to look for potential hazards or simple improvements that would reduce the risk of lawsuits. After all, both you and your insurance company would like to reduce your chances of a lawsuit as much as possible.

Chapter 13

Why Properties Fail

*D*o you remember studying all night for an exam and being completely ready for it, but when it came time to take it, nothing on the exam was what you studied for? You probably threw your hands in the air and asked, "Why did everything go wrong? How did I fail so miserably?"

That's exactly how coauthor Peter Harris felt when his first real estate failure happened. As he coped with this failure, he took several real estate and life lessons from it. For instance, he discovered that every failure in his life had a cause. And he gained more insight through these failures than he did through his successes. He also realized that he could come back stronger, smarter, more humble, more appreciative, and more successful from any failure. And he has. Countless other investors and entrepreneurs have done the same.

Having said all that, we want to remind you that properties do fail occasionally. And these failures come in many ways, sizes, and circumstances. So, in this chapter, we go through real-life real estate failures, what causes them, who causes them, how to avoid them, and how to survive them (and thrive despite them!).

This chapter could very well be the most important chapter you read. Only by going through many failures and painful experiences in our years of real estate investing can we write this chapter. We like to believe that we went through it all so you won't have to. But the absolute best part about this is that we lived and prospered through it all!

What Is a Property Failure?

To understand what a property failure is, first consider the dictionary definition of what it means to fail. There are three common definitions: to "lose strength," to "fade or die away," and to "stop functioning normally." Now we'll put property failure into perspective regarding these dictionary definitions. For example, when a property begins to lose strength, its financial condition is probably in distress. This may mean that as an owner you're losing money on a monthly basis. When a property starts to fade or die away, its desirability factor is usually gone. The property no longer has curb appeal and no one wants to move into it. And last, when a property stops functioning normally, a significant part of your operations, such as rent collections or leasing, likely isn't working properly or at all. All these factors can lead to property failure.

With property failure, the owner obviously suffers some consequences. For instance, as an owner, you may have to do the following:

✔ Sell the property for a loss.

✔ Fix your ruined credit and credibility.

✔ Handle damaged business and partnership relationships.

✔ Foreclose and give the property back to the bank.

✔ File for bankruptcy.

✔ Incur lawsuits from vendors and contractors that you used.

✔ Deal with investors who lost their investments.

But there is good news in all of this! You don't have to experience any of this to be successful in commercial real estate investing. The purpose of this chapter is to prepare you to find, acquire, and own the best real estate possible. We set out to show you both sides of the equation so you can spend the rest of your time on the positive and lucrative side of investing. Use our life lessons to catapult your investing to greater levels; use them as a road map to success.

How You, the Investor, Can Cause Failure

The number one cause of property failures is inexperience on the investor's part. For example, overenthusiasm and a lack of knowledge from start to finish can kill investments. Here are the three main ways that you, the investor, can cause a property to fail: by making bad deals, accruing too much debt, and staying in denial regarding property problems. We explain each of these in the following sections.

Especially if you're new to real estate investing, don't be a Lone Ranger. Get help. Do what you're best at and hire out the rest. For example, Peter Harris was absolutely horrible at running the accounting books and he hated it. But, running the books is a crucial part of any real estate business. So, he hired a bookkeeper to handle the books. Because the bookkeeper was great at her job and had a passion for accounting, his business grew. And as the business grew, he realized that he needed partners to help him get to a higher level.

You made a bad deal

Coauthor Peter Harris's very first mentor, Nick, gave Peter some great advice during an intense negotiating session. He said, "As emotions go up, intelligence goes down." He was so right. Inexperienced and first-time investors often get wrapped up and emotionally attached to their properties. They want a first deal under their belt, so these newbies end up making costly mistakes.

Performing poor due diligence

Because they want their deal to go through, many new investors aren't look-ing at their due diligence checklists with an eye of a detective. Instead, they're looking at them with an eye of an impatient and anxious investor. Because of this impatience, they miss things, such as property income and expense discrepancies, hidden repairs, and bad market data.

This mistake has failure written all over it. A big concern for businesses is zoning. It's important to make sure that the property used in the business is properly zoned and also that the zoning of your neighbor's property isn't going to be a problem. Properties and businesses fail because they don't investigate the land use and zoning issues carefully enough. To avoid this problem, find yourself a real estate attorney and have her thoroughly investi-gate land use and zoning. But remember that even if you do your homework, issues can come down the road if governmental agencies or neighbors try to change the zoning on your property to limit your use of it. Check out Chapter 6 to find how to do thorough due diligence.

Having insufficient market knowledge

Many new investors go into a deal without finding out about the market they're buying into. This is a huge mistake because to invest in out-of-state properties successfully, you need to understand the demographics and economics of the city that you're investing in. For instance, if a city has rent control laws and you purchase a property there with the intention of raising rents as often as you like, you're in for a rude awakening because you won't be able to.

To avoid costly mistakes, do thorough research of rent laws, rent levels, vacancy rates, and crime statistics. It also helps to know what other owners are doing to attract and retain tenants. Chapter 4 details the ins and outs of market research.

Paying too high of a price

Paying too high of a price is a surefire way to lock up your cash flow and profits. New investors tend to overpay because of fear of losing the deal to the next investor waiting in line if you don't buy it. When you pay too much, it typically means that your debt on the property is too large. For the most part, three expenses on a property remain fixed (or increase, but never decrease) for an extended time: taxes, utilities, and the mortgage. And these are by far the property's largest expenses. If you overpay, you have nothing left after you pay for these expenses. Paying too much also means that making a profit on a sale may take longer (or may never even happen!).

The causes of overpaying are not knowing how to crunch and analyze the numbers properly and not researching what similar properties have recently sold for in the same area.

Having exit strategy tunnel vision

You've likely had tunnel vision sometime in your life, but when it comes to your career and your exit strategies, take your blinders off — the world is your oyster. That's Peter's motto when he's planning his own exit strategies. Even though he's focused on executing his investment strategies, he leaves an open mind for all possible exit strategies. And here's why: Local markets and personal circumstances can change, and after a while, you may find that a particular exit strategy may not be possible after all. So don't focus on one exit strategy. Instead, keep three or four in mind. That way you avoid having the conversation with your buddies as to "the one opportunity that got away." (See Chapter 7 for more information on exit strategies and closing deals.)

Forgetting to run your properties like businesses

Real estate investing isn't a hands-off business. So being passive with your investments inevitably leads to failure. Would-be investors (or new investors) often and mistakenly think that they can buy a property, and then kick back and watch the monthly checks roll in. We wish it were that easy. But instead, just like in any other successful and prosperous business, you have to keep up with the day-to-day tasks. You have to monitor the budget, manage the cash flow, make sure tenants are satisfied, maintain a nice property appearance, and know the competition well.

You have too much debt

If you've leveraged yourself too much into the purchase of a piece of property and have taken on too much debt, you need to plan for a rainy day. In fact, you need to know what happens if the storm lasts for more than a few days. Do you have a cash reserve until the storm passes? Here's what we mean: If your monthly mortgage is very large and you encounter an unexpected property problem that requires extra cash on a monthly basis to fix, it's just a matter of time before cash-flow problems occur. Consider the following:

✔ **Putting all of your available liquid cash into one deal or property investment is risky.** Yes, you may hit it big, but why take the risk if you don't have to? Stuff happens after you own the properties and you need cash to fix that stuff. If you have no cash available because you used it all in the purchase, you're setting yourself up for a cash-flow headache. Go for the base hits rather than the home run! Then make sure that you have cash reserves ready to keep you healthy and afloat.

✔ **The most common mistake made in property evaluation is underestimating operating expenses on the property, and the second most common mistake is overestimating the income of the property.** New investors many times fail to set realistic and achievable financial targets because they just don't know how. Here's what to do to avoid financial trouble: After you set your property's financial targets, find someone who's a lot more experienced than you are to review your projections. Or have a professional property management company do the same. These second opinions are great reality checks because they keep you from going into cash-flow dreamland. The best advice anyone can give you is to give yourself some cushion in your projections.

Proformas, which are "best-case" or "perfect-world" financial reports on a property, are prepared by the real estate agent and given to you. Often times, proforma financial numbers are unreachable. So, don't purchase or make offers based on the financial picture that the proformas paint. Proformas should only be used to draw attention to prospective buyers; never use them as actual financials. To avoid getting duped by the numbers, double-check every bit of data given by a Realtor and construct your own financial projections of the property.

✔ **It takes time (years!) to build a real estate fortune.** Acquiring too many properties too fast and highly leveraging yourself too quickly is a sure-fire way to collect many properties that perform at average or below average levels. Being debt-heavy is too stressful. Instead, strive to collect a smaller number of properties that all perform well and have smaller, more manageable debts. To do so, start smartly and within your comfort zone.

You're in denial regarding problems

Say, for example, that your significant other stops calling and replying to your e-mails. And then your birthday passes without even a word or gift. Is the writing on the wall? It sure is! You must have messed up somewhere and now he or she is trying to get rid of you! In situations like these, you can't be in denial; you have to face the truth.

The same goes for real estate. When you start having problems with a property, something has to be done. Simply ignoring the problems or denying that they're there won't make them go away. Even your authors have fallen prey to denial. Just remember that the denial of property problems is a major cause of property failures. Here are some of the most commonly denied symptoms:

- ✔ **Poor curb appeal:** The most important part of keeping your property occupied with paying tenants is to keep it looking nice, clean, and attractive. Imagine looking for an apartment to rent for yourself and having a choice between a bright, shiny, and nicely manicured apartment building and one with an overgrown lawn, missing screens, and loose shingles. Which one would you walk into? A property that resembles the latter is showing symptoms of financial distress. Being in denial in your property's appearance goes straight to the bottom line.

- ✔ **Missed monthly mortgage payments:** This symptom of distress is a pretty obvious one. Consider those who have had trouble paying the mortgage on their homes. The reason they had trouble was because they had money problems. They had too much month at the end of the money! The same trouble applies to owners of a commercial property — they can have money problems too. Just remember that missed mortgage payments serve as the writing on the wall. Something's obviously amiss if the owner can't come through with the payments.

- ✔ **High vacancy levels:** When a property has experienced higher vacancy levels than its comparable neighbors for months on end, don't be in denial, and consider yourself forewarned. A high vacancy level generally means that the owner doesn't have the money to prepare the vacant space for a tenant, let alone market it efficiently. In this case, tenant turnover is likely to be higher as well.

- ✔ **A struggling market:** Even if your property is in good physical shape, there's no guarantee that the leasing market will be strong. The problem with a struggling market is that you can't place paying tenants into your property if the tenants or their businesses don't exist. We have been in this situation before and we were forced to deeply lower our lease rates and offer huge incentives to attract tenants. When this happens, supply simply outweighs the demand, and then you run into greater competition for a smaller number of tenants. Face the truth sooner, by getting aggressive in your leasing strategies by deciding whether to have zero rent in a soft market or a little rent in soft market.

A way to spot high vacancy levels and struggling markets is to research market *concessions.* Concessions are incentives given out by the property to entice people to lease from you. An example of a concession would be one month free rent or a reduced move-in security deposit. If you see a lot of concessions in a market, you know that quite a few vacancies need to be filled. A market that's full of vacancies is called a *soft market.* If you invest in a soft market, be prepared to operate a property with a larger vacancy factor than usual.

✔ **Lack of lease renewals:** Because leases are the lifeblood of the commercial real estate business, tracking lease expirations and renewing them becomes crucial to your survival. If the property's leases are expiring and not being renewed or extended frequently, you're headed for trouble.

Managing your lease expirations is as critical as the leasing itself. So make sure to stagger your lease expiration dates across the property. Avoid having a bunch of leases expire in the same month. Consider what the consequences would be if 10 of your 12 tenants' leases expired all in the same month. Instead, stagger the dates to spread out your risk.

✔ **Inability to pay normal bills:** When bills such as landscaping, phone, elevator service, security, and advertising go unpaid, you've come across a danger sign. And when your leasing manager is handling more bill collector calls than leasing calls, trouble has arrived. Instead of living in denial, strategize on a new cash-flow management system that includes working with vendors by making partial payments for a while.

There is no shortcut on avoiding denial, even in real life. It comes down to taking ownership and responsibility of what you're in charge of. Facing cold hard facts of the matter is what makes truly successful people successful.

How Management Can Cause a Property to Fail

Most people can recall or know of a once-prosperous company that either made major management changes or brought in new management and the result was a disaster. The company had everything going for it — great staff, great product, great operations, great brand, and the list goes on and on. But, unfortunately, the management made mistakes and ruined the company's success.

The number one reason that investors fail is because they poorly manage their property or hire incapable property managers (and don't forget that this failure can happen to both inexperienced and experienced investors!). No matter who fills the position, the property manager must be an effective leader. An effective leader does the following:

✔ Works from a business plan

✔ Sets goals and takes responsibility for the results

✔ Defines the roles of the staff under him or her

✔ Confronts operational problems head-on and finds workable solutions

✔ Encourages the staff

✔ Provides direction when needed

✔ Knows his or her capabilities and knows when to ask for help

We highly recommended that when beginning your quest for acquiring a property you "lead" with a professional property management company. What we mean is that you find reputable property management for the type of asset that you're pursuing in that city before you even make offers to purchase. If you can't find experienced and trustworthy property management in that city, don't buy the property. It's that simple.

If you spot any of the following management warning signals, take action immediately:

✔ **Your management is failing to manage.** This warning sign is dangerous and sets a precedent. If your management is failing to act, you may notice that it isn't holding the onsite property manager accountable to the expected promises and actions, it isn't calling and meeting with the managers consistently, and it isn't reading the property reports regularly. The performance of a property like this one is headed for a crash and burn. You, as the owner, can take action by starting at the top of the food chain. Get the property management company's management in conference immediately. Be very specific going over your concerns. Don't depart until action items have been agreed on and delegated.

✔ **Your management seems to be clueless at times and is always ineffective at operating the property efficiently.** With ineffective management, you'll have higher than market vacancies, higher expenses, late property reports, poor communication, and arguments. In the end, you won't have a chance to be profitable. So what do you do? Start interviewing other companies for hire and cut your ties with the current company as quickly as possible.

When hiring professional property management, make sure that the candidate has extensive experience in managing the type of property that you're acquiring. For example, if you're acquiring a 100-unit apartment building, don't hire a company that only has experience in managing retail strip centers. Managing, marketing, and operational strategies are different as night and day.

✔ **Your property manager is ripping you off.** Yes, your property manager can rip you off. It's unfortunate, but true: They can steal from you, lie to you, and hide things from you. The consequences of this disrespect can be devastating — it can set you back financially for months or years. It can even send you into foreclosure. How do you spot a thief? First of all, have your finances audited at least once per year. You can also monitor the cash like a hawk by verifying bank deposits and receipts to checks. It's also smart to visually verify completed work and physically verify rented space or units.

To avoid getting ripped off, consider getting some of your employees or your property management's employees bonded. *Bonding* is an insurance contract in which an insurance agency guarantees payment to an employer in the event of unforeseen financial loss because of the actions of an employee. You don't have to get every employee bonded, but it's smart to at least bond the ones who have access to money or accounts. Luckily, bonding isn't very costly.

✔ **You're being managed by your own property.** If you're managing a piece of property yourself, it's easy to start losing perspective of who *you* are. You're the owner and you're in charge. When your property begins to run you instead of you running it, you'll start making business decisions based on your current circumstances rather than from your set business plan and financial goals. You'll easily get off track, and that's when things can start to unravel and fall apart. To avoid having your property run you ragged, set appropriate boundaries. Don't take work or your work attitude home. Have a phone dedicated for work and shut it off at quitting time. Have an after-hours service set up or have others on-call for after-hour service calls or for other non-emergencies.

✔ **Your property doesn't have a business plan.** A business plan guides you and your property in the right direction when it comes to making business decisions. It can help you determine when to study the competition, it can help figure out your property's strengths and weaknesses, and it can set performance benchmarks that keep other management members on track. If your property doesn't have a business plan, from what basis are you making business decisions? Every property goes in a certain direction, but it may not be going in a profitable and sustaining one. A business plan can be your compass. A good and well-thought-out business plan has a property summary, a market analysis, a sales and marketing plan, a management summary, and a financial plan.

Property management is a favorite topic when commercial investors get together. We like to collect horror stories and then brainstorm ways to systematically remove the possibility of having the same issue come up again. To get mentoring help with your property management challenges or to read some of the recent solutions, go to www.commercialmentoring.com.

How the Market Can Cause Failure

Owning commercial real estate can be more dynamic than you ever thought it would be. For instance, you may not have ever imagined that you would have to concern yourself with levels of inflation, interest rates, job growth, and population growth as an investor of an apartment complex or a downtown office building. And you may not have realized why it's important to know where your market is headed if you plan to develop a strip mall on a 10-acre site. But deal making and daily business decisions need to be made and carried out. And if you don't take these market issues into consideration, you might choose investments that miss their financial targets.

The behavior of your market can cause your property to fail. So, you need to know what influences your market and how to spot and identify these influences. The next two sections break things down simply.

The ups and downs of real estate cycles

As you're probably well aware, our nation's economy is cyclical. For a few years, we're going like gangbusters, and then for a few years after that, we slow down to a snail's pace. Luckily, for the most part, economists can tell us when the economy is growing, stagnating, or shrinking. Real estate undergoes the same type of cyclical pattern. At times your market may grow and at other times it doesn't. In fact, it may even shrink back a bit sometimes.

Just don't forget that it's possible to misunderstand your market's real estate cycle, and this misunderstanding can cause your property to fail. For example, if you buy property at the following times, you're likely setting yourself up for failure:

✔ **Buying at the end of a boom:** Buying at the end of a boom (or at the top of the real estate cycle) sets you up for failure in more ways than one. At this point, the market is saturated. Rent prices level off and drop a little. The supply of new buildings outweighs the demand and then vacancies increase. After vacancies increase, you have to drop your rent prices and offer incentives. This starts the downward financial spiral because as your income decreases, your expenses stay the same (or get even higher). And as your income decreases, you obviously have less money available to keep the property in tiptop shape.

✔ **Buying during a recession:** It pays to know if your market is in a recession or if it's headed for that part of the cycle. In a recession, you can expect new supply on the market (more competition) and demand for rentals and space to decline. You can also expect rent prices to fall and vacancies to reach all-time highs. Your typical investor flees from this market, which means that property values will plummet and foreclosures become more apparent. Not a pretty picture for most.

✔ **Buying at rock bottom:** Call yourself a bottom fisher if you buy property in this part of the cycle. If you invest here, your hope is that you have reached the bottom of the cycle and the market is starting to recover. In real estate, there's a fine line between the end of a recession and the beginning of the recovery period. You may catch it perfectly and reap the benefits or you may miss it and experience more recession or years of delay waiting for recovery to start. Because you're rolling the dice, having a sizable cash reserve is suggested when investing at this time in the cycle. Cash gives you holding power.

The best way to spot one of the previous three cycles is to know the vacancy rate in your market. In a recession or down market part of the cycle, for example, the vacancy rate is at an all-time high. In a recovery part of the cycle, the vacancy rate is decreasing towards neutral. As the cycle heads toward the top to the expansion or new construction cycle, vacancy rates reach an all-time low. So before you invest, do your research and make your phone calls to property management companies and leasing companies to find out what the vacancy situation is in your market.

There's no such thing as an all-purpose real estate cycle that you can use for your everyday commercial real estate investing decisions. And there's no national market either. Cycles differ for apartments, retail, office, industrial/warehouse, and leisure in each geographic area. Each type has its own set of unique dynamics. What this means is that you can't take a real estate cycle study of offices and use it for the cycle study of your apartment deal. In addition, real estate cycles differ in locale and geography. For example, a small suburb outside of Chicago could have a stark difference in real estate cycles compared to the city of Chicago itself. And likewise, Chicago's real estate cycles could be much different than our national real estate cycle. Be specific when studying real estate cycles in your market — research the property type and the exact property location.

The influence of demographics

In real estate investing, we define *demographics* as "the movement of people." Where the people go, we go. Where the people are not, we're not. It's that simple. If you have a lack of people in your market, who's going to lease and rent from you? Or if you see a trend of people moving out of your market, how bright does the market's future look? Consider the following few demographic pieces, which if not followed and accounted for can lead to property failure:

✔ **Negative population growth:** If your market is experiencing a wave where more people are moving away than are moving in, that's a red flag you need to watch. Why? The movement of people away from your market negatively impacts home prices, retail sales, and the overall economy. As your pool of possible tenants decreases, the competition for tenants also increases. After the competition for the limited number of tenants increases, you have to lower your rents and offer incentives to keep your property full of paying tenants. The result is lower income, which doesn't bode well for the future success of the property. Trouble looms if the trend continues long term.

To attain the population growth data for your market, it's okay to start with the U.S. Census Bureau. However, remember that it only presents data every ten years. For more up-to-date data, go to the local chamber of commerce and request population growth data up to the present year. Population data can change quite drastically over a five-year period.

✔ **No job growth:** When job growth is missing from your market, you're likely to see a slowdown in single-family home sales and retail sales. A lack of job growth also causes most commercial real estate to experience higher vacancies. Have you, for example, ever been to a small town that's very quiet and still and has no growth? If you contrast that town with one that's lively with new construction and people and cars buzzing around, you can easily see the difference. To find out job-growth data, start with the local chamber of commerce and the office of economic development.

To get up-to-date demographics information for your specific market, contact the city's office of economic development. Usually, you can find the office's contact information online. When you contact the office, you might consider asking the following questions:

✔ What has been the percentage of job growth during the last three years? And what do you forecast for this year?

✔ What companies are causing these new jobs?

✔ What new companies are moving in or have moved in?

✔ What incentives do you provide to these new companies?

✔ Do you have any upcoming city revitalization programs? If so, in what areas and when? Who's funding the program?

✔ What new building construction has been approved?

✔ Are there any plans for new highway or freeway off-ramps or on-ramps?

After you gather this information, you'll have a good feel for the market's direction and the amount of growth that has occurred.

Folding Up and Walking Away

Let's face it. Some properties headed for failure can't be saved. Some are just too far off the deep end. In this case, you have to let it go. Your alternative is to continue pouring money and time into the property. That alternative is usually pretty bleak because most people don't have an endless stream of money and time to give to a property. However, we believe that the most difficult part is facing the feelings of failure. But instead of spending more time and money and spinning your wheels, you have to make a decision, and usually that decision involves folding up and walking away. When we say "fold," we mean making preparations and doing the things necessary to walk away.

Knowing when to fold

Knowing when it's time to fold up and move on is never easy. After all, how do you know when the property is truly hopeless? Here are a few clues:

- ✔ The property is vacant.
- ✔ You're paying the mortgage out of your own pocket.
- ✔ You can no longer pay the employees.
- ✔ Your mortgage is in default.
- ✔ You're in foreclosure.
- ✔ Your cash reserves are gone because you've been in a negative cash-flow position for an extended period of time.

Choosing to walk away honorably

Folding up shop and giving in is tough to do. Indeed, walking away in defeat after you've tried everything possible is an investor's worst nightmare. But, how you choose to walk away from the property affects the overall outcome. You can either walk away honorably or dishonorably. Obviously we suggest that you walk away with honor and dignity.

Here's how you, the investor, can honorably walk away from a failed property:

- ✔ **Inform everyone who's impacted by your fold.** You don't need to have all the answers right now. You simply need to make the call as a professional courtesy.

    The call, for example, may go something like this, "Hi Bob, it's me. I just wanted to let you know that I'm folding up shop here. My project failed and we're closing down, so I'm calling everyone who's affected. I'm not sure what's going to happen or how things will go from here because I don't know myself, but I felt that the right thing to do was to inform you. Thank you. I'll be in touch soon."

- ✔ **When engaged in conversations concerning the property's failure, tell the truth and admit that you blew it.** People who are affected by the failure will be upset already and will be more upset if they sense that you aren't telling the truth. Being dishonest sets you up for more trouble, whereas a good portion of the disappointment can be defused by being straightforward and truthful.

✔ **Remember that it isn't all your fault.** When properties fail, some of the causes may be beyond your control (for example, hidden mold problems or hard-to-find structural defects). So don't place 100 percent of the blame on yourself, the property manager, or the local economy. Do take some responsibility, but also explain how certain circumstances caused the failure.

✔ **Never speak a word or make a promise that you can't back up.** Your words can be used against you legally, and they can also force you to be on the defensive, which simply adds fuel to the fire. Just be honestly remorseful and listen.

An investor who walks away dishonorably usually is guilty of

✔ Not quickly delivering the bad news to everyone who's been impacted (for example, employees, partners, investors, contractors, and service providers). You would be amazed as to how quickly rumors can travel and cause unnecessary damage to your reputation and integrity.

✔ Being dishonest in telling those who are impacted what really happened. Tell them the truth upfront because they're sure to find out through someone else anyway.

✔ Putting the blame on everyone but himself.

✔ Skipping town, hiding, and avoiding everyone.

Walking away from a deal is tough. If you need some help or encouragement, connect with our mentoring group some evening. To see the schedule of events or online discussions go to www.commercialmentoring.com.

Tried and True Tips on Surviving and Thriving

Because this book is about investing successfully in commercial real estate, and this chapter is about why and how properties fail, we need to discuss ways to avoid failure. But we have to do this with caution. We don't want to put too much impetus on failure or even avoiding failure because there's a big difference between *winning* at something and *not losing* at something. Some may think they're of the same focus, but they aren't.

Consider it this way: When you go into a game to *win,* your focus by definition is "to be the victor." When you go into a game to *not lose,* your focus becomes by definition to "not suffer deprivation" or to "not bring forth

Failure is really just the beginning

One day, Peter Harris was sitting with a well-known and highly successful investor over lunch, discussing the subject of making it big in business. He told Peter, "In order to end up being really, really successful, you'll have to lose it all at least once." He explained that he had heard a statistic of the ultra-wealthy that shows that they have all lost their fortunes at least once. Peter's question, of course, was, "You mean in order to be wildly successful, I have to go through a major failure first?"

As Peter inquired further, the life lesson he learned that day was two-fold. Most important,

he learned that those ultra-wealthy and successful people took huge risks and lost big time at some point. But they also eventually won big time. Big risks equal big rewards. The second lesson he learned was that their failures didn't stop them after they fell on their faces. They got up, brushed off the dirt, and got back into the game as a different person altogether. They were wiser, more determined, and more humble. And in the end, those are the people that you want to learn from. To them, failure is really just the beginning.

destruction." You're after the same result, but your focus is different. Of course, *winning* is more fun and more rewarding. So, we want to focus on how to invest in winning properties. Here are some tips for successful investing:

- ✔ **Fall in love with the deal, not the property.** In other words, remember that the most beautiful property could be a part of the worst deal you ever make. Real estate investing is all about the deal, the terms, and the return on investment.

- ✔ **Be an investor instead of an accumulator of commercial properties.** The whole idea of making investments is to produce an income or a profit. So, if you buy a property that produces no income or profit, you really just acquired a property (instead of making an investment).

Educate yourself so that you can negotiate smartly, know how to crunch the numbers, and perform thorough due diligence. You also need to know how financing works so that you can get the best deal available. Know how to hire and handle property management, and be sure to follow your exit strategies. Know how to do all of this before you invest in or purchase *any* property.

- ✔ **Understand that every property has a lifetime.** Just as human bodies have a lifetime, properties do as well. When properties get older, they start to fall apart and need repairs (just like us!). One of the biggest mistakes that you can make as an investor is to ignore the fact that over time, you'll have to spend money on the cosmetic upkeep of the building, inside and out. The building may need a roof replacement and the electric or plumbing systems may need to be updated. All of this can cost thousands of dollars. Every building goes through these phases and some more so than others. It really depends on the age and condition.

So make sure that you have a long-term plan to handle such repairs. To prepare ourselves for this, we have a reserve account or you can call it a savings account for each property. Or we'll refinance the property and pull money out to do these upkeeps.

If you don't have such a plan, be prepared for a slow downward trend in the performance of your property, because a property that's old-looking, has antiquated systems, and needs a roof will be undesirable. Prospective tenants will simply go down the street to the "nicer" property.

✔ **Focus on one investment type at a time.** Especially when first starting out, we highly recommend that you focus on one type of investment: apartments, offices, retail, land, or whatever your preference may be. Having an apartment deal and a land deal at the same time is too much to handle and oversee. Each deal needs and deserves your undivided attention. It's better to be master of one than average over many. And who wants average-performing properties anyway?

✔ **Remember that environmental problems can shut you down.** A huge potential concern when owning commercial property is hazardous waste problems. Property owners have the primary responsibility for fixing such problems, even if the current property owner didn't cause them. These problems may not be obvious or apparent to the naked eye, and they could arise from anything ranging from an underground storage tank to the remains of an old U.S. Navy shipyard.

If at some point you held an ownership interest in a property, you're potentially responsible for paying for the clean up of it. The costs for an environmental cleanup and disposal can run into the millions of dollars. Obtain an environmental report from environmental assessment companies as part of your due diligence if needed. The reports cost a bit, but as the saying goes, "It's expensive being cheap."

✔ **Get a mentor so that you can learn from his or her mistakes.** Mentors can save you from making huge mistakes and miscalculations, they can identify when you've missed due diligence items, and they can connect you with resources that you otherwise wouldn't have immediate access to. To find a mentor, go to www.commercialmentoring.com.

We once mentored a new client who came to us with a property already under contract for $1.8 million. We reviewed the deal and discovered that the contract price was too high. We had her renegotiate the price down to $1.2 million and it closed right on time. Mentoring saved her $600,000 and gained her thousands in cash flow per month.

✔ **Determine whether you and your assets are adequately protected.** Unfortunately, as life happens, so do lawsuits. Tenants and owners sue each other. That means you need to do everything you can to protect yourself. Ask yourself the following questions to determine whether you're protected:

Why we included failure in this book

How many books on real estate investing have you read? Probably quite a few. And how many of those books have chapters dedicated to *unsuccessful* real estate investing? Probably none.

The truth is that not every single real estate investment that you invest in or hear about will be successful. Some inevitably fail. That's just a fact of life. Some of the huge ones make the news, but most do not. Our goal with this chapter is to provide real-world truths to you. Anyone who tells you that it's impossible to go wrong in real estate is just plain dishonest.

But what you'll discover is that successful investing is not magic, but is more common sense. It's getting ahead of ourselves and foregoing attaining knowledge that gets us into trouble. Any investment you make is as risky as your level of understanding. So go out there and get knowledge, start within your comfort zone, and invest sensibly.

- What do you have at stake if you lose a lawsuit?

- How is your property protected?

- Is your property in an LLC?

- Is your personal property (for example, your home) protected?

- Are your other investments totally separate from each other so that one lawsuit doesn't affect the other investments?

- Are you sure that your investments are protected? How do you know? Can your attorney vouch for this?

Don't guess when it comes to the answers to these questions. Talk to a lawyer to ensure that you're protected if you're sued. (See Chapter 12 for more on protecting your assets.)

✔ **If you're in a partnership deal, do your best to finance your deal with a non-recourse type of loan.** *Non-recourse* means that you aren't personally guaranteeing the loan. This gives you two distinct advantages: it allows you to be taken off the loan if the partnership goes sour and, if the property fails, it won't be tied to you personally.

Part V
Kicking Your Investing into High Gear

The 5th Wave   By Rich Tennant

"Don't worry, Mrs. Morse. As soon as the plumber's done patching the roof I'll have him call the electrician to finish wallpapering the dining room."

In this part . . .

*I*f you're looking to find out more about commercial fixer-uppers, you've come to the right place. In this part, we also help you discover the insider secrets to taking a piece of land through the approval process so that it can be developed. The advice in Chapter 16 can save you tens of thousands of dollars in taxes every single year. Finally, we discuss how to jump into a commercial real estate career.

Chapter 14

Making a Success Out of Commercial Fixer-Uppers

*W*ow, we are so excited! We get to talk about a subject that's fascinating and has made us a lot of money over the years. Normally, when an investor thinks of a fixer-upper, he or she thinks about a little house on the corner that needs a new fence, new paint, and a remodeled kitchen. But now it's time to think big and consider fixer-uppers in the commercial real estate world — large apartment complexes, office buildings, strip malls, industrial projects, and the list goes on. The main differences between investing in residential real estate and investing in commercial real estate are that commercial projects have larger potential profits and the property needs to be leased with tenants to give it full value.

In this chapter, we cover what commercial fixer-uppers are, how to locate them, how to turn the opportunities into sizable profits, how to spot costly pitfalls, and why commercial fixer-upper opportunities will be around forever and ever.

We hope that after you read this chapter you'll get as excited as we do when you spot a possible fixer-upper opportunity. Your creative juices and can-do attitude will turn on automatically as you drive through town with a new perspective on those run-down buildings.

Just What Is a Commercial Fixer-Upper?

To understand what a commercial fixer-upper is, watch while we take the term apart and put it back together. *Commercial* refers to commercial real estate that can be defined as a retail strip mall, an apartment building, an office building, or an industrial project, to name a few. And *fixer-upper* is something you can buy at a discount because of its poor condition with the intent of fixing it up and selling it for a profit. Therefore, a *commercial fixer-upper* is an underperforming piece of commercial real estate that you acquire at a discount, fix up, lease, and sell for a profit. (Or keep for cash flow.)

Here's an example of a typical fixer-upper. Your favorite grocery and hardware stores sit in a neighborhood strip mall. But because the owner didn't spend any money on cosmetic improvements or new and better-placed signage, tenants have relocated elsewhere. Three years ago, that same strip mall had a beauty supply shop, a chain pet store, a family restaurant, and a dry cleaner, but since then, those shops have moved out and those spaces have sat empty and untouched. We're sure that you can drive around your town and spot such properties. They're everywhere.

Here's another common example. A two-story apartment building located in a decent neighborhood was sold five years ago, and the new owners have never been seen. A partly torn-down chain-link fence surrounds the sides and back of the property. You know some of the units are occupied because you can see curtains in the windows, but at least a third of the units have boarded-up windows. This one makes you scratch your head because five years ago, this complex was one of the nicest in the neighborhood.

Once-proud neighborhood commercial properties turn into fixer-uppers when

- ✔ The property falls into disrepair and doesn't bring in the revenue the owner had hoped for.
- ✔ The owners fail to keep up with the property.

Distressed and poorly performing property

A *distressed property* is a property in a state of desperate need, both externally and internally. For instance:

- ✔ External needs can include improved landscaping, new paint, a new roof, or maybe a complete reface.
- ✔ Internal needs can entail updated electrical and plumbing systems, an interior remodel, or an earthquake retrofit whereby the structural integrity needs to be strengthened.

When maintenance and upkeep aren't completed in a timely manner, the property becomes distressed. As these needs go unmet, the property becomes less desirable for its tenants who either live there or run businesses from it. As the property deteriorates, tenants move out, and no one wants to move in. This, of course, affects the property's financial performance and sends it into distress mode. With no money to pay for maintenance, the owner struggles to pay the property's operating expenses, and the likelihood that the property will become a fixer-upper is right around the corner.

Signs of a distressed and poorly performing property include

- ✔ Overgrown grass and weeds and very poorly kept landscaping
- ✔ Lots of vacancies more than 90 days old
- ✔ Boarded-up windows and/or evidence of fire damage
- ✔ A good percentage of mailboxes without names on them (this indicates vacancies)
- ✔ A property line fenced off with a chain-link fence
- ✔ Obviously deferred maintenance
- ✔ Lower-class and a lower quality of tenants attracted to the property
- ✔ Abandoned appearance

Distressed and poorly performing owner

Once-profitable neighborhood commercial properties can turn into fixer-uppers because of distressed and poorly performing owners. Properties fail and become fixer-upper candidates when an owner lacks experience. Often, new and overenthusiastic owners get in over their heads. They may have too many repairs to make and not enough money and skills; they may mismanage the property; or they may take on too much debt. All these scenarios, as well as others, lead to property distress.

Signs that a property is being poorly managed include the following:

- ✔ You find out that the property is in preforeclosure status.
- ✔ The property is for sale and the real estate agent tells you that the owner is very, very motivated and will consider all offers (hint, hint).
- ✔ You find out the owner can't pay normal bills such as water and electricity. In fact, you find shut-off service notices taped on the entry doors.
- ✔ You've noticed over the last year that the property's exterior condition has worsened to the point of "Wow, what happened to that place?"

When you see "owner financing available" that's a good sign for you. Get excited and inquire quickly. Usually, when an owner offers to finance all or part of the deal, it means she's really ready to sell the property. One of the reasons why she's offering to finance the deal herself is because the property doesn't qualify for a traditional loan (where the buyer has to ante up a 20 percent down payment) because of the property's physical condition, financial situation, or both. When you set up the financing with the owner, you don't have to undergo the usual lender qualifications. You can create whatever type of deal you two agree on. Deals like this allow you to create incredible deal-of-a-lifetime, win-win results. (See Chapter 9 for more details on creative financing.)

Uncovering Diamonds in the Rough

Finding commercial fixer-uppers isn't a tricky endeavor. In fact, there are more opportunities than there is demand. Why? Because not many investors want to buy other people's problems if they don't have to. Here's a disclaimer, however: Not every commercial fixer-upper is for you. We discuss this a bit later in the chapter.

How to find fixer-uppers

You can locate commercial fixer-uppers in several ways: scout out properties yourself or hire someone to do the legwork for you. It's also possible to find these properties by looking where no one else is. We cover each of these options in the following sections.

Look for yourself

When you're on the hunt for commercial fixer-uppers, you need to open your eyes and open your mind. Look at each building and ask whether that property has the signs of being distressed. (See the earlier section "Distressed and poorly performing property" for a list of signs.) Do this as you drive around town or view for-sale listings. Look for preforeclosure and foreclosed properties through the same resources you'd find foreclosed homes. Make it a habit to always be on the lookout. In fact, we're almost obsessed with looking for potential properties when we're out driving around. It's all about mind-set. When we do find a potential fixer-upper, we obtain the owner's contact information by either calling a title company or going down to city hall and looking through the recorded deed records.

Never assume that a distressed property without a For Sale sign isn't for sale. Quite often, unlisted properties are the best deals around because they don't have the baggage of a real estate agent's advice and marketing. The price you pay will reflect this. Find out who the owner is and start the communication process. You never know where he is in his life. He may be ready to retire, there may be an illness in the family, or his partnership may be falling apart. This could be your diamond in the rough.

Hire someone to look for you

Another way to find commercial fixer-uppers is to get someone to find them for you. You can get help from the following folks:

- ✔ **Real estate agents:** The key to success in working with a real estate agent is twofold. One, find a real estate agent who can help you find the type of fixer-upper deals you're looking for. The agent should be knowledgeable about the area — especially concerning recent closing prices — and should know of lenders who can provide favorable financing on properties in the area. A good agent will filter out the bad deals for you so you won't waste his or your time.

  The second key to working successfully with your agent is to develop a good relationship. How you interact with your agent is critical to the flow of deals coming your way. To be straightforward, if your agent likes you, deals will come your way. If she doesn't, she may withhold them. From the agent's perspective, your loyalty means a lot. Don't switch from agent to agent. Also, don't make offers just to make offers and never close a deal. Agents are paid via commissions and will develop a nose for "closers." Be a closer. Also, don't make your agent do all the work. Volunteer to help out with researching a property that's sent to you. She's on your team, and that's what successful teammates do.

  As for finding an agent to work with, we recommend working with a commercial real estate agent rather than a residential real estate agent. Their training, industry knowledge, and resources are much different from each other. The best way to find a reputable commercial real estate agent is by referral. Ask a fellow investor who he uses and is happy with.

- ✔ **Online services:** Numerous online services can get you started with locating a commercial fixer-upper. You can choose from free services or paid subscriptions. The unseen value of online services is the networking you can do from the comfort of your office or home. Many times coauthor Peter Harris calls the agent and finds out that the property is no longer available, but he remains in touch with the agent to hear about future listings and deals. His list of agent contacts and sources of deals vastly increased because of this.

- ✔ **Property managers:** Property management companies have the inside track on which properties are in distress or appear to be in distress. Because they're managing the property themselves, they already know that it's failing and may be able to tell you why. Certain property management companies have relationships with lenders that are about to or already have foreclosed on properties. This is your "in" before the property makes it to real estate agents.

The world of property management is a small one. Everybody knows everybody, and a lot of talk happens in the properties they manage or know of. We recommend that you go out and find a property management company to work with, even if you have no properties yet. How to interview (and hire) management companies is covered in detail in Chapter 11.

Many times, our property manager approaches us when his owners are ready to sell or if he knows of fixer-upper opportunities in his managing area. If you're already working with a property manager, make it known to him that you're interested in buying if he comes across such a deal. Of course, it would benefit him, because he would manage it when the deal closed. Reward the manager with a finder's fee as an incentive, if possible.

✔ **Attorneys and accountants:** Professionals who handle estate affairs can be a solid source of leads for you as well. Attorneys handle estates that contain numerous properties that their clients may want to unload for various reasons — death, divorce, inheritance, or change in investment or goals, for example. Accountants prepare financial statements for their clients who are about to sell their properties for different reasons. Here's a word of advice: It's much easier getting deals from these two professionals if you're a client yourself.

✔ **Lenders:** Most properties that a lender forecloses on are placed in a foreclosure auction. If the auction isn't successful, the property reverts to the lender and becomes bank owned or, in more common terms, a *real estate owned property* (an REO property). At this point, you can attempt to purchase the property from the bank. The purchase will be "as-is," so do your homework. Contact your lender and talk to someone in its REO department to find out more about their purchase procedures.

In some markets, you'll see REOs listed at market price levels. But you want a bargain, right? You should take your chances and wait for a better price. The REO property isn't an asset to the bank; it's a liability and has costs associated with it, such as paying a management company, property taxes, and hazard insurance. Our suggestion is to be patient, even if your offer was rejected. Let the property and its high costs simmer in the bank's portfolio for a while. Pretty soon, we bet the bank will be willing to listen to your offer.

Look where no one else is looking

You can also find commercial fixer-uppers by not following the crowd. By the time you get to where everyone else has either read about or visited, you're probably too late. Move away from the herd. Look for fixer-uppers in places that make your investor friends say, "Where in the world is that? I've never even heard of that city?" Be a trailblazer. Be an original. There's a handsome reward awaiting you.

Where to buy

Just like every other type of real estate, you can choose where to buy, depending on your investment goals and means. As your search narrows and you begin to focus, you want to choose the right neighborhood. You have the following four choices, and each has unique pros and cons that you need to pay attention to:

- ✓ **Bad part of town:** Investing in commercial fixer-uppers in this neck of the woods is riskiest. Prices are the cheapest here, and there's a reason for that. The relative costs to complete the rehab process are roughly the same in each neighborhood, but you have to think about some big questions: Where is the neighborhood headed? Is it in the recovery cycle, or the down-and-out cycle? If you do manage to fix up the property, will it be desirable to tenants? If you can catch the neighborhood on the upswing, buy at a good price, successfully fix up the property, and lease it, this may be your home run!

- ✓ **Lower-middle class:** This is where most of the successes happen for apartment complex fixer-uppers. In these neighborhoods, lower-income tenants abound. And because it's too costly to construct new apartments for them to occupy, and they can't afford rents on a newly built property, you don't have to worry about losing your tenant base. They'll always be there waiting for the spiffy, remodeled, and fixed-up complex. This is where we consistently see the biggest dollars made.

- ✓ **Suburbs:** This is the middle of the road because it's less risky than the previous two. More than likely, your return on investment will be a little lower because of the higher entry prices, but that may be okay with more conservative folks. The one thing you can count on here is stability because the real estate cycle swings are less volatile.

- ✓ **Downtown:** Fixer-uppers here can be very lucrative if you know what you're doing. The majority of opportunities here involve office buildings and *mixed-use properties*. Mixed-use properties are buildings that contain residential and retail or residential and office space. Typically, you need deeper pockets here because of the size of the projects. We've seen tons of money made here when investors changed the property's use to something that the downtown needed more of. For example, does that particular area need more retail centers and restaurants?

Taking action before those great opportunities disappear

Peter Harris's mentor taught him a lot about business, but one thing Peter couldn't anticipate was the importance of anticipating his needs and skills. He truly believes that you need to go through an entire transaction from start to finish to completely and honestly appreciate the process. Here are the needs and skills you need to anticipate through the process:

- ✔ **Your management skills:** This is first on the list because it's the most important. Management has two levels:

  - • **Project management** involves managing the overall rehabilitation of the property.

  - • **Property management** involves managing the operations such as leasing, maintenance, accounting, marketing, and so on.

  If you don't have these skills, we urge you to find a partner who has them or hire a professional property management company.

- ✔ **Your availability:** How much time can you honestly devote to your first fixer-upper project? Is most of your daytime taken up by a full-time job? Is investing in commercial fixer-uppers going to be a part-time job for you? If so, can you afford to hire out the things you can't do? Set realistic time commitments and budget in the hired help. Do the numbers still pan out?

- ✔ **Your sweat factor:** Investing in fixer-uppers pays off hugely if done effi- ciently and smartly, but it involves hard work and risk taking. Are you willing to go the extra mile and put in a full day's work on minor details? Do you have the fortitude to hold your position when things don't go just right? You're going to reap the rewards of what efforts you sow in every project you take on.

- ✔ **Your financial firepower:** Do you have the means to go to a lender and get construction financing for the project? Do you have private money resources to get money quickly? Do you have cash readily available to get the ball rolling on a project? What is your cash position?

- ✔ **Your personality:** Who are you? Are you the type who can deal with ten- ants and contractors one on one? Are you a number-crunching, spread- sheet junkie, or are you the smooth-talking relationship guy? Do what you do best and either partner with or hire out the rest if you can afford it. Focus on your strengths.

- ✔ **Your goals:** Set realistic goals and timelines that everyone involved agrees with. A surefire way to start off on the wrong foot is to assume that you're in agreement with your partners or contractors when you're not. In the fixer-upper business, one thing is tied to another, so delays in one area can affect the entire project.

- ✔ **Your exit strategy:** When you come up with your plan on how to profit from this project, make sure that your real estate agent nods his head "yes" when you ask him if he thinks you'll be able to sell the property for a certain amount. Also, if your plan is to refinance the property, ask your lender the following question: "So, Terry, in order for me to refinance this property in _____ years, where do the financials have to be in order for me to refinance out _____ dollars?"

Figuring Out What a Fixer-Upper Is Worth

As we've said before, the name of the game is to buy smart and low, fix up, lease up, and sell high. But a couple of questions always come up. What's considered low, and how do I figure out how much the property is worth before I fix it up? And how high can I sell it for, and who sets the price?

Here we start with how to figure out the worth of a commercial fixer-upper. Valuing a single-family home fixer-upper and a commercial fixer-upper is much different. A single-family home fixer-upper is valued on what similar homes in the same market have recently sold for. That's it. But a commercial fixer-upper is valued on how much income it brings in yearly. That's priority number one. Priority number two is what similar commercial properties in the same market have recently sold for. In a nutshell, commercial properties are valued on their income and location.

Determining your cash flow

Say you own a 2-story, 20-unit apartment building, and you've collected the rent from your tenants for the month. This is your *gross income.* Now, you have to pay normal property expenses such as property taxes, hazard insurance, maintenance, repairs, water, electricity, and trash. These are your *operating expenses.*

After you subtract your expenses from your income, what's left over is called your *net operating income* (NOI). And from the net operating income, you pay the mortgage. After the mortgage is paid, what remains is your *cash flow.* That wasn't too difficult, right? Cash flow should be one of your main goals in maximizing the value of the fixer-upper after it's fixed up and leased. Generally speaking, the higher the cash flow, the higher the value. Check out Table 14-1 for a quick example.

Table 14-1	20-Unit Apartment Building Analysis: What Is This Property Worth?	
Description	*Monthly*	*Yearly*
Gross income (rents)	$6,000	$72,000
Operating expenses	$2,400	$28,800
Net operating income (NOI)	$3,600	$43,200

(continued)

Table 14-1 *(continued)*		
Description	*Monthly*	*Yearly*
Mortgage payment	$2,000	$24,000
Cash flow	**$1,600**	**$19,200**

Figuring your NOI, cap rate, and sales price

Commercial properties are valued by their income and location. As for the income, you want to pay special attention to the NOI, which determines a commercial property's value. The NOI is simply the gross income minus the operating expenses. Please note that mortgage payments are not included in the NOI.

Another term you need to understand in valuing commercial properties is *capitalization rate*. The cap rate, as it's often called, is the return on your cash investment as if you had paid cash for the property. Cap rate measures a property's performance without considering the mortgage financing. If you had paid cash for the investment, how much money would it be making? What's the return?

The equation for cap rate is NOI divided by the sales price. See the following formula:

Cap rate % = (NOI ÷ sales price) × 100

Cap rates vary not only from state to state or city to city, but also from market to market. The real estate industry uses cap rates in different ways. Here are two:

- ✔ **A high cap rate** (typically 8 percent and higher) usually typifies a higher-risk investment, higher potential returns, and a low sales price. High cap rate investments are typically found in low-income areas.

- ✔ **A low cap rate** (7 percent and below) usually typifies a lower-risk investment, lower potential returns, and a high sales price. Low cap rates are typically found in middle-class to upper-income areas.

Markets within cities are assigned cap rates. For example, the nice part of town may have a going cap rate of 6 percent (because prices are relatively high), but in the bad part of town, the going cap rate may be as high as 10 percent (because prices are relatively low).

You can find out what cap rates run in your market by asking a knowledge-able and experienced local commercial broker, commercial lender, or commercial appraiser.

If you know a property's NOI, and you know the typical cap rate for your market, you can calculate what the *sales price* of the property should be when you're ready to sell the property and walk away with a tidy sum of cash. Here is the equation for it:

Sales price = (NOI ÷ cap rate) × 100

For the example in Table 14-1, you can calculate what the property is worth. For instance, say that we asked a commercial broker and an appraiser what the going cap rate was for the market; they told us 8 percent. Use the previous equation to figure out the property's worth:

Sales price = ($43,200 ÷ 8%) = $540,000

Therefore, based on the given market cap rate and the NOI, the property is worth $540,000.

After you know what the property is worth, your next step is to find out what similar properties have sold for in the area in the last 12 months. That way you can make sure the sales price you calculated ($540,000 in this case) isn't too far off.

Running the numbers on an example property

To help you better understand the numbers game when determining how much a commercial property is worth, we're going to walk you through a real-world example by using Cool Heights Village, a 120-unit apartment community.

Cool Heights is located in a middle-class neighborhood, about 2 blocks from downtown and about 3 blocks from the town's mall. The new owner, Abe, bought it from a family who had owned it for 17 years. When Abe bought the family-managed property, it was in poor physical condition and, for the last four years, had never achieved better than 75 percent tenant occupancy. The property looked run down. There were two other apartment complexes in the area; one was slightly larger and one slightly smaller, and both were about a half-mile east. Both properties were nearly 100 percent occupied and in decent condition. Abe bought Cool Heights with the intention of fixing it up, getting the occupancy up to the market level, and then selling it.

Abe confirmed that the other two complexes also were recent purchases. The purchase price for both of those properties averaged $37,000 per apartment unit. Abe paid $3 million for Cool Heights, or $25,000 per unit. Abe planned to put the complex back on the market at around $37,000 per unit when the property's rehabilitation was complete. After 12 months of hard work, the rehab was complete ($260,000 worth), and the property's occupancy had hovered around 96 percent for the last 3 or so months. Thanks to the improvements, Abe increased the rents of each apartment by $25. He also cut operating expenses by getting new insurance and hiring higher-skilled maintenance people. Take a look at the before and after scenarios shown in Table 14-2.

Table 14-2	Cool Heights Before and After Fix-Up			
	Cool Heights Before Fix-Up		*Cool Heights After Fix-Up*	
	Monthly	*Yearly*	*Monthly*	*Yearly*
Potential rental income	$50,400 @ $420 each unit	$604,800	$53,400 @ $445 each unit	$640,800
Actual rental income	$37,800 (75% occupied)	$453,600	$51,264 (96% occupied)	$615,168
Operating expenses	$27,500	$330,000	$22,864	$274,368
Net operating income (NOI)	$10,300	$123,600	$28,400	$340,800

When Abe was ready to sell the apartment complex, he found out what the going cap rate was for the area, which was 8 percent. Then Abe found two comparable and recent property sales to measure his property with. Here are the numbers:

Market cap: 8 percent

Value at 8 percent cap: $4,260,000

Cool Heights was put on the market by a local real estate agent, and it sold within three months for $4.26 million, or $35,500 per unit. Abe's profit was $1.26 million before subtracting costs of $260,000 for fixing up the property. So in the end, Abe profited $1 million for his efforts. Cool Heights turned into a cool deal.

Profits at sale (before costs of fix-up): $4,260,000 (sales price) − $3,000,000 (payoff of loan) = $1,260,000 − $260,000 = $1,000,000.

Mapping Out a Fixer-Upper Game Plan

For us, figuring out whether we can turn a profit with our fixer-upper is the most exciting part of the process. We see if we're likely to make a whole lot of money, a little bit of money, or if we need to pass on the deal. Mapping out a game plan involves knowing your comfort zone, selecting an area, choosing a property type, doing due diligence, understanding the financing options available, and most important, knowing how to get the profits out of your property.

You need to check four factors when considering a commercial fixer-upper. Because each factor affects the others, give some serious thought to the viability of the project if one factor is deficient. Here they are:

- ✔ **Speculation factor must be low:** One of the most dangerous things you can do when investing in fixer-uppers is to speculate. Don't invest in a fixer-upper where the majority of your profits depends on your speculation of falling cap rates or yearly appreciation. This is a cash-flow business where appreciation is a bonus only. If you get it, great. If you don't, no part of your exit strategy changes. Don't roll the dice. Commercial properties are valued on the ability to produce income. More income means higher value. Therefore, do your evaluation based on today's cap rates.

- ✔ **Location factor needs to be sound:** Ask yourself, "If this property were in a different location, would it have been successful?" If yes, what would those ideal location characteristics be? Now, take those characteristics, and ask yourself, "Can I neutralize those needed characteristics by modifying the property, or can I see those favorable characteristics taking place in the neighborhood today?" Location is critical to your timing of the purchase and sale. You can make tons of money fixing up shopping centers if you understand that location is the most important factor in maximizing value. You can fix a shopping center, but you can't fix a location.

- ✔ **Physical condition factor:** The property must be physically sound. If it has extensive defects or shortcomings, the project may be financially unfeasible. Defects may include structural foundation, electrical, or plumbing issues, just to name a few. Take on a project within your comfort zone. If your prior projects involved new paint, new sheetrock, and new appliances, think twice about taking on projects involving replacing a foundation on a vacant property. These are two different animals, and two different skill sets are needed. Creative solutions to physical problems can create huge profits.

- ✔ **Owner readiness factor:** The owner must be ready to sell. He must admit his best solution today is to remove this property and its problems from his portfolio. To help in his decision, come up with a few good and compelling reasons for the owner to sell.

Does your prospective commercial fixer-upper favorably satisfy these factors? If so, you're ready to move on to the next level: due diligence. If not, consider finding another deal for now.

Perform due diligence

Due diligence is the process of doing your homework on a potential investment. You're looking to find out whether it's a good buy, an average buy, or a bad buy. Because we have dedicated Chapter 6 to the subject of due diligence, we recommend that you review it again.

Due diligence is not only a fact-gathering mission, but it is also a mind-set. You must think like an investigator on one of those detective television shows. Leave no stone unturned. Expect the unexpected. Expect drama. Expect the twist in the story. The one thing you want to avoid is a surprise ending, right?

A proper mind-set also means being "present" with what's going on around you. You need to be as distraction free as possible when going through the due diligence process. What are the consequences of being distracted during due diligence? Not good, that's for sure. Not being present may cause you to overlook important property expenses or not follow up on a severe physical defect in the property's structure.

The due diligence process usually has three areas of focus: physical inspection, financial investigation, and legal inquiries. In the following sections, we touch on these topics as they pertain to commercial fixer-uppers, but we add another area: sales and marketing strategies, which are often overlooked.

Physical inspection

Hire a professional property inspector to do the physical inspection. These professionals are trained to spot apparent and potential problems. They'll get on the roof, check out the building's foundation, walk through every unit of occupyable space, including storage and garage areas and laundry facilities, check for building code violations, and see if the electrical and plumbing systems are up-to-date.

Keep in mind that during a physical inspection, your goal is to take note of every broken piece of the property that's going to need fixing. For example, jot down if there is evidence of a roof leak or if a section of the sidewalk is a safety hazard and needs replacing. Remember, your goal is to buy at a good price, fix it up, lease up, and sell. Knowing how much the fix-up is going to cost is a major piece of the puzzle. After you have your list of items that need fixing, you're in a position to add everything up to see if the costs outweigh the benefits of buying.

During the inspection, it's a good idea to have your roofer and general contractor there, walking around with the property inspector. An inspector will give his best guess on what it will cost to have a roof replaced or what it will cost to have siding replaced. With the roofer and general contractor there, you can get more accurate costs immediately.

Although a professional property inspector can give you the overall picture of the property's condition, you should consider bringing in a specialist if the inspector's report turns up a potential problem that's beyond his experience.

Financial investigation

You'll run into different financial scenarios with a fixer-upper than you would if you were buying a normal, ready-to-take-over commercial property. First of all, because the property is distressed, the financial records will show it. Typically, the income is much lower than its potential, and the expenses are higher than normal, proportionally. Don't be surprised. Second, expect the financial records to be incomplete, nonexistent, and maybe really unprofessional looking. This is why it's a fixer-upper. This is where you make your profits.

When you do your financial investigation, crunch the numbers as-is by evaluating the cash flow of the property in its current condition. Of course, you'll see a horrible, negative cash-flow condition. Make a note of that negative cash-flow number. Now crunch the numbers as if the property is fixed up and 90 percent occupied or at market occupancy with great tenants. What does the cash flow look like? Hopefully it's great. Make a note of that positive cash-flow number. See the big difference between the two? Now, you have to ask yourself these questions:

- ✔ How do I go from that huge negative number to that great positive number?
- ✔ How do I bridge the gap? Is it attainable?
- ✔ How long will it take and how much will it cost?

All of these issues are discussed later in the chapter.

Legal inquiries

Everything that you read about "legal" due diligence in Chapter 6 applies here. However, with fixer-uppers, you need to look at a few things a little more closely. First, because the property is distressed, we would be concerned about liens from contractors, subcontractors, workers, and materials suppliers. Make sure that your purchase contract agreement states that the seller is responsible for clearing up all liens placed against the property before closing occurs. Also pay close attention to building code violations. Because the property is distressed, what corners did the owner or management cut? Last, but not least, pay extra attention to the insurance policy, and obtain a claims history report. You'll find out about things such as past fires, past water-damage claims, and prior tenant claims.

Sales and marketing strategy

Part of your due diligence is to come up with a sales and marketing plan to lease your spiffy new property with great tenants and great leases as quickly as possible. Just as any new forward-looking, successful business has a business plan, your project needs one too. This part of due diligence is often overlooked because the person managing the update has his hands full with those challenges. And most great project managers don't have a salesperson's mentality. They're usually very analytical, but not the salesperson you need to have on the team.

If you're creating a plan for a retail center, start off by asking these questions:

- ✔ How are other retail centers doing in this area?
- ✔ Is the population trend upward or downward?
- ✔ Is there job growth in the city?

Do enough research to solidly quantify any trends that you discover. Next research and find out if there will be a strong market for your fixer-upper after you finish. Will your finished product be in demand? Do this work upfront. Then figure out the most effective ways of marketing your completed fixer-upper. Implementing a strong plan with the right salespeople on the front lines makes all the difference. For more help on this topic, check out *Marketing For Dummies,* 2nd Edition, by Alexander Haim (Wiley).

Before fix-up and after: Bridging the gap to payday

After your due diligence is complete, you have to make a decision. Do I pull the trigger on this deal? Your due diligence holds the answers to some key questions: Can I take this property in its "before" condition and transform it into its desired "after" condition? Can I do it profitably and within a reasonable time frame? In other words, do I have the skill, know-how, and resources to take this mess of a property, this great opportunity, and cross the bridge to a property that attracts the best tenants, gets good lease rates, improves the area, and makes me money? Here are tips for bridging that gap:

- ✔ **Know your break-even point.** Know how much income you need to bring in to break even after paying operating expenses and the mortgage. Get to this point as quickly as possible. (We discuss breaking even in detail later in the chapter.)

✔ **Find out the cause of the distress.** Find the root causes of how the property got into trouble. Property problems go two to three levels deep. For example, if the property's distress is blamed on a weak rental market (level 1), it's probably because the owner is marketing to the wrong type of tenants (level 2). The owner may be misdirecting her marketing because she's out of tune with what's happening in the market today (level 3). As you can see, each level has a root cause (as well as a solution).

✔ **Rate the seriousness of each problem.** After examining the causes of the distress, prioritize each one on a scale from one to five, with five being very serious. Immediately address the fives first, and then work your way down.

✔ **Total your financial needs.** You need to figure out as best you can how much money you need to purchase and fix up the property. Your total should include any long- and short-term loans, including construction loans, rehab loans, bridge loans, hard money loans, or lines of credit. And as a safeguard, add a cash reserve.

✔ **Figure out how long it will take to complete your game plan.** Although this may be difficult to pinpoint, sketch out as best as you can how long it will take to acquire, fix up, and sell the property. Don't just throw out a number of months or years. Instead, make an educated guess. For instance, if the purchase process takes 3 months, the fix-up takes 12 months, and positioning and selling takes 6 months, you're talking almost 2 years for the project completion. The months can really add up quickly. It's best to be on the conservative side.

✔ **Decide who's going to do the work.** Who's on your team? You'll have to develop your team of professionals — general contractors, attorneys, property managers, leasing agents, maintenance personnel, project managers, accountants/bookkeepers, and various other folks.

Determining your break-even point

One of the first things we like to know before jumping into a deal is how much income we need to bring in each month to at least break even in cash flow. It's stressful owning and managing negative cash-flow properties, so the question is, where do you need to be occupancy-wise to at least break even? You want to get to this condition as soon as possible. Getting to the break-even point allows you to predictably turn the corner to positive cash flow and profitability.

Here's a quick and easy formula to use to figure out your break-even point:

1. **Calculate your potential gross income.**

   Potential gross income is defined as the most income the property can make when it's 100 percent occupied. For example, if you have 60 apartment units renting at $555 per month each, your potential gross income is $60 \times \$555$ or $33,300 per month. Now, multiply by 12 to get the annual total, which is approximately $400,000.

2. **Calculate your total operating expenses.**

   Add up all of your monthly expenses, including taxes, insurance, maintenance, repairs, utilities, landscaping, accounting, management fees, salaries, and so on. Then multiply that number by 12 to get your annual total.

3. **Calculate your total mortgage payments for 12 months.**

   This is called this your *annual debt service*.

You can use this formula to find your break-even point:

Break-even occupancy % point = (operating expenses + annual debt service) ÷ potential gross income × 100

Here's a quick example: Suppose the fixer-upper is currently 50 percent occupied. Say at 100 percent occupancy, the property brings in $400,000, and the operating expenses run you $185,000. The annual debt service is $95,000. See the break-even point calculation below:

Break-even occupancy % point = ($185,000 + $95,000) ÷ $400,000 × 100 = 70%

This means that when the property reaches 70 percent occupancy, it will break even. Below 70 percent occupancy, the property will operate in negative cash flow. Any occupancy above 70 percent will produce positive cash flow.

In this example, the property is currently 50 percent occupied. After it reaches 70 percent occupancy, it will have a positive cash flow. Given these numbers, you need to ask yourself these questions: How long will it take to reach a 70 percent occupancy break-even point? And can I support the property financially until it reaches 70 percent occupancy?

Creating checkpoints for the renovation process

It's a given that when you purchase a fixer-upper you'll have to do some work on it, and for that, it's best to have timely checkpoints. Start your checkpoints by identifying the main pieces of the fix-up puzzle: financial, rehabilitation, property management, and lease-up.

You need to think about many questions and tasks to establish checkpoints for your commercial fixer-upper project. What follows are the various checkpoints to consider for putting together each piece of the timeline puzzle.

Financial checkpoints

You need to answer three questions to come up with a financial timeline. If you have all the necessary funds to fix up the property, you're all set. But if you need to obtain the money from other sources, such as a lender or investor, you need to plan accordingly. Ask yourself these questions:

- How much do I want to profit and in what time period? You may have to expand your rehab tasks and spend a little more to achieve a greater profit.
- How much is it going to cost me to fix up the joint?
- How fast can I get a hold of the money I need?

Rehabilitation checkpoints

When planning the rehab work on the property, keep these points in mind:

- **Identify the rehab items that will give you the highest rate of return on your rehab dollar.** Start on those first. For example, if all you need to do is minor drywall work to make your downstairs office space lease ready, and there is a ready market for that space, do that first.

  Curb-appeal improvements provide the highest rate of return on your rehab dollar. The easiest way to fix up and turn around a property is to make it look "pretty." It's amazing what a little sprucing up at a retail strip mall does to increase its occupancy and desirability. Before you start implementing your ideas for marketing, do your most important curb-appeal-type tasks. You can't sell on promises. Rarely will a tenant sign a lease because you verbally promise that the property will look "pretty" within a few months.

- **Set up a spending budget with enough detail to show how many tools and supplies you plan on using.** Include items like rags, towels, and rolls of masking tape. You need to be that detailed. You may not know exactly how many rolls of masking tape you're going to need, but have them in the budget. Simple cost overruns can turn huge in a heartbeat if you don't take every single line item into account. Be a penny pincher.

- **Get your skilled helpers ready to get to work.** Do they have their own tools? Will materials and supplies be ready for them? Do you have enough help to get the job done in the amount of time required? Have you budgeted for a little extra just in case you need more help?

- **Have a system of monitoring progress of the rehab work.** We use project management software. Many choices are available online.

Property management checkpoints

Keep these issues in mind when determining your property management needs:

- ✔ **Do you have extensive property management experience?** If not, hire someone who does. This is a critical part of the fix-up process. The property manager makes sure that all the projects and the overall timeline stay on track and checkpoints are checked off.

- ✔ **Make sure that your means of reporting information or obtaining information from the property is consistent and reliable.** We use Web-based property management software for all of our properties. Information is available to us 24/7 with a touch of a keystroke. So at anytime, we can find out about project accounting costs, budget monitoring, profit and loss reports, payable and receivable reports, tenant information, and maintenance status. Depending on the project, we create our own spreadsheets by using a program such as Microsoft Excel. For more expansive projects with multiple people and where sharing is involved, we'll use an online program such as Microsoft Groove.

- ✔ **Put the focus on customer satisfaction.** Keep in mind that the purpose of fixing up the property is to attract paying tenants and keep them for a long time. To measure customer satisfaction, look at the property's tenant turnover ratio. A turnover ratio of greater than 70 percent means that 70 percent of your tenants are leaving within 12 months. Not good for your bottom line. Chances are that they're leaving because they aren't being served satisfactorily.

Lease-up checkpoints

When it's time to starting leasing, consider these points:

- ✔ **Be ready for the Saturday drive-by and visit.** Put on a good first impression for the person who's just driving by. Make sure the grounds are clean and well landscaped, keep your signs and buildings painted, and have convenient parking. It's a lot easier to lease up your property if you can get potential tenants to come through the front door or call the number on the sign outside. We can't overemphasize enough how important it is to have the completed fixer-upper look dazzling from the outside in.

- ✔ **Set your marketing efforts to the type of tenants you want.** Know who you want as your tenants. Know their socioeconomic status, income, and lifestyles. Then figure out where to find these people and focus your marketing strategy there. If your newly renovated property is ripe for doctor's offices, forget about marketing in apartment rental guides. If your newly renovated downtown office building is ready for lease-up, consider hiring a leasing company that specializes in placing downtown office tenants.

✔ **Motivate your marketing and leasing staff with money.** We routinely give bonuses to our leasing agents as each new lease is signed. Rewarding our leasing agents with a bonus equal to half of the first month's rent isn't out of the question when we need to be really aggressive. Don't be cheap. Being cheap can be expensive!

✔ **Check out the competition.** When was the last time you went shopping? No, not grocery shopping. When was the last time you went shopping to peek at your competitor's offering to the public? Before you lease one bit of any space, make sure you perform lease and rent surveys of your competition. In addition to finding out what they're charging for rent, see if they're giving out incentives such as one month rent free or a reduced lease rate if the tenant signs a longer lease. What amenities do your competitors have that you don't? Being a shopaholic is encouraged here!

Avoiding Headaches and Pitfalls (Or at Least Minimizing the Pain)

Experience is the best remedy for the headaches of taking on a commercial fixer-upper. We wish we would have had a book like this to lay out the groundwork for us when we first started. We've heard that mentoring means getting wisdom without the pain. In an effort to offer you some mentoring, here are a few nuggets about how to avoid common pitfalls (yes, ones we've experienced ourselves). We also include some tips for hiring out your headaches — oops, we mean projects.

Recognize hopeless situations

Not every commercial fixer-upper can be fixed. That's right. Some deals out there are just too far gone to make a profit from. Sometimes you can spot them upfront, but most times you'll have to go through some due diligence to really find out. Here are a few signs and situations that tell you that your prospective fixer-upper deal is hopeless and you should move on to the next opportunity.

Avoid obsolete properties

In commercial real estate, properties can be deemed obsolete in three ways. When the property is obsolete, it can be very difficult and very expensive — and sometimes impossible — to make right. An enormous loss of real value can occur if a property becomes obsolete. Here are the ways in which a property can be obsolete:

- ✔ **Physically:** This is a loss of value due to Mother Nature and old age. Or the property is just plain worn out. Physical deterioration is another name for it. A property with a foundation made out of crumbling bricks and located in an earthquake zone is a good example.

- ✔ **Functionally:** In this category, a property can't be used or it loses value because of its poor design or lack of modern facilities. An example would be a warehouse that doesn't have enough electrical power to accommodate today's advanced electronics and circuitry.

- ✔ **Economically:** Here a property loses its value because of external forces, such as a change in zoning or changes in traffic flow. A good example would be having an airport or freeway constructed too close to your property. Another great example could be the loss of a major employer in your immediate area.

Avoid an owner who doesn't want to play

If the owner isn't serious about selling or isn't willing to be reasonable, don't fool around. Move on to the next opportunity. Maybe give the reluctant owner a call 30 days from now to see if his motivation has changed.

Avoid properties that have too much debt

We have seen properties that have been refinanced many times and now have huge mortgage balances on them. The large mortgage payments have sucked the cash flow from the properties and now the owner wants to sell. But here's the problem: The amount we're willing to pay for the property is lower than what is owed on the property. Unless the owner can do a "debt workout" with the lender, we're passing.

Avoid buying properties with bargain-bottom prices

Don't invest in an area experiencing a downturn. The price is low for a reason, especially in areas where the economy is declining. Because typical real estate cycles run on ten-year curves, you may have to wait for ten years for a turn-around or peak, if one happens at all.

Hire good contractors (and think like one when you do projects yourself)

Contractors make a living by estimating the costs of a project, adding extra to it for profit, and then doing the work. As a commercial fixer-upper investor, you should think the same way. When a contractor takes too long to finish a job, he'll start "running in the red," meaning that he's no longer making a profit. When you take too long to complete a fixer-upper, you can easily wipe out your profits.

When you've done all the right things — bought low, fixed up under budget, and improved the financial situation — don't hesitate to get out. Don't wait around for new challenges and problems — they'll cost you your profits. Sell as quickly as possible. Think like a contractor: get in, do good work, and get paid.

As for hiring a contractor for your commercial fixer-upper, it's different than hiring someone to remodel your home's kitchen. Commercial real estate investing is a business, so you need to think like a highly skilled and professional businessperson.

We may sound like a broken record, but treat your commercial real estate business like a business and hire only the best and most cost-effective people or companies of the highest integrity. Don't take any shortcuts and never compromise. Your future will thank you for it.

Be leery of contractors who ask you to make payments in their personal name, ask for cash only, or want large payments upfront. All of these are red flags, and they indicate that the contractor's license may have been revoked or suspended, that his insurance is cancelled, or that he's having financial problems.

Why commercial fixer-uppers will be around forever

Want a career with never-ending possibilities and an endless flow of money-making deals? Commercial fixer-uppers will always be around as long as real estate exists. The real estate cycle continuously creates distressed properties and distressed owners. At the peak of the cycle, where you have seller's market conditions such as high price and low inventory, you find buyers who have gotten in over their heads because of over-enthusiasm and lack of experience. Within a few years (sometime less) of owning the property, these owners want out at all costs because of distress. So here's your start of the fixer-upper opportunities.

At the bottom of the cycle are buyer's market conditions. High inventories and low prices are signs of the times. In this market, you have countless opportunities. Somewhere in the world, a buyer's market always exists.

We see quite a bit of "uneducated" money chasing after the same properties a seasoned and experienced investor would. The uneducated investors end up paying too much and buying with unrealistic investment goals. This results in two things: First, prices get inflated. Second, these same owners become owners of distressed properties over time because they're in over their heads. Do you see the cycle?

For those of you who want to invest in commercial fixer-uppers, more money is available to you than ever before in the history of real estate investing. Lenders want to lend you money to fix up commercial properties that will enhance an area or city. Every time you fix up a property, you add jobs to the city and increase the tax revenues.

Timing Your Fixer-Upper for a Quick Sale

You've transformed your fixer-upper into a profitable, respectable place, and now you're ready to cash in on all of your hard work. Planning well plus efficient management equals a handsome payday for you. It's time to pat yourself on the back and celebrate. Payday is around the corner!

But first things first — how do you know it's time to sell? Well, you went into this project with certain goals to meet, and you told yourself you'd sell after they were met, right? Realistically, when the property reaches its maximum potential, you want to sell at the top.

 Getting emotionally tied to a project not only delays your profits, but it can erase them as well. Markets can change on a whim, the economy is ever changing, and the consumer mentality is always in flux. Plan your profits. Work for your profits. See your profits. Sell and get your profits.

Timing the sale just right isn't rocket science. In fact, it's pretty simple to decide to sell:

✔ When you see the profits, it's time to sell.

✔ When you're ready for more growth — both businesswise and personally — it's time to sell. You may need the profits from the sale to move into the next project. If your goal is to become a bigger investor, it usually requires bigger money and bigger plans.

To figure out how much to ask for your revitalized property, see the "Figuring your NOI, cap rate, and sales price" section earlier in the chapter.

Chapter 15

Land Development: The Heart of Commercial Real Estate

*L*and development is a way to take a small amount of money and turn it into a fortune. If you can see the vision, stay the course, and make friends with plenty of city planners and other governmental types, you can have a new and prosperous career in land development.

In this chapter, we take you on a winding journey through the ins and outs of developing raw dirt into the property of your dreams. We show you where to find land deals, how to deal with stubborn government bureaucrats (who you need on your development team), how best to negotiate, and how to get your deal approved.

The Pros and Cons of Investing in Land

Land development can be a wonderful thing, but it can also be quite challenging at times. In this section, we show you both sides.

The pros

When you take a 5-acre piece of raw land that's worth a million dollars (because of its location), and you change its use (better known as *rezoning*), there's a very good chance that the value of that raw land can go up 25 to 100 percent in value. If you know how to raise the funds by using private investors (see Chapter 10), you buy the property and, in a couple of years, depending on the community, you can double what you paid for it. Land can be an incredibly profitable investment. Plus, you can do really big deals without using much of your own money. All you need is desire, determination, and guts.

The cons

Here are some of the downsides of investing in land:

- **As a beginning developer, you typically aren't paid until the end of the project.** Of course, as in everything else, after you've established a track record, getting paid for your services along the way is easier.

- **Land development typically requires upfront money to cover the costs of doing your due diligence, environmental studies, and/or a market suitability report.** For example, in a deal that our team members put together recently, we put up almost $300,000 of investor money, set at a high rate of return because they contributed fully at-risk money. If we had decided not to do the deal, they could have lost it all.

- **You have to gain the trust of people in the community, which can be pretty tricky sometimes.** Any one community governmental or neighborhood association can put up a roadblock to the completion of your land development project, so you have to be sure to make lots of friends.

- **With land development, you can make massive chunks of money, but you can also lose money swiftly.** For example, in one of our projects, we didn't foresee a huge problem with building in an existing community that was almost complete. Specifically, 35 townhouse buildings had been built; we were planning to build the last 5. The homeowner's association opposed our involvement, but we weren't smart enough to see this burning issue going into the deal. When all was said and done, we pulled out and got our earnest money back, but we lost $37,000 in the *soft costs* (fees paid for surveys, research, and inspections) that we had put into the deal.

- **With commercial real estate, your biggest concerns can be potential environmental problems.** When you're buying land, you're basically buying dirt, and if that dirt has been raw for 200 years, there's a chance that somebody dumped oil or gas or fertilizer on it back in the 1930s or

1940s when no one thought or cared about it. Here's the problem: If you have contaminated dirt or other environmental problems, you need to remedy all those problems as part of your land development project. Even though environmental problems aren't necessarily showstoppers, they do add to your costs, so you definitely need to be aware of them.

Understanding What Makes Land Worth More

Certain things can cause a land's value to increase (or decrease if the situation isn't right). Here are the three factors that affect value:

- ✓ **Location:** Land that's close to where people live, work, and play is worth more than land out in the middle of nowhere. You may have heard this before — and with land development it's absolutely essential. The most valuable land is typically close to people — lots of people.

   One of the best places to own land is "on the water." The value of waterfront property continues to climb over time because that's where people want to live and play.

- ✓ **The approval to build:** The reason that land is developed is so that it can generate more income. Land that's used for farming brings in much less income than land that has an office building or shopping center on it. When you change the zoning or take a piece of land through the approval process, it becomes more valuable simply because you now have the ability to build and create more income from the land.

- ✓ **Availability of utilities:** In order for land to be improved, you need to make sure that the water, electricity, gas, and sewer systems are available. Land that's several miles away from these services will require you to spend hundreds of thousands of dollars in additional costs to develop the property. Because of this, land that's next to existing utilities, or that already has utilities in place, is worth much more.

Knowing Whether You're in the Right Market

When you're looking for the right piece of land to develop, you need to pay attention to what surrounds the piece of land that you're interested in. For instance, ask the following questions:

Changing zoning

Several of our Commercial Mentoring Program students found a property that included some office buildings, warehouses, and also about 900 acres of undeveloped land. They used our agreements to get the property under contract and worked hard to review all the due diligence that was needed to purchase a mixed-use property like this.

They were able to put together a presentation that convinced a group of friends they had met at one of our trainings to provide the funds needed for the deal. Their exit strategy is to sell off the office buildings and warehouses but to keep the land. If the contract that's in place right now closes, they'll have made enough money from selling the pieces with the buildings on it to pay off all the investors and the remaining 900 acres of land.

Because it's zoned agricultural and is just beyond the edge of a large growing metropolitan area, this land is worth about $2 per square foot. This means that within the next five to ten years, this land will become more and more valuable. When the zoning is changed on this land to allow residential development, the value goes from $2 per square foot up to about $7 per square foot. This works out to a huge profit. Are you starting to see the potential in land development?

✔ Is the area growing and population coming in?

✔ What kinds of residences or businesses are already in place?

✔ What are the demographics of the area?

✔ If you intend to build a commercial enterprise, is there plenty of housing or apartments going into the area?

In other words, assess the local economy; it needs to be strong for you to make the venture profitable. What you're looking for is the right spot to put up houses or build your retail shopping center. Of course, you wouldn't just buy a piece of land because you got a good price — unless you had a way to support it. What happens if you put up 55 townhouses, but no one is around to fill them? You may have just created a perfect situation for a foreclosure property. And the last thing you want to do is build a negative, depleting asset, so be extremely careful about both the surroundings and demographics of the piece of land you're looking at.

One of our Commercial Mentoring Program coaches, Stephen, is building a $45 million project in Winter Park, Colorado. He spent $15,000 to have an independent comprehensive market study done to find out whether what his team thought about the marketplace was indeed true. Stephen says, "I'd rather spend $15,000 now than spend $45 million to realize we were wrong because our egos got mixed into our calculations." To watch Stephen as he shares "How to Explode Your Net Worth with Land Development" go to www.commercialquickstart.com.

Getting an outside expert's opinion

No matter how good you think your land development project is, always get an outside expert opinion. Every land developer that we know has either a mentor or a close-knit group of experienced friends who can provide that outside, third-party viewpoint. Check out www.commercialmentoring.com to find people to help with your project.

Recently, one of our team members hired an outside company to do a market study on the town he was considering investing in. The company flew into town, interviewed all kinds of people, and sent back a 122-page market study. The study validated everything that our team member was thinking about the market — that it was, indeed, a great time to invest. This information boosted not only his own confidence, but also the confidence of the investors he was bringing in to fund the project.

Examining the path of progress

If you were to look back at the history of most cities, you'd find that many of them started off as small encampments along riverbanks or other convenient places for people to gather and live. As a town grows over time, it spreads farther and farther away from this central area. If you look at any town or metropolitan area, you can see which direction the city has grown and which direction it's most likely to continue growing in.

When you buy land outside the city limits, you're investing in the path of progress. As the city continues to grow, your land will become more and more desirable as other projects and developments move out toward your property.

Taking advantage of zoning acres

Commercial real estate brokers talk about an acre as typically being 43,560 square feet, so if you were to purchase a 40-acre lot, you'd have a total of 1,742,400 square feet (40 × 43,560). However, when you're talking to the planning department in an area where this land is located, check the list of definitions they use to see the number of square feet in an acre. You'd think that it would be the same 43,560 square feet as commercial brokers use. But you may discover something called a *zoning acre*. To keep things simple, many municipalities define a zoning acre as having a nice even 40,000 square feet. That means if you're subdividing your 40 broker-talk acres into house lots that are each 1 zoning acre in size, you'll end up being able to sell 43.5 lots. Using this tip, you just picked up an extra 3½ acres of land for free. How's that for a return on your investment?

Many cities have an outer development boundary that's drawn on the planning maps. This boundary is outside the city line, and it defines the areas in which the city expects to be developed over time. Ask your planning department where you can find out more about this.

Identifying the Three Ps for Successful Projects

If you want to be successful in your land development project, you need to follow what we call "the 3 Ps." Here they are:

- ✔ **Position:** What's your position in the marketplace? Is there a demand for the type of development that you're contemplating? You can have the best project in the world, with the fanciest architecture, and many more people than your mom can love it. However, if you can't sell it over time, you'll make a mistake buying it in the first place.

- ✔ **Profits:** What profits is the land likely to make? This includes making a great return on your time, energy, and personal capital that you contribute to the project. In addition to money in your pocket, most good-sized land development projects end up using bank financing, private investors, or a combination of the two. Banks want your project to be profitable so that they can get paid. Your investors want not only to be paid back, but also to get a high rate of return.

- ✔ **Politics:** What does politics have to do with land development? *Everything.* Why? Because before you break ground to build something, you need the approval of several different governmental entities, including the city council, the planning commission, the zoning department, and several other bureaucratic departments that you may not even think about — like the neighbors, the homeowner's association, and even the U.S. Postal Service.

Mess up in just one area here and your land development project could be delayed, denied, or defunct. This is why you need to be good at making friends fast in high places when you do land development.

To be successful, it's also important to know your exit strategy before you get in. Typically for land development, your exit strategy is to sell to another builder. Or you may decide to get the right land in the path of progress and wait for the other developers to work their way out to you. Before you jump in, however, make sure that you understand what you'll eventually do with the property. You can sell to another builder, hire a builder and manage the project, or build it yourself.

Investing in Land with a Team

Yes, we understand that it's difficult to invest in land on your own, which is a key reason why our commercial investing trainings keep getting bigger and bigger. Our Commercial Mentoring Program students return not only to refresh their knowledge and get little nuggets of new information, but also to rekindle relationships and meet other students. We've seen many of these relationships turn into joint ventures over time.

With a big land development project, it makes sense to have a number of people on your team. When you're picking the right people, recruit those who have different talents and characteristics than you do. For example, it doesn't make sense to recruit only detail-oriented people and no one who's able to see the big picture. (See Chapter 10 for more on creating partnerships.) Here's a list of the people that you want on your team:

- ✔ Civil engineer
- ✔ Commercial broker
- ✔ Geologist
- ✔ Homebuilder
- ✔ Landscaping architect
- ✔ Marketing consultant
- ✔ Mentor or coach
- ✔ Project manager
- ✔ Real estate attorney
- ✔ Structural architect
- ✔ Surveyor
- ✔ Tax attorney
- ✔ Tax strategist and/or certified public accountant

Picking the right experts to work with is essential. When you don't have the right people on the team, it can be a painful learning experience. But we also recognize we wouldn't be where we are today if we didn't have those experiences. For more information on land development consultants in your area, visit www.commercialmentoring.com.

We've found a little tool, the Kolbe Index (www.kolbe.com), that's helpful for determining within 20 minutes someone's characteristics and talents. It tells you if someone is good at starting things, following through on things, implementing things, or taking care of details. It can help you choose the right people to work with.

Finding the Best Places to Invest in Land

One of the best places to develop land can often be right in town. Do you know of any areas of open land that may be big enough for five to ten houses? These are called *infill projects.*

Another good place to invest in land is in the direction in which the city is expanding. For example, the Denver metropolitan area is bordered by mountains in the west and mostly open space in the north. This leaves areas to the east and the south as obvious places that will be developed over the next 10 to 20 years.

Denver is a good example of how a major transportation hub, such as an airport, can affect the path of progress. Denver International Airport was built about 20 miles directly northeast of the then current city line. The city of Denver annexed all that property. Because businesses and associated housing for workers is filling in the area around the airport, a major path of progress lies between the city and the airport.

The path of progress is often determined early on in a city's development and continues for decades. So consider the path of progress points, combined with job growth, migration, and new construction, when deciding whether to pursue a project.

One way to reduce your risk with land development is to look for where other big businesses are going in (which is usually in the path of progress). With commercial properties, every other piece of land that's developed helps to attract more people to the area. When a big box store goes in, it's much more likely that other commercial projects are going to succeed. The more people that go by your tenants' stores, the more successful your tenants will become — and successful tenants will make you rich. The trick here is to make sure that you get into the game before all the other investors want to jump onboard.

With Land, Time Really Does Equal Money

When you're developing land or putting a project together, the more time you have, the easier your job is and the more money you'll typically make. The reason for this is that extra time gives you the ability to

- ✔ Do more throughout due diligence to allow you to avoid potential pitfalls
- ✔ Go back and negotiate with the seller over time to get additional concessions
- ✔ Research the marketplace to come up with more exit strategies

ANECDOTE

You gotta know when to hold 'em

Rob, one of our Commercial Mentoring Program coaches, used to work as a corporate warrior. He traveled out of town every week from Sunday night through Thursday. His marriage was looking pretty shaky and his kids hardly knew him. Rob read our book *Making Big Money Investing in Real Estate without Tenants, Banks, or Rehab Projects,* and decided to quit the corporate rat race and join our Residential Mentoring Program. He began investing in single-family houses and, over 18 months, worked up to the point where he had almost 50 properties. Then Rob noticed that some of our other students were getting involved in commercial real estate. He had been happy up to that point simply investing in single-family homes.

Rob went to his father-in-law, David, who was a commercial broker and said, "Pop, I want to do what you do. Would you be willing to take me under your wing?" Fast-forward two years. Rob has found a 12-acre piece of land that appears to be located in the path of progress. Rob did some quick research and then had his father-in-law and his other mentors check his assumptions.

David told him, "It's not a for-sure deal, but if that area develops like I think it will, then that land is going to be worth quite a bit more over the next few years." Using some of the creative ideas from the Commercial Mentoring Program, Rob effectively got the land under contract with an agreement that he didn't need to close for 12 months.

His plan was to control the property and sit back to see what happened in the marketplace. About eight months later a broker friend of Rob's came by the office. "Would you want to sell that 12-acre lot Rob? I can get you $500,000 more than your purchase price. You can make a cool

half a million and never even have to own the property."

Although this sounded enticing, Rob told the broker that he was going to think about it overnight. He arranged to meet the broker for lunch the next day. Rob went to his mentor at this point to get his advice. His mentor said, "I can see definite signs of development out there, Rob. If it's worth that much more today, just think how much more it will be worth in a year or two. Hang on to it if you can."

The next day at lunch, Rob let the broker know that he'd decided to keep his 12-acre lot rather than sell it. The broker said, "That sounds like a good decision on your part, Rob. " He smiled and said, "If I owned it, I wouldn't sell it right now either."

Over the next month, Rob had 17 other people approach him about buying his land. He couldn't get any of them to share with him what was going on. All he knew was that something big was going to happen. At the end of the year, Rob brought in some other investors to help him close on his contract to purchase the land. His price worked out to $2 per square foot.

Several months later, Rob was sitting with his wife and kids one morning when he saw an article that caught his eye. The headline said "Factory Outlet Mall Coming to El Paso." Then Rob realized that the mall was going to be right across the street from his 12-acre lot! Rob and his wife had been waiting for a big hit like this. When we talked to Rob several weeks ago, he said that other land nearby was selling for close to $10 per square foot and that he had a number of offers in the $9-per-square-foot range.

The lesson here is that it only takes one commercial deal for you to be set for life. Rob and his family stand to make several million dollars on this one deal before it is over.

✔ Shop around with various lenders to get the best rates

✔ Find all the investors you need to fund the cash needs of the project for you

✔ Allow local market activity to push the value of your land up

ANECDOTE

Stretching the time you have to close a deal: A real-life example

One of our clients, Roger, came across a property that was owned by a national corporation that had moved its offices and manufacturing facilities to another area of the country. The owner was annoyed at the time because another investor had tied up the property for 11 months and then used an escape clause to get out of the deal. Even though they were asking $7.5 million for the property, this was a tiny little thorn in their sides compared to everything else the corporation had going on. At this point they wanted to sell it and sell it quickly.

Roger went to the selling agent and asked a very good question: "What's a good offer going to look like?" The agent said that it would probably take the full $7.5 million because there were two other offers on the table. In addition, the broker said that the seller wanted to close in 60 days. Now, 60 days is about what it takes to close a deal on a house. But on a big property like this, it was highly likely that it would take more time for Roger to check everything out and line up his investors.

Roger said, "My offer is $7.6 million. Here's $100,000 earnest money and I'm okay with writing down the closing date as 60 days from now." Roger was smart enough to make sure that his money didn't become nonrefundable before the 60 days was up. He had two months to find a way to figure out how to make this deal work.

Roger got busy at that point. He talked to his partners and enlisted their help in moving through the due diligence process. He also found a way to connect not only with the selling broker, but also with the people from the corporation who were in charge of the deal. He knew that it was going to be next to impossible to close within 60 days, so he started dropping little hints that they may need some more time.

He ended up doing a number of other things to stretch out the time to close this deal — things like asking about a previous environmental problem that had been completely taken care of. But Roger said, "Well, obviously we need some time to review that just to make sure it's all completely taken care of." How could a seller say no to that? Roger also used language like "Gosh, these buildings are actually quite a bit bigger than I thought — we're going to need an adequate amount of time to check out the property, just as any other serious buyer would." By doing this, he was able to extend the time to closing from 60 days all the way to 9 months.

And during those nine months, Roger was able to find a bank that would loan him $5 million and also line up investors who put in another $5 million. This gave him a total of $10 million to work with. He now had the money to cover the payments on the property during the next several years in case he didn't get it leased or sold right away.

Roger says that he's had several offers that are in the $20 million range. And he has only owned the property for about seven months. He doesn't want to sell it right now, because if he does he's going to have to pay short-term gains tax on his $10 million profit.

The big picture is that all of this allows you to make more money and also helps to reduce your stress levels.

Using contracts to get more time

When buying any type of commercial property, you're going to need time to check out the property, look at the title work, and line up any investors that you may be using. One of the easiest ways to get more time is by using some special language in your contracts.

One of our favorite approaches is to list a bunch of things that we need to see as the buyer, such as a recent survey, all the title work, complete copies of any environmental reviews, and so on. In the contract, you can ask for a certain number of business days after you receive all these items to complete your due diligence. The clock doesn't even start ticking until the seller gets you all these items.

Another way to get more time is to ask for an extension upfront. You can say, "We probably won't need this, but in case we do, would it be okay if we had a one-time extension of 60 days, just in case the lender has a delay or some other minor problem comes up? We'd hate for the entire deal to fall through due to some little detail like that." When you get agreement on this, put it into writing in the contract.

Here are two key points to remember for stretching out the time that you may need on a deal:

- ✔ The connection and rapport that you have with the broker and seller is absolutely critical.

- ✔ If you're going to ask for an extension, don't wait until the day before the closing to bring it up. The worst thing you can do is go right to the end of the time when they're expecting that you're ready to close and say, "We can't close. We need more time."

Buying time with options

After you close on the purchase of the land, you have to pay real estate taxes and costs on any mortgages you have until it can produce income to cover these expenses. How can you buy time until you're able to fully develop the land?

Our favorite way to do this is by using options to control your ability to purchase the property without actually having to make payments on it. An *option* is a fee paid to the owner. That fee allows you to have the property under contract while you have time to move the development ahead. Your option also gives you the time to do your due diligence and get approval from various agencies.

Changing the Property's Zoning and Getting Approved to Develop

If you change a property's zoning from something like an agricultural property to mixed use or residential, its value can go up, often by a factor of ten. The challenge is making sure you meet the community requirements enforced by the local town, county, and/or state agencies.

Determining what to build on your land

When you look at a piece of land, what do you want to build on it? Do you want to go commercial, such as strip centers or strip malls? Or do you want to settle on single-family units or multiunits? When trying to decide what to build on your land, be sure to look at the surrounding neighborhoods to see how your project might fit in.

Just like other commercial real estate, the value of land is directly related to the income it produces. This means that open agricultural land that's good for growing crops or grazing cows will be worth a lot less than a piece of land on which a skyscraper has been built in the middle of a city.

Taking master plans into consideration

Most municipalities work off a master plan. A *master plan* (sometimes called a *comprehensive plan*) states the community's goals and objectives. It helps to establish the rules and policies that relate to growth in the community, including both new development and modifications to existing areas.

The master plan typically represents the opinions and suggestions for both the community and governmental attitudes and goals. The suggestions in the master plan are based on analysis of the local economy and demographic studies, along with other factors that affect community. The master plan attempts to provide a vision of what the community will look like as it evolves over the next 5, 10, or 20 years.

In most places, a master plan is created as a way to provide direction, not legally binding laws such as zoning regulations. In a few areas of the United States, the master plan actually requires conformance, which gives it the

ANECDOTE

How it took eight months to make a million overnight

Leta, one of our students, purchased a mobile-home park from owners who weren't doing a good job of managing the property. The park was losing money because it was only half occupied. She found a way to buy it "subject to" the existing mortgage, which meant that she could get in without using any of her own money.

The park ended up taking up all of Leta's time and attention for the next eight months as she worked hard to attract mobile-home owners into the park. She even went out and bought some used mobile homes just so that she could get the rent for the lots. There were a number of times when she came to us ready to quit.

After she finally had the mobile-home park turned around and making money, Leta realized that the same owner from whom she had bought the mobile-home park also owned some land that was right next to the mobile-home park.

After talking with the owner of the land, Leta realized that she didn't have the money to buy and that the owner really didn't want to sell because of the taxes he would have to pay. Because she had taken the time to get to know the owner from the mobile-home park deal, Leta felt like the owner trusted her enough to perhaps do another creative deal. Leta asked the owner if she could have an option to buy the land at any point in time over the next 12 months if she paid the real estate taxes for the owner.

The owner agreed to this and Leta asked a relative of hers to provide the funds needed to pay the taxes in exchange for one-half of the deal if and when she ever bought the property. During the next year, a new shopping center went in behind Leta's land. This made the value go from $1 million to over $2 million overnight.

A million bucks overnight? That's how it may look to some people. We think that Leta's willingness to take on the mobile-home park and work hard to turn it around, as well as her connections with the owner, made all the difference.

power of law. In most areas, however, the local bureaucrats and agencies do their best to follow the master plan and meet the needs of their community. If any of their decisions are questioned, those in line with the master plan are most likely to be confirmed as correct.

For the people who live in an area of the master plan, the plan allows them to know what to expect in terms of quality of life in that area. It identifies the services people expect to get and helps create a common theme for the various neighborhoods. Most people don't like change. The master plan gives people the certainty of knowing what can happen in an area. Ideally, this lets them avoid any changes that can reduce their property values. The master plan allows business owners to see the future locations of new areas for employment or where residential communities may be located in order to support workers who need to come and work in their business.

The future of a labor force and also areas where businesses are likely to succeed can be determined from the plan. From the land developer standpoint, the master plan helps to protect the project's value. In addition, a developer can look at the plan and find new opportunities for development. After all, the developer is in the business of finding land that can be converted to a higher and best use.

A *land-use map* shows a picture of both existing and future land uses such as residential, commercial, industrial, and centers of employment. It may also show the various densities of zoning, which tells a land developer where it may be good to put in a new project. The land-use map typically shows proposed highway interchanges, locations of regional shopping malls, schools, and churches. This is important information to have in your planning.

When existing zoning on land is different from the master plan, the existing zoning will actually take precedence over the master plan. Because of this, as a developer you'll have the option of moving ahead by using the existing zoning, or requesting a change to the zoning shown in the master plan. Although no zoning approval is ever final until it's done, if you ask for something that's already in the master plan, your project is more likely to be approved.

Going after entitlement

Entitlement means taking a piece of land that formerly wasn't approved for development and getting all the necessary zoning changes, applications, and approvals in place so that the land can be developed and built upon. As an entitlement specialist, your exit strategy is to sell your land project to a builder; this strategy is called "taking it to the map."

So what exactly does this strategy mean? It means that you're improving the raw land so a builder can come in and build on the property. The developer often provides roads, sidewalks, underground utilities, and landscaping, but this isn't always the case. On one of the projects we're selling, for example, we're putting in infrastructure on one side but on the other one, we're not. We're just getting the final map showing approved lots — about 43 lots altogether. Each one will have its own separate title. So we've done all the approval process and then it's up to the builder to put in the road, sidewalks, and utilities. You can do it either way.

Jeff, one of our Commercial Mentoring Program coaches, has two projects requiring entitlement. When he went into these two projects, his initial exit strategy was to build out both projects. After these projects were under way, Jeff found another area that was ripe for land development. He started on several more deals there. As a result, Jeff decided to take these two projects "to the map," but not to build anything. So he'll sell these to a builder and focus his attention on the bigger fish he found.

The approval process and why it frustrates many would-be investors

Here's an example of what zoning and the approval process is all about from the municipality side: The mission statement from the planning department says:

> *We will actively promote a diverse, safe, and dynamic community and enhance the living, working, and recreational choices for all of our citizens and visitors.*

Now let's translate this into what this mission statement looks like from the land developer side:

> *We will create a complex, confusing, and frustrating experience for any and all developers who attempt to build or improve any area of our community. To keep the developers guessing, we will change our minds often, and write our regulations in a way that they are very difficult to interpret.*

We're kidding, of course. Sure, dealing with the various agencies that can make or break your deal can be a challenge. But it's a lot more fun if you turn it into a way to meet interesting people, as opposed to thinking that you're going to have to fight with city hall.

Here's an example of some of the different boards and agencies that you may have to deal with on your development project (see Table 15-1 for a more complete list):

- ✔ **Building and fire code review and appeals board:** These folks are charged with the responsibility for reviewing and updating the city's building codes for public safety and best practices.
- ✔ **Common council or zoning department board of public works:** They advise on any matters concerning public lands or structures.
- ✔ **Community development authority:** They act as an agent of the city to perform, operate, and administer the city's housing rehabilitation services.
- ✔ **Landmarks commission:** They regulate construction or reconstruction, exterior alterations within locally designated historic districts, and demolition of historic structures. They also recognize landmarks.
- ✔ **Planning commission privilege in streets committee:** They make recommendations to the board of public works and the common council on applications for encroachments into the public right of way.
- ✔ **Pedestrian/bicycle/motor vehicle commission:** They deal with policies on pedestrian, bicycle, and motor vehicles systems and facilities.

✔ **Urban design commission:** They review matters of aesthetics, design, and appearance of specific building proposals.

✔ **Zoning board of appeals:** They hear and act on applications for zoning variances, appeals to alleged errors in orders, and requirements or determinations in the enforcement of the zoning ordinance. They also make the final determination on these issues and appeals to their decisions are made to the courts.

You'll also meet with the water department and the sewer department to determine answers to the following questions:

✔ Is there enough water?

✔ Is there sewage removal?

✔ Is it well water? Is it septic?

✔ If it's septic, how much waste is allowed?

These are all crucial things to find out within five or six business days of identifying the property you put under contract.

One of our commercial clients came to a training we had in Hawaii. She got a piece of land under contract where she thought she could build 68 townhouses. When she went to the water department, she found out that she'd never be able to get more than 13 taps. (One tap is required for each townhouse in a project like this.) So she went back to the drawing board and came up with a way to develop the land with 13 houses on it so that she was able to get approval.

You'll also want to meet with fire officials in the area of your land and ask:

✔ Does the property have fire facility usage?

✔ Can they provide fire protection for the areas that your project is going into?

If your property is outside the growth boundary to be serviced by the fire and ambulance, your project probably won't be approved by the city council. It doesn't matter if all the other agencies like your project — if you don't have access to emergency services, your project will get shot down.

Table 15-1 The Departments You May Need to Consult in Land Deals

Department	Issues addressed
Engineering	Erosion control; flood plain; parking lot drainage; plat review; sanitary sewer; storm sewer and drainage; storm water management; street name and address; street layout and size; utility easements; water detention; wetland zoning

Department	Issues addressed
Fire	Fire passage; fire flow requirements; fuel tanks; hazardous materials; service stations; screening over windows; zero-lot line
Metro Transit	Bus stop requirements; easements for operation and infrastructure; pedestrian/handicap access and circulation; plat review; street layout and size; transportation and demand management plans
Parks	Open space; park areas; wetland zoning
Traffic Engineering	Access control; impact on streets and neighborhoods; parking lot geometry, layout, and circulation; pedestrian/bicycle access and circulation; plat review; rights-of-way; street layout and size; traffic generation; utility easements
Water/Utilities	Costs (assessments) distribution; easements; hydrants; main locations; service; water supply
Planning and Development	Access to buildings; building code compliance; circulation; demolition; design; easement dedication; environmental hazards; flood plain; floor area ratio; grading plan; handicap access; heating code compliance; landscape plan; lease of city property; lot coverage; lot size; national electric code compliance; parking requirements; plumbing code compliance; sale of city property; screening; soil erosion; signs; site design; special districts; street encroachments; street graphics; street occupancy; title; trash pickup enclosures; units (number of); usable open space; yard setbacks; zoning

Getting the Green Light on Your Deal

Part of doing land development is understanding how local planning, zoning, and other rules may affect your project. You can expect to deal with government agencies on everything from the amount of square feet you can build and permitted uses to the drainage of storm water. In some areas, you may need to provide a detailed review of the traffic that will be generated by your development.

According to the U.S. Constitution, local zoning and planning is left up to the states. You'd think that at least within one state, there would be some consistency in how they deal with developers. Unfortunately, that isn't the case. Each county or municipality has its own rules and regulations. Sometimes even in one area, different projects fall under different guidelines and add confusion.

As an urban area matures over time, the citizens and their political leaders want to have more specific rules for development and construction. As a result, the local government fine-tunes the zoning regulations and procedures to deal with priorities brought up by community leaders. Sometimes, some of these new regulations may even take effect after your land development project is underway. This requires adjusting your development and construction budgets during the rezoning process as well as throughout the life of your land development project.

Coauthor Peter Conti's parents have a small home up in Sydney, Maine, where they spend their summers. His brother works there on a dairy farm milking cows. Even though Peter's brother's house is on a small piece of land, his backyard view across lush green fields and trees is spectacular. Looking out off his back deck, you'd never guess this area has absolutely no zoning. This means that if someone wanted to rebuild a school bus in their front yard, there are no regulations to stop him or her from doing so. Luckily, most of the neighbors work together to keep the community looking nice. In effect, the zoning and planning departments of any municipality work like the community of Sydney works to make the best of any development that happens in their area.

You may want to take on several projects in one area omce you become familiar with the land-use planning, zoning, and regulations in that jurisdiction. As strapped as cities are these days with their budgets, they aren't able to do much to help developers through the jurisdictions, regulations, or review procedures. This leaves it up to you as the land developer to understand and know the local regulations. So make sure that your project meets all the guidelines the first time without having to go back and make multiple changes.

Dealing with bureaucrats

As soon as you have a property under contract, plan to talk to officials at the city council and planning department. Don't waste any time. If you have the idea today, within the next day or two, you need to be in front of the planners to find out the actual use of the property and its zoning.

Tell the planners what you're contemplating. Get their opinions, and see if they think the municipality would allow you to change the zoning to provide for different use. If you want to divide the land up into smaller lots, for example, get their opinions on whether they think it would be possible. Ask about similar projects that have either been approved or disapproved. Doing your homework early pays off.

Don't wait until you have a deal under contract to get to know the people at city hall. Ideally, they should know you by name when you walk in the door. When talking to city council people, keep in mind that they're volunteers who have normal jobs. Take them to lunch, run your idea by them, and ask, "What do you think the members of the city council will think about my idea? Will they like it or not like it?" If the councilperson says, "We hate this idea," the proposition will never get passed when it comes time for a vote.

Lifestyle development policy: An idea whose time has come

There's a movement to create lifestyle commercial and mixed-use development through public policy and land use ordinances. Instead of just developing property to make a profit, the idea is that everyone works together to have a nice place to live and meet the needs of the community.

This concept is based on the following lifestyle development principles:

- **Efficient use of land resources:** This means that, especially when developing in urban areas, the development is compact, using only as much land as necessary.

- **Full use of city or county services:** This requires planning developments in order to fully use existing and planned services.

- **Mixed use:** Mixed-use development brings land uses that are compatible closer together. An example would be a shopping complex that includes condos on the second and third floors.

- **Transportation options:** Wouldn't it be great to live somewhere where you could get around by walking, bicycling, or using public transit? It seems like everyone riding around in cars is a throwback to the Old West when everyone had his own horse.

- **Detailed, human-scaled design:** Lifestyle design means the development is attractive, design-friendly to pedestrians, and takes into account the community's character and history.

These principles make up smart ways of building a community because they provide benefits to everyone who lives there while making intelligent use of financial and natural resources. Lifestyle development helps support most states' land use and transportation policies. It also provides a number of benefits including:

- Economic development and improved tax base

- Revitalization of downtowns, main streets, and neighborhood centers

- Housing that's close to jobs and services

- Job creation, allowing people to walk to work

- Choices for transportation and the ability to connect between different methods of transport

- Communities in which people can actually walk rather than drive (Wow, what a concept!)

- Reduction of that hated bumper-to-bumper traffic

- Ways to use existing urban services and facilities, instead of continuing to expand into new areas

- Energy saving by not relying as much on cars

If after hearing several different opinions you're still being told that your idea won't ever get through, you have your decision right there. All that negativity makes it easy to decide not to move. Either come up with a project that the council likes or find a different piece of land. Whatever you do, don't fight city hall.

Avoiding neighborhood opposition

One of the most important keys to getting your land development projects approved these days is making sure that you're going into an area where people will approve of your project idea. This means working *with* your prospective neighbors rather than *against* them. Conduct some investigative meetings to get their suggestions. Doing this can go a long way toward avoiding mob-type crowds who get mad and want to kill your deal. Get to know the leaders and people in the community as much you can. If you get a feel for how they want to develop the area, you'll be much more successful.

Because the process of dealing with your neighbors is going to differ in every municipality, predicting what can happen is difficult. But here's a good example: Before filing an application, the land developer provides written notice to neighborhood associations and the municipality. After the application is submitted, the following procedure is used to notify neighboring property owners and the neighborhood association of the pending application and the upcoming public hearing on the application:

1. **The zoning staff posts a sign.**

   At the time of application, the zoning staff provides a sign to the land developer indicating the time and place of the public hearing. The sign is required to be posted on the property that's the subject of the public hearing.

2. **Notice is given to the neighborhood.**

   Following the submittal of the application, the planners send a notice to the neighborhood association saying that the application was submitted and indicate the pending public hearing dates.

3. **A public hearing article is printed in the newspaper.**

   Public hearing notices are typically published in the local newspaper, which carries legal notices.

4. **Notices are mailed to property owners and occupants.**

   Ten days before the public hearing, the planner's staff sends a notice to the neighborhood association and all property owners and occupants or residents within 200 feet of the perimeter of the property subject to the public hearing.

5. A public hearing is held.

A public hearing is held by the commission or agency that has final authority to approve or reject the request for rezoning or development. Depending on the area, you may need to deal with one, two, or sometimes even more agencies.

Our bold challenge to the press

Because we have been called the "World's #1 Greatest Commercial Real Estate Mentors," it's not a surprise to anyone that we get attention from two very different types of people. The first category is people like you, who are serious about taking big steps in their life and aren't afraid to search for knowledge or guidance to make sure that you get where you want to go.

The other category contains those who say they want to do big things, but when push comes to shove, they quickly come up with a thousand reasons why they can't do something new: I don't have the money yet. I'm going to wait for a better time. Real estate would be great but only if I got started ten years ago. And they go on and on. By coming up with excuses to give to other people, they convince themselves in the process that they are doing the right thing by playing it safe.

We believe to the core of our being that a willingness to step up to the challenges life offers us is what makes champions of us all. To prove that successful commercial real estate investing is really possible, we recently took the bold step of issuing a challenge to the press to prove that anyone, and we do mean anyone, can make

$1 million or more by investing in commercial land development.

After all, if your authors, a former auto mechanic and introverted engineer, can make a fortune investing in commercial real estate, then you can too. Here's the challenge that we sent out to 3,159 TV stations, radio stations, and newspapers:

> Give us a team of people who are committed to going after their dreams, and within 90 days they will have a land development deal under contract and within 180 days the project will be fully underway. By the time the team is done, they will have developed the knowledge and confidence to be able to put together commercial deals on their own and they will have made $1 million or more.

We believe that the key to making things happen is in making a commitment that you can't back down from. We have publicly put ourselves on the line and now the pressure is on. We are going to win or lose with the whole world watching us. To watch those we've picked to be on the challenge team in action and cheer them on, go to www.landdevelopmentchallenge.com.

Chapter 16

Expert Tax Advantages and Strategies

● ●

In This Chapter

▶ Using tax benefits to maximize your wealth

▶ Choosing an entity based on the expected tax benefits

▶ Discovering the tax advantages of owning commercial real estate

▶ Determining how depreciation can save you thousands in taxes

▶ Avoiding taxes with a 1031 exchange trade

▶ Saving money with commonly overlooked loopholes

● ●

*O*ne of the biggest expenses you'll face owning and operating commercial properties will be your tax bill. So, doesn't it make sense to have a plan to pay as little tax as legally possible? And what if you found a way to defer paying taxes on profits for just about forever? If you're interested in knowing more — and we bet you are — read this chapter.

As a commercial real estate investor, you have a partner in every single deal you do — even if you think that you're investing by yourself. Sorry, you have no choice: Uncle Sam is your partner whether you like it or not. Fortunately, there are ways that you can use the existing laws to reduce (or sometimes eliminate) the shares that your partner, Uncle Sam, takes away from your commercial real estate profits.

In addition, you can actually get benefits from owning commercial real estate, and these benefits allow you to offset or pay less tax on income from other sources. The government does put limitations on this benefit, and it's also important to know how you can use real estate to pay less tax on your profits from commercial real estate investing and realize those benefits as quickly as possible.

An Overview of Money-Making Tax Strategies

When you buy real estate, be sure to look at the tax consequences of buying because it affects your real estate purchase. In fact, remember that the "go" or "no go" decision on commercial real estate often boils down to the tax benefits. So, you want to include this info in your property analysis. When we look at a commercial property, we include the tax benefits right along with its cash-on-cash return. Taxes are part of the total return calculation — positive or negative — that the property will have for you.

You can make money investing in commercial real estate — without paying taxes — with the following four tactics:

- ✔ Appreciation
- ✔ Depreciation and other tax advantages
- ✔ Paying down the mortgage
- ✔ Rolling over

Appreciation

Appreciation occurs when the value of your commercial property goes up over time (or maybe even overnight!) because you've increased the net operating income. Or, over time, the value increases simply due to the economic factors in the marketplace such as supply and demand and/or falling capitalization rates. The value can also go up quickly when you find a property where rents are below market and you jump in to increase the rents. Make sure you use the techniques in Chapter 18 to increase the net income of your commercial properties. You see that when the net income on a property increases, its value does also.

Tapping into the appreciation in your commercial property without paying taxes on it is simple: All you have to do is refinance the property or take out another mortgage. You won't owe any taxes on the money you receive because borrowed funds aren't taxable.

The downside to borrowing equity out of your commercial property is that when you sell it, you have to pay tax on any money that you've borrowed out of the property. So, be careful and understand that tax benefits like this are great to have, but you must plan carefully so that you aren't surprised by a tax bill when you least expect it.

Depreciation

Depreciation occurs when the value of an asset declines because of wear and tear or obsolescence. *Obsolescence* is a fancy word for saying that something no longer has the same value as it did because needs change over time. For example, the computer you bought 15 years ago — even if it's in brand-new condition — isn't worth the same amount as a computer you can buy today. In the same way, a commercial property that was designed 30 or 40 years ago won't meet the standards that you're looking for in a commercial property today. In commercial real estate, this change in value is called *economic obsolescence.*

The Internal Revenue Service (IRS) allows you a deduction for depreciation "on paper" whether your commercial property is profitable or not. So, in effect, you can have a commercial property that makes money every year, yet on your tax return, you get to pretend it had a loss (and pay no taxes). What an awesome benefit! This deduction is one of the most important reasons that high-income earners have quality commercial properties in their portfolios.

In addition to the benefit of depreciation, as a commercial property investor, you get other benefits just by being in business as a real estate investor. For example, you can deduct the mortgage interest and a variety of other deductions for rental properties. And because you're in business, as long as you follow the rules, you can deduct expenses such as driving to your properties from your office, purchasing a computer, and all kinds of other cool things you couldn't write off if you weren't in business for yourself (we discuss all these deductions later in the chapter).

Paying down the mortgage

Another tax benefit is when you use the income from your tenants to pay down the mortgage or loan on a property. As you pay down the loan balance, your equity increases. Not only are you increasing your wealth that way, but also the interest amount of the loan that you pay every year is tax deductible. The higher the loan amount, the more interest there is to deduct. This deduction is the reason it makes sense to leverage your way into a property. You can *leverage* by using a small amount of your money as a down payment on a property and then borrowing the rest from a lender. Sometimes you can even borrow most of the funds you need from the owner of the property through an *owner-carry agreement* (see Chapter 9 for more on these agreements). As a result of this leverage principle, you can make tremendously high rates of return.

Rolling over

With commercial real estate, you can take all the profits that you've made in a property — including all of your appreciation, depreciation benefits, and mortgage reduction equity and roll them over by trading into another property. This is called a *1031 tax-deferred exchange*. With this exchange, instead of paying taxes when you sell a property, you can take your profits and reinvest or *roll* it into another property over time. That's just like getting an interest-free loan from the government!

Being an Investor or a Dealer: The Difference Is Huge

Depending on how you run your commercial real estate investing business, the IRS puts you into one of two categories: You're either considered an investor or a dealer. What's the difference between these two? Quite a bit as you'll discover in this section.

In the end, you may find it best to be considered an investor, not a dealer. Or you may love the idea of building and flipping deals so that you get to play the role of a dealer in the eyes of the IRS. Whatever route you take, understand the path that you're on, and take the tax effects of your decisions into account. It's not how much you make that counts; it's how much you keep that's really important.

At some point you may end up buying and selling commercial properties quickly so you can make some quick cash. However, you're probably also going to invest in long-term-hold properties. To avoid running into problems, we suggest putting these different business activities into two different business entities. Doing so enables you to be treated as a dealer and as an investor. Be sure to consult your tax strategists on this. After all, we can give you our ideas and opinions, but it's up to you to check with your own tax counsel to see what's most appropriate for you.

Holding real estate long term as an investor

As an investor, you're a passive owner who holds real estate for long-term cash flow and appreciation. In other words, you buy and hold rental or other income property, and then you sell or exchange it after a number of years.

Benefits of being an investor include the following:

- ✔ Your long-term gains are taxed at a capital gains rate, which is likely lower than your personal income tax rate.

- ✔ Your gains aren't subject to self-employment taxes.

- ✔ You can defer your gains and pay no tax when you do a 1031 tax-deferred exchange.

- ✔ You can deduct the depreciation expense.

To take advantage of the lower long-term capital gains rates of 15 percent, you must keep all of your properties for at least one year and one day before selling. When you hold a property this long, it demonstrates your intent to operate as an investor rather than as a dealer.

Buying and selling quickly as a dealer

A dealer is someone who holds real estate for short-term resale purposes in the ordinary course of a trade or business. Usually as a dealer, you're into building, rehabbing, and possibly flipping properties (buying and selling them as quickly as possible). Benefits of being a dealer include the following:

- ✔ When you have a loss on the sale of the dealer property, that loss is fully deductible against ordinary income. As a dealer, your losses aren't subject to passive loss limitations regardless of what your adjusted gross income is.

- ✔ You can get in and out of a deal so that you capture your profits right away.

Here are the downsides of being a dealer:

- ✔ All the profits you make as a dealer are to be taxed at ordinary income rates, which are currently as high as 35 percent.

- ✔ You can't get depreciation deductions.

- ✔ Your profits may also be subject to self-employment taxes of 15 percent.

- ✔ You can't take advantage of the 1031 tax-deferred exchange or an installment sale to delay paying taxes.

Naming Yourself a Real Estate Professional: It Pays

One of the really cool things about commercial real estate is that a property can show a tax loss yet still be putting cash in your pocket money every single year. The tax loss is created by the paper deduction of depreciation as well as all the interest and other deductions that you're entitled to (see the earlier section "An Overview of Money-Making Tax Strategies" for details). Under the current tax code, these losses that you can claim from your commercial real estate are called *passive losses*.

The tax code says that passive losses can only be deducted against net income in the same passive category. This means passive income — money made from rentals and gains from your commercial rental property activities. In other words, you can use the losses from your commercial real estate to offset the gains from other real estate investing, but not to offset the gains you've made from income in other areas, such as working your regular job.

The rules say passive losses are limited to $25,000 per year, in most cases. However, as your income exceeds $100,000, this limit gets phased out. In fact, it actually disappears completely at the $150,000 income level. But these rules don't apply to those folks who are considered real estate professionals. So, make sure that you meet the strict IRS requirements of being a real estate professional. Then you can take an unlimited amount of passive losses as a write-off each year.

One way to qualify as a "real estate professional" is to own more than 5 percent of a business involved in real estate activities (you can't be classified as an employee). Some examples of qualifying activities could be selling real estate as a broker, leasing real estate, being an architect or a developer, and running a management company or structural engineering firm.

One of the easiest ways to qualify as a real estate professional, however, is to have your real estate broker's license and operate as an independent business that you own (instead of working as an employee for someone else).

The IRS considers the amount of time you spend on real estate activities compared with other work you do. To be called a professional, the regulations require that you spend at least 750 hours a year on real estate activities. You also have to work more on your real estate activities than you do on any other job you have. So, if you're working 40 hours a week as a dentist, you'd have to work 41 hours a week in your real estate investing activities to meet the requirements of a real estate professional. Wow, 81 hours a week — that may not be the lifestyle you want to be living.

Some people have accused the IRS of showing unfair benefits to married people (all you married people out there better listen up!). For example, a single person who's making high earnings in a non–real estate business, such as an investment banker, wouldn't be able to qualify as a real estate professional. However, if the investment banker's spouse meets the requirements for a real estate professional, the couple can take the deductions because the spouse qualifies. In this way, all the income from the high earner can be offset without limitations when it comes to paying taxes.

Choosing Your Entity: An Important Tax Preparation Before You Buy

Your tax planning and preparation needs to begin even before you buy your first property. Putting your latest property into a corporation may cause you to be taxed doubly. Closing your deal as a sole proprietor causes you to be taxed at the highest possible rate. The most popular choice for entities is the limited liability company (LLC). It provides the liability protection of a corporation and the flexibility benefits of a sole proprietor. But never decide on using a particular type of entity because everyone else is using it. There is no one-size-fits-all entity.

One of the first tax planning choices you need to make is determining the type of entity you should use to hold title to your properties. The word *entity* is a fancy term that pretty much refers to your company. An entity can be any of the following:

- ✔ A sole proprietorship
- ✔ A corporation
- ✔ A limited liability company
- ✔ A limited partnership

Many real estate investors like to use limited liability companies because they're easy to get started and they offer good liability protection. They have proven to be one of the best entities for holding real estate because of their ease of use, asset protection qualities, and favorable tax treatments. (Check out Chapter 12 for more on how you can use entities to protect your assets.)

We suggest meeting with your attorney and tax strategist to decide which entity is best for you. When discussing entities, be sure to consider these four things:

- ✔ **Liability protection:** Ideally, having a separate entity prevents any problems from your commercial property from affecting your other assets, such as your house and cars.

- ✔ **Tax benefits:** If you're buying this property as a tax shelter of some sort, make sure that both of your advisors agree that you actually can. If you have partners in your deal, ensure that your entity of choice is the best fit and provides the best tax advantages.

- ✔ **Costs and administrative requirements:** You need to know what requirements there are to run your entity over time. Entities, for instance, may require annual meetings among partners, tax returns, and payment of annual fees in order to remain in good standing with the state.

> ✓ **Exit strategy planning:** What are the tax consequences of selling? What if the partnership breaks up? What if one partner becomes ill? Or dies? Is the property transferable between entities without incurring a tax hit?

No matter which type of entity is used to hold your commercial real estate properties, be sure to have adequate liability and other insurance protection in place. These protections are your first line of defense to avert disaster. (Flip to Chapter 12 for more on protecting your assets.)

Sole proprietorships

A *sole proprietorship* is one of the easiest ways of putting together a business because it requires no organizational filings or annual paperwork. You don't even need to file a separate tax return. Instead, your business reports its income or loss on Schedule C of your federal income tax return.

Having a sole proprietorship doesn't give you any liability protection. You're completely exposed to lawsuits. With commercial real estate, accidents and other liabilities can happen during the construction phase and from having people on or living in the property. Without protection, these liabilities can be disastrous to your wealth-building strategies. For this reason, you'll probably want to use an entity other than a sole proprietorship for your commercial property.

Corporations

Corporations give you good liability protection. But in most cases, they aren't the best entity for holding real estate properties because of double taxation. They are taxed as separate entities; as a corporation and then again at their individual rates. Corporations aren't that flexible, accounting-wise, compared to LLCs and require, but are not limited to, annual reports, boards of directors, and federal reporting. We like to use corporations to either manage LLCs or to run businesses out of, but not to hold real estate.

If you're set on using a corporation, we highly recommend that you check with your tax strategist and your attorney to find out if it truly makes sense for you and your situation. There are actually two types of corporations — one is called a C-corporation and the other called an S-corporation. Each has distinct functions and uses that depend on your and your company's setup and investment objectives. Consult an entity expert.

Limited liability companies

Limited liability companies (LLCs) are one of the best entities you can use for investing in commercial real estate. Why? Because these entities give you a lot of flexibility with respect to dividing up the benefits related to a property. In other words, they allow you to divide profits and tax benefits unequally if you want to. For example, the high-income earning professional may want to tap into more of the tax benefits than some of the other owners (who may want to take more profits). Dividing tax benefits and profits unequally can be tough to do with a corporation, so if you need to do this, an LLC may be the better choice for you. LLCs are fairly easy to run. For example, you don't need to hold annual meetings and you don't have as much paperwork as you do with corporations.

Limited partnerships

A *limited partnership* (LP) is a popular form of holding real estate for investors who want to be limited partners. They basically invest their money while having liability protection and limited liability from the partnership's debt, creditors, and lawsuits. A limited partner doesn't get to participate in the management of the business. But there is one partner, a general partner, who assumes liability for the partnership's debt as well as controls the company's day-to-day operations. In most cases, the general partner is an LLC, which provides a layer of liability protection for him. LPs are popularly used to attract investors who want to participate in the profits, but desire to limit their risks (their cash investment only) and want no part in the daily operations. Limited partners may also be replaced or leave the partnership without it having to be dissolved.

Digging into Depreciation

We've mentioned depreciation a few times already in this chapter. In this section, we dig a little deeper and explain how depreciation can save you tens of thousands of dollars in taxes. Depreciation, as you may know, is the tax term that lets you pretend that *all* the improvements made to the raw land in commercial real estate properties are wearing out. Think of the improvements as the buildings, the roads, the landscaping, and so on. But remember that you can only write off or depreciate the improvements on a property. This includes the building and other improvements but doesn't include things that don't wear out — like the land itself. Depreciation allows you to write off or deduct a portion of the value of all the improvements according to the schedule below:

✔ Over 27½ years for residential homes and multiunit properties

✔ Over 39 years for commercial nonresidential properties

So, for example, the tax code for commercial property allows investors to depreciate ⅟₃₉th of the value of the improvements on your commercial property over time. This means that over 39 years, you get a deduction on your taxes every year "on paper." Now, the "on paper" part is important because normally to have a deduction you have to spend some money. You have to have an expense in order for the IRS to let you write it off. After the 39 years, the depreciation is used up and you can no longer take it. But few properties stay with a single owner for that long.

With depreciation, however, you don't need an expense in order to get the deduction (though some day you'll need to eventually replace the property when it really does wear out). So, it's possible to have a property that loses money on paper while making money in real life. The end result is that on your tax return, you get to take a loss, which lets you pay less money in taxes — yet the property still brings in money for you. How cool is that?

Any time you have an asset that's being depreciated, when that asset is no longer usable, you can fully write off all the remaining depreciation and get all the tax benefits right away. For example, if you have a computer that you're depreciating on a five-year schedule, and two years after you bought it, your hard drive goes up in smoke, you can fully depreciate the computer at that point, instead of waiting another three years (see the later section, "Cost segregation: Saving thousands more by separating your property parts," for more on depreciating personal property). You did back up your computer files, didn't you?

So, you plan on selling?

Let's say you decide that you'd like to sell the commercial real estate property that you have owned over the past few years (and we'll assume also that you have a huge pile of profits to go along with that property). Before you sell, spend time with your tax strategist to find out what the effect of the sale will be for you tax-wise. Specifically ask how you can structure the sale to take maximum advantage of all the loopholes in the tax code available for you as a commercial real estate investor.

Your tax strategist will likely ask you, "Has this been a long-term or a short-term property for you?" A long-term investment requires that you hold a property for at least one year and one day. This way, you pay capital gains taxes rather than ordinary income taxes on any gains you make. So by holding it for over a year, you pay a lot less in tax. You will also be asked, "Have you considered doing a 1031 tax-deferred exchange?" This strategy allows you to defer paying any capital gains taxes as long as you meet certain presale criteria. See www.1031taxcodesecrets.com for more information on 1031 exchanges.

In the following sections, we explain all you need to know about taking full advantage of depreciation.

The magic of depreciation

The magic of depreciation is that it isn't based on your down payment or on the amount of money that you invest in a deal. Rather, it's based on the value of the commercial property minus the value of the land.

Here's a simple example: Let's say you bought one or two smaller commercial properties over the first year or so of your investing career. Then you really wanted to knock one out of the park, and so you bought a property by using other investors' money. In fact, let's say that you purchased a large office complex worth $50 million.

Assuming that you're the only owner, you now have the ability to depreciate or write off ¹⁄₃₉th of the value of the improvements on the property (not the land) over each of the next 39 years. So keeping it simple, let's say the value of the land is $11 million. On that land is your large office complex and all the other improvements valued at $39 million. So, for the next 39 years, you have an annual deduction of $1 million. We know we're stretching the numbers a bit to have some fun here, but we hope it opens your eyes to various possibilities involving tax savings.

Depreciation applies also to capital improvements such as putting in a new parking lot or placing a new roof on your commercial property. So, when you put on a new roof, you get to start depreciating that roof over the next 39 years. And if you replace it again in 17 years, you can write off the remaining years left as one big chunk and then start over again with 39 years for the new roof.

Don't "recapture" your depreciation

When you sell your property, make sure that you talk to your tax strategist about the effects of the depreciation that you've taken over the years. Investors who receive tax benefits such as depreciation over time and then borrow money out of the property to either reinvest in other properties or to buy a big boat may get a surprise when they "recapture" all that depreciation when the property is sold. Recapturing is a fancy IRS name for: "We gave you a break back then and let you out of paying taxes. Now you owe us all the taxes. Tough luck, buddy."

To avoid recapturing your depreciation, consider doing an exchange of property, which is known as a *1031 tax-deferred exchange.* An exchange such as this occurs when you take your profits out of the property and instead of putting them in your pocket, you reinvest them in another property. This well-known process allows you to take all the taxes that you would have had to pay on your profits and invest them into other commercial real estate, which will continue to make you income for years to come. A 1031 exchange is such a great benefit that we call it "the golden goose." In fact, if you *don't* use 1031 exchanges, it's like killing off the golden goose that lays the golden eggs of passive income for you.

If one day you decide to sell and not perform a 1031 exchange, you'll pay taxes. So make sure that your heirs (spouses, kids, estates, and so on) understand this as well. Include a copy of this book in your estate planning to educate whoever is next in line to own your property.

Cost segregation: Saving thousands more by separating your property parts

It's important to understand that by separating different parts of the improvements to your property, you can actually depreciate some at a much faster rate than others. This means that you can realize those tax savings sooner rather than later. And that means more money in your pocket sooner.

You already know that you can depreciate a property over either 27½ years or 39 years, depending on whether it's considered residential or commercial. But just wait — it gets even better. When the many components of the building are broken out and listed separately, which is called *cost segregation,* you can get even greater tax savings. How? Through a faster depreciation schedule. By accelerating the schedule, all the money you save taxes on comes to you sooner.

Some of the improvements can actually be written off over 5 to 7 years or over 15 years, depending on what they are. These improvements include things like stoves, refrigerators, carpeting, counters, cabinets, shelves, light fixtures, plumbing fixtures, and even the value of landscaping that's been added to the property. When considering cost segregating, break up the property into three parts — personal property, land improvements, and the building itself. Personal property can normally be depreciated over the five to seven year period. Land improvements such as sidewalks and fences can be depreciated over 15 years. And the building itself is depreciated over the full 39 years.

Here's a typical list of land improvements that you can depreciate over 15 years:

- ✔ Curbs
- ✔ Docks

- ✔ Drainage
- ✔ Driveways
- ✔ Fences
- ✔ Landscaping
- ✔ Sewer lines
- ✔ Shrubbery
- ✔ Sidewalks

And here are just some of the personal property items you can depreciate over five to seven years:

- ✔ Carpets that aren't glued down
- ✔ Drapes
- ✔ Fire extinguishers
- ✔ Miniblinds
- ✔ Refrigerators
- ✔ Stoves
- ✔ Wiring for the building's electrical system
- ✔ Plumbing fixtures

The really cool thing with cost segregation is that it applies to anything that's movable. If you think we're kidding, consider what our CPA and tax strategist was able to write off within five years: walls! When he moved into his new office, instead of dividing up the offices by using walls that were secured to the floor and ceiling, he chose to use movable walls instead. (And if you were go into his office and look at the walls, you probably wouldn't even notice the difference!) From a tax standpoint, the fact that the walls are movable means that he can write off the cost of the walls over 5 years rather than over 39 years.

It's ideas like putting up moveable walls that can make you tons of money over the years. If your CPA or tax strategist isn't investing in commercial real estate and doesn't use the ideas that you're gleaning from this book, it may be time to look for a new CPA. That advice may seem kind of cold, but it's real-world advice. Or buy him a copy of this book as starters!

Coming up with the value for cost segregation

Instead of picking values out of thin air as far as what you think the various pieces of personal property are worth and what the land improvements and building are valued at, perform a formal *cost segregation study*. This study documents how you come up with accurate values for the items that you're depreciating faster by using cost segregation.

If the value of all the personal property is $1 million or more, CPAs recommend that you hire an engineering firm to do a cost segregation study for you, because cost segregation is closely watched by IRS auditors. Hiring a firm does require putting in some extra effort and expense upfront, but it's absolutely worth it in the end because of the great tax savings you'll realize. When considering cost segregation for your property, weigh the costs of the firm's study with the first year of tax savings. Our CPAs recommend at least a 2 to 1 ratio of first year savings to costs.

If you plan to flip a property right away, you may end up spending more on the cost segregation study than the benefits that you're able to get. So don't bother using this loophole if you're only going to own the property for one or two years. Because cost segregation studies can cost tens of thousands of dollars on large properties, you may not be able to capture the costs of the study and reap the full benefits of it if you sell too quickly.

How cost segregation puts cash in your pockets

Sure it's more work to sit down with your tax strategist and separate out the values of all the stoves, refrigerators, carpeting, and so on that are part of that 300-unit property you just bought. But the upside is that by using cost segregation, you get extra tax deductions, which can help put more cash in your pocket — right here and right now.

We believe that any money that you can make immediately is worth more than the same amount of money that you may make many years from now. Can we hear an "Amen" to that?

The 1031 Exchange: Avoiding Taxes by Trading In for Another Property

With commercial real estate, when your property has increased in value, you have the choice of simply selling the property outright and getting a big check at the closing table (after taxes, of course) or using the magic of a 1031 tax-deferred exchange, which allows you to make even more money. A *1031 tax-deferred exchange* allows you to roll over money that you get from the sale of your old property into a new property while deferring paying taxes. So, if you've made $200,000 in the first commercial property that you've invested in, you can sell this property and buy a second one by using the $200,000 as a down payment.

When it comes time to sell your second property, you can take your original $200,000 in profits from the first property, along with whatever you made in the second property and continue to roll over the gains again into yet another property. There's no limit to the number of times you can do an exchange in this manner. Clearly, it's a great way to build your real estate wealth without paying taxes on it as you go. However, if some day you don't want to buy another property and want to sell the one you have for profit, you're going to have to pay taxes.

To meet the requirements for a fully tax-deferred 1031 exchange, the new property must cost more than the old property, and the loans on the new property must be the same size or bigger than the loans on the old property. In addition to this, you can't get any cash from the sale.

When you're involved in a 1031 exchange, you can sell any type of investment property and buy any other type of investment property. In other words, you can sell an office building and buy a warehouse or you can sell an apartment building and buy bare land. The properties both must be real estate investments, though. You can't sell a rental property and buy personal property like a motor home or boat.

Before anything else, get expert help

To avoid having your exchange disqualified by the IRS, you need to be sure to follow the rules correctly when doing a 1031 tax-deferred exchange. How? You need to hire an expert called an *exchange accommodator*. The accommodator shows up when you sell your old property, takes all the money you would have received, and then leaves. Then the accommodator brings your cash to the closing when you purchase your new property. The accommodator also helps to make sure that you follow all the rules so that your exchange isn't disqualified by the IRS. Make a mistake here and you'll end up paying those pesky taxes. Ouch!

Exchange accommodators are unregulated by the government. You'd think that given the tremendous amounts of money that they hold, they would need to be licensed, bonded, and regulated, but that's not the case. People who want to present themselves as accommodators may do so, even if they're convicted felons. Obviously, you really need to know who you're dealing with. This is where the strength of your relationships and connections with people in your network pays off for you. When choosing an accommodator for your exchange, make sure to consider the following:

- ✔ **Experience:** Make sure your prospective accommodator has at least ten years of experience.

- ✔ **Tax law knowledge:** The 1031 exchange is an IRS tax code, so deep knowledge in tax law is a must.

- ✔ **Fidelity-bonded:** Your accommodator should have a sizeable fidelity bond as well as adequate liability insurance.

✔ **Members of the Federation of Exchange Accommodators:** Ensure that your accommodator is a member of this national trade organization specializing in 1031 exchanges. His or her membership provides credibility and reputability.

Surveying the exchange rules

The first time that you're involved in a delayed exchange, you'll find it a bit weird to see your accommodator walk out of the closing with all of your profits. You may be a little unclear as to what's going on. But don't fret, here's a summary of the 1031 tax-free exchange rules, courtesy of our personal accommodator Gary Gorman:

✔ **Property that you hold for investment or that's used in a trade or business qualifies for a 1031 exchange.** *Held for investment* means that you intend to hold the property for future appreciation, or for the production of income. Property that you intend to resell quickly doesn't qualify for an exchange, so make sure that your properties, both old and new, are held as an investment for least one year and one day.

✔ **From the day you close the sale of the old property, you have 45 days to come up with a list of properties that you want to buy.** You must follow these three rules when coming up with a list of properties:

   • **Three Property Rule:** You can identify up to three properties regardless of their market value.

   • **200% Rule:** You can identify as many properties as you want as long as the cumulative total of the market value do not exceed 200 percent of the property value that you're selling.

   • **95% Rule:** You can identify as many properties as you want as long as the cumulative total of the market values is at least 95 percent of the property value that you're selling.

The list of properties absolutely must be sent to the accommodator on or before the 45th day or you will not be allowed to proceed with the 1031 exchange. You'll have to pay the taxes if you don't.

The 45-day rule must be adhered to even if the 45th day falls on a weekend or holiday.

✔ **From the day you close the sale of your old property, you have 180 days to close on the purchase of your new property.** You have to buy one of the properties on the 45-day list that was sent to the accommodator. Failure to close on or before the 180th day means that your exchange is hereby cancelled — hello taxes!

✔ **You can't receive or have access to the money between the sale of your old property and the purchase of your new property.** By federal tax law, you're required to use the services of an independent third party, which is your accommodator.

✔ **The old and new property ownership must be the same.** This requirement means that the name or entity on the tax return of the owner of the old property has to be the same person or entity who owns the new property. For example, you can't sell a property that you own in your name personally and buy the new property in the name of your limited liability company.

✔ **In order to avoid paying tax, the selling price of your new property must be equal to or greater than the net selling price of the old property.** The *net selling price* is the selling price minus the closing costs.

✔ **You must reinvest all the cash.** Any cash that you access becomes taxable to you. In the eyes of the IRS, if you take cash, you've sold something. So, no matter how much cash you invested in the old property, if you touch any cash at all, you pay taxes on it.

If any of these rules are not followed exactly, your 1031 exchange is null and void. Uncle Sam will be at your door happily waiting for what's due to him. Don't bother with excuses, just pay the man.

Our accommodator, Gary Gorman, has written an excellent book called *Exchanging Up* (Success DNA, 2005), which goes into all the detail you need to do a 1031 tax-deferred exchange. We like this book because it's a simple-and-easy read, not complicated or confusing as many books on tax issues are. Visit www.1031taxcodesecrets.com for more information on Gary's book or to get your questions answered by the 1031 experts.

Taking Advantage of Some Commonly Overlooked Deductions

Throughout this chapter, we discuss depreciation, mortgage interest, and itemizing expenses, all of which can significantly reduce your tax burden. But other tax loopholes are out there.

The following list is only a partial one showing what's typically deductible. This topic is far reaching and can only be maximized by a tax professional. Get the advice of an experienced tax professional who understands tax implications of commercial real estate not just single-family residences.

Accounting expenses

Be sure to deduct your accounting and bookkeeping expenses, and don't let us catch you doing your own accounting or bookkeeping! Your time is much more valuable than that! Instead, hire someone to take care of your books for you. And remember that everything you spend in this category is completely deductible as an expense in your real estate business.

Consulting expenses

From time to time, you'll likely want to bring in consultants to help you strategize or to guide you through an area in which you don't have expertise, such as condo conversions. Paying these consultants is an expense to your business and therefore fully deductible. Here are some consultants who you may use and whose payments are deductible: appraisers, financial planners, mentors, and architects.

Many tax advisors cost of researching your business and educating yourself is deductible as well. Going to real estate-related seminars, buying books, tapes, trade magazine subscriptions, and dues to professional organizations usually are too.

Home office expenses

For most real estate investors, it's great working from home. Our friends often tease us about walking into the kitchen and grabbing a cup of coffee, and then arriving at our offices about 30 seconds later. The good news is that all of your expenses for your home office are completely deductible. That includes the cost to heat or cool your office, to clean your office, and other things that people have to pay for even though they don't have a commercial real estate investing business. (By the way, your dog and the family piano can't be considered expenses — no matter how much better they help you work.)

Office equipment such as computers, fax machines, copiers, and phones can be fully deducted. And don't forget the beautiful leather office furniture and mahogany desk and shelving!

Here are some ways to support your home office deductions:

- ✔ Use a separate room for business use only, and perform most of your administrative and management activities in that home office.
- ✔ Spend a substantial amount of your office time in your home office.

✔ Use your home address as your business address and put it on your business card.

✔ Get a separate phone and fax line for your home office.

✔ For IRS auditing proof, document everything by keeping logs of time spent in your home office and take photographs of your office and its furnishings just in case you move and are audited years later.

All property-related expenses

When running commercial real estate properties, you incur month-to-month expenses (traveling, cellphone, and business meals, for example) and even surprise expenses such as maintenance and repairs. The good news is that you'll be collecting income from your tenants to cover these expenses. Plus, the really good news is that nearly all these expenses are fully deductible for you as a business owner.

Transportation to and from your properties

It's important to go by and check on your properties from time to time. If they're in town, keep track of your mileage so you can write it off as a travel expense. If you're traveling across the country to look at your properties, make sure you maintain a list of *all* your expenses including your rental car, airfare, business meals while eating with or entertaining someone, and the hotel that you stayed in while looking at your properties.

Expenses for your technology gizmos

When running a business, you need to keep up with the latest technology and stay in touch, right? Well, you can't do it without all the latest tech gizmos, such as a cellphone or PDA, a computer with Internet and fax capabilities, and software programs for keeping your business organized. All these expenses are tax deductible as long as you're using them completely in your real estate investing business. These items should not be mixed with personal usage.

Of course, you can't go overboard and claim that everything tech-related in your house is part of your business. But if you purchase a phone system to use both for your business and for your residence, and you have two business lines and one home line, you have a good argument to claim two-thirds of the cost of the phone system as a tax deduction.

Chapter 17

Leaping into a Commercial Real Estate Career

In This Chapter

▶ Helping others buy and sell commercial property

▶ Managing commercial property as a career

▶ Lending money to commercial real estate investors

▶ Appraising commercial property

*E*ntrepreneurs live a life of action and risk and can be rewarded hand-somely for it. A good portion of us who make a living in the commercial real estate business have been afforded great lifestyles because of the risk we took at some point in our lives. We invite you to do the same.

Leaping into a commercial real estate career is exciting because you can venture into so many different areas. It doesn't matter your personality type, background, and most times, even your education. It's a wide-open field of opportunity. Of all the successful people we know and work with in commercial real estate, we see three success traits in every one of them: integrity, perseverance, and understanding the value of relationships.

In this chapter, we discuss the many career choices in commercial real estate, from starting out as a commercial sales agent, to becoming a property man-ager of commercial buildings, to doing big loans on large pieces of property, to getting paid to give your opinion on the value of real estate. Most of these wonderful professions require a certain entrepreneurial spirit, but the life rewards as well as the financial rewards are limitless.

Becoming a Commercial Sales Agent

You're about to enter a realm of the elite. Becoming a commercial real estate sales agent is a huge commitment, but it pays off in so many ways. The opportunities in this field are numerous. You can work in office buildings, retail centers, multifamily apartment complexes, or industrial parks. And even those categories have their own subcategories. Commercial sales agents are seen as the "cream of the crop" in real estate sales because of their ability to put together big deals that involve tens of millions, if not hundreds of millions, of dollars. It's difficult to describe the feeling you get when you close on a transaction for a multimillion-dollar commercial property that took four to five months, countless meetings and teleconferences, and the coming together of buyer and seller. Now it's time to see if you have what it takes to succeed.

Four myths of commercial real estate sales

Here are a few misconceptions about selling commercial real estate:

- ✓ **Residential real estate sales is a steppingstone to commercial real estate sales.** You have two different products and two different consumers. Focus on one or the other. You can compare this myth to a salesperson who believes she must know how to sell U.S.-made passenger cars before she can sell high-end European sports cars. But really, it just doesn't matter. A salesperson is a salesperson, period.

- ✓ **Commercial real estate is too complicated.** Commercial real estate isn't more complicated than residential; you just have to know different information. Consider the U.S. car and European car example. Finding out about U.S. cars takes the same effort as finding out about European cars. The content is very different, however.

- ✓ **You can make more money in commercial sales than in residential sales.** Although this can be viewed as potentially true, income generation comes from having your act together. If you don't know what you're doing, regardless of which field you're in, your income will suffer. As they say, "You'll get out what you put in."

- ✓ **You need a broker's license to be a commercial sales agent.** Commercial sales agents fall under the same licensing requirements as residential sales agents. In most states, any sales agent, commercial or residential, must work under a real estate broker. But you don't need a broker's license to do big deals in commercial real estate sales. All you need to get started is a sales agent license and to be under a broker.

Four truths of commercial real estate sales

Here are some surprising and also tough truths about commercial real estate:

- ✓ **You can make a great living from commercial real estate sales.** How much money you make really depends on how hard you work and how focused you are. Your earnings potential is unlimited. We know of agents who make several millions of dollars per year. But don't forget that a great living also includes having great relationships. Those are attained by operating with integrity and professionalism.

✔ **Commercial real estate sales is all about "the relationship."** Bart, a good friend of ours, loves commercial real estate sales and makes several million dollars per year in commissions. His success comes from putting the relationship and his clients' success before any commissions. We have personally watched him walk away from commissions to maintain his integrity and the relationship with the client. Bart clearly sees his clients as his lifelines to wealth.

✔ **Commercial real estate sales isn't for the fainthearted.** This is a tough business that's highly competitive with very driven people. Things move fast. Decisions are made quickly, impersonally, and seemingly without much time to think them through. If you take failure or rejection personally, this business isn't for you.

✔ **No single commercial real estate brokerage firm dominates the U.S. market.** In fact, the nation's five largest firms account for only 13 percent of the nation's commercial real estate sales volume. The U.S. market is fragmented, meaning that no one firm can claim to have significant market share. Do the math. That means 87 percent of U.S. sales is yours for the taking.

Real estate agent versus real estate broker

Just what is the difference between a real estate agent and a real estate broker? This section gives you the facts of the matter, although some answers may differ in your state. Check your state laws if you decide to pursue a career in this field.

What distinguishes a real estate broker from a real estate agent is the licensing. There are two types of licenses — a salesperson license and a broker's license. A person with a salesperson license (generally called a real estate agent) can only perform salesperson duties, like representing sellers and buyers while earning a commission. Someone with a salesperson license must have a broker's supervision to perform those duties.

Someone with a broker's license has a few more rights and privileges than a person with only a salesperson license does. A broker can do what a sales agent does, plus the following:

✔ Start his own office and hire and manage other sales agents

✔ Receive commissions or referral fees (a sales agent can only receive fees through his or her employing broker)

✔ Manage property (in most states)

These are the only real advantages of having a broker's license over a salesperson license. Having one or the other doesn't give you more skills, credibility, or increase your business volumes.

Getting your foot in the door

If you think commercial real estate sales is for you, take a minute to do some honest-to-goodness self-examination. This potentially lucrative business is at-heart, entrepreneurial. Therefore, ask yourself the following questions:

- **Am I a self-starter and self-disciplined?** Every morning, you have a choice to go out there and make things happen or to pull the covers over your head and go back to sleep.

- **Am I competent and trustworthy?** These are traits of a successful and prosperous salesperson. Are you willing to put in the hours of study time to be a walking encyclopedia of your market? Can people rely on you? Do you show up on time for meetings?

- **Am I a competitor?** Do you thrive or just try to survive when business gets tough? This industry is very competitive by nature because of what's at stake — big dollars. You have to be a go-getter.

If you answered "yes" to all of the above, you're ready to get your real estate sales agent license (or in some states you can jump right into getting your broker's license). To get your licensing, go to your state's department of real estate and check out the requirements to take the license exam.

After you've passed the licensing exam, it's time to find a commercial real estate brokerage firm to work for. First, decide your area of expertise: office, retail, multifamily, or industrial. If you love dealing in apartments, you don't want to work for a company that's known for downtown office investments. After you select your field, locate those companies that handle the properties you'd like to focus on. The best way to get started on finding them is by word of mouth. Big-name firms can be just as good as the smaller local firms.

Next up, you need to interview the firms. You'll find that even though the firms you've chosen may sell the same product, the inner workings of each firm can be dramatically different. The following are some tidbits to consider and ask about when interviewing firms:

- **Commission splits:** Understand what the commission splits are with your broker. Usually, new agents start off with a 50-50 split. When your income reaches a certain level, the split should decrease in your favor.

- **Training program:** Ask if a training program is available. Some of the larger national firms offer structured training. We know of one firm that offers boot camps for new agents. Or the firm may let you "hang out" with an experienced agent.

✔ **Management structure:** As you know, a company's success starts from the top. Ask about the top management's visions, its experience, and its street reputation. See if the answers line up with the management's actions.

✔ **Office support:** This will differ from large national firms to smaller local firms. But make sure that critical forms and agreements are readily available. Ask what type of technological support is available and whether you have to pay to use it. And last, find out whether someone who's more experienced than you is available to answer simple questions.

Living the life of a commercial sales agent

Attending your kid's basketball games and karate tournaments. Having a lunch date with your loved one on a whim. Taking off on a mountain bike ride midweek to escape for a few hours. Flexibility and freedom. Potentially, these are all possible after you make it as a commercial sales agent.

But in the beginning, life as a commission-only salesperson can be quite stressful. It can take up to four months just for a deal, from start to finish, to close and get paid. Therefore, having a lot of deals in the works at once is how life goes. Having several months of savings for living expenses and living on a budget are important for the beginning agent.

Here are a couple of tips that can help in your early days:

✔ **Get a mentor.** Having a mentor at this stage of your career is all about exchange. In exchange for your mentor's time and knowledge, what are you offering? Of course, you don't have much to offer right now, correct? We recommend putting on your "servant" hat and volunteering to take care of any small tasks that bog him or her down. You can discover a great deal about the inner workings of the business this way. But most important, be a good student. Show up on time. Have a grateful attitude. Be present. Be respectful.

✔ **Get a good grasp of the nuts and bolts of the profession.** You should study and become familiar with the fundamentals of real estate law, taxation (including 1031 exchanges), contracts and agency, title, surveys, property analysis, appraisals, financing, zoning and land use, environmental issues, and property management. Knowing the basics of at least these things should give you a little credibility in the field, especially when first starting out.

Most newbies start out by representing buyers or investors. Buyers are easy to come by. Finding properties that fit their criteria will be your challenge, but you can do it. This is how most new commercial agents close their first deals while working on building their client database and planning marketing efforts in the meantime.

After you're engrossed in the "everydayness" of your new career, you'll discover that the most successful and highly paid sales agents put a lot of focus, energy, and dollars into two things: leads and listings. These two things keep the commission checks rolling in and enable you to run your business instead of the business running you.

Getting leads and listings

Getting leads and listings are at the roots of success in this business. Of course, the two are related. You can have the greatest sales skills this side of the Mississippi. You can also have the keenest knowledge of real estate negotiations (see Chapter 5) and be a master of your market. But if you have no one to talk to (leads, that is), all that skill and knowledge is for naught. The key to generating leads is to go out and capture an audience of interested potential clients who own property and know of others who own. You can't get listings if you don't generate leads.

Getting leads and listings starts with studying your brains out to get industry-specific knowledge. Your goal is to attain laser-like knowledge of your area of expertise. If you're going to work in multifamily properties, you should know the most recent closed sales transactions, whether you closed them or not, and you should also know the going cap rates for your area (see Chapter 3 for more on cap rates). If your area of specialty is in retail, you should know locations, specific demographics, and price per square foot. Market your expertise and know-how to generate leads. You want your leads turned into potential clients, and then into clients, so they need to feel confident in your competence as their advisor and agent.

Focus on becoming an expert in one field. Today, generalists are few and far between because the markets are huge and have a lot of moving pieces. You'll find that the most successful sales agents are known for one type of asset. This is where they make their names and reputations known. Being a "jack-of-all trades" doesn't work effectively in this business. Being a specialist does.

After you have your knowledge quotient up, it's time to focus on a certain geographic territory. In the commercial real estate sales business, this is called *farming* an area. The theory behind farming is to market your expertise to clients in a particular territory, with the hope that the better you know the territory, you'll become the territory's expert, and more leads will come in. Effective farming gets your face known in the territory.

Farming involves sending out strategic and interesting marketing materials such as postcards and market info sheets with your name and contact information. It is a well-known fact that when a mail campaign is taken on, only 2 percent of the mailings actually result in a lead. Therefore, if you send out 1,000 pieces of mail, you'll get maybe 20 responses on average. Another part of farming is the dreaded *cold call;* calling someone you don't know personally. Cold-calling is a very effective way to generate leads as well as pick up new and interesting tidbits of data on your market. The easiest way to generate a cold-call list is to get a list of property owners from a title company.

The National Do Not Call Registry prohibits telemarketers from selling goods and services through interstate phone calls to those consumers who register their phone numbers. This means that you can't cold-call someone who's registered on the National Do Not Call List. We urge you to go online to retrieve a list of registered callers, cross-check it against your list, and mark any names that appear on both lists as "do not call." A consumer who receives a telemarketing call despite being on the registry can file a complaint with the Federal Trade Commission. Violators can be fined up to $11,000 per incident. Go to www.donotcall.gov for details.

Taking your new listing to payday

Hooray! You got your first listing! Here are ten easy steps that can help you take it to closing and get paid:

1. **Prepare your marketing blasts for the new listing.**

   Get your marketing repertoire in full swing — e-mails, mailings, call lists, and subscription listing services.

2. **Market-blast your new listing to everyone every which way you can all at the same time to give it maximum exposure.**

   The more exposure you give the listing, the higher the value you'll get in return. It's proven. The more money your seller makes, the happier he'll be, and the more likely the next listing — or at least some referrals — will come your way.

3. **Follow up on all inquiries.**

4. **Show the property to the interested and potential buyers.**

5. **The buyer submits a sales and purchase contract. You and the seller negotiate with the buyer and his agents.**

6. **When everyone has agreed on the terms of the deal, finalize the contract.**

7. **The buyers go through their due diligence and check out the property thoroughly. Your role as the agent is to make sure that the buyer and seller deliver to each other what the purchase contract calls for.**

8. **The buyers get approved for their new loan on the property. You should confirm that everything else is on track, such as the title work and contract contingency removals.**

9. **Closing the transaction is on schedule and will take place in 15 days. Again, your job as the agent should be to make sure that your client has everything he needs at this point.**

10. **Closing day is here. The closing goes smoothly. Clients are happy. You receive your commission check from the title or escrow company. You're happy.**

    Congratulations! Now, do it again!

We know, we know. Selling property doesn't happen this smoothly all the time, but every once in a while, you'll get to enjoy a transaction like this.

Being a successful independent broker

At some point in your successful career, you may want to make a go of it on your own and start your own company. You'll be required to obtain your real estate broker's license as you venture out on your own. There are obvious pros and cons in becoming an independent broker.

The pros, the way we see them, are

- ✔ You'll have no one to answer to — you get to be your own boss. You'll have more freedom and leeway in your listings, and you'll have more control over the quality of your work.

- ✔ You won't have to split any commission fees. That's huge dollars earned and saved. Say you have a 3 percent commission on a $2 million deal coming to you. That equals $60,000. As an independent broker, 100 percent of that comes to you. If you work for a firm, you'd have to give up maybe 10 percent to the firm, and then 50 percent for your broker's split. So you'd end up with $27,000.

- ✔ You probably won't have to transact as many deals because you won't have to split commissions.

- ✔ As an independent broker, you'll tend to form relationships with other independent brokers. That's a good thing because the camaraderie developed favors doing future deals together. After you develop a reputation for smooth closings, other brokers want to do business with you.

But wait, we see a few cons as well:

- ✔ You'll be a business owner with business-owner responsibilities, such as possibly hiring and overseeing employees, paying for overhead costs, carrying liability insurance, and finding office space to lease or setting up a home office.

- ✔ Start-up costs will include office furniture, office equipment, phones, and stationery.

- ✔ You may lose a few clients who are loyal to your old firm.

When becoming independent, don't forget what made you successful. It wasn't the name brand of the firm you left behind. What got you where you are today were solid salesmanship, hard work, focus, integrity, and professionalism. Often when independents first start off, they forget about their area of expertise and go after "any commission" because they're afraid of not succeeding or not making ends meet. Resist this mind-set as best you can. Stick to what worked for you.

Making a Go of It as a Property Manager

Plainly put, the primary goals of a property manager are to

- ✔ Meet the objectives of the property owners
- ✔ Maximize income and reduce operating costs
- ✔ Strengthen tenant retention and relations
- ✔ Enhance the property's visual appeal and increase property value

We explain all the nuts and bolts of achieving these goals in Chapter 11. Here, we're going to open your eyes to the seemingly endless career opportunities of commercial property management.

As you drive through downtown or cruise around your neighborhood, every commercial property you whiz by is managed by the owner or a third party, called a *professional management company*. Apartment complexes, office buildings, shopping malls, shopping centers, ministorage centers, warehouses, and mobile home parks must be managed in some fashion. Open your mind to the possibilities for yourself.

A quick look at the different property manager hats you can wear

From the outside looking in, all property managers look alike, vocationally speaking. But this is far from the truth. In fact, property managers come in many different ranks. What we mean is that when you call someone a generic property manager, it's like calling a soldier a soldier. That soldier may be a private, a sergeant, or a lieutenant, and with the differing ranks come levels of management, responsibilities, and duties as well as compensations. Here's a look at the breakdown of property manager levels:

- ✔ **Property management company:** You hire this company to manage your property. It's sometimes called *third-party management*.

✔ **Property manager:** This is the actual person assigned to or contracted to run the operations of your property. This person may be responsible for overall operations of several properties simultaneously. She often has a real estate broker's license, and in some states, a broker's license is required. Check your state requirement.

✔ **Assistant property manager:** This person assists the property manager and is usually in training to become a property manager. She may handle leasing, collections, and following up on scheduled maintenance while in training.

✔ **On-site property manager:** This person, who is usually employed by the property management company, usually works in an office set up on the premises. Typical responsibilities involve overseeing the day-to-day operations of the property, including but not limited to leasing, overseeing maintenance and repairs, record keeping, and evictions. Another name for this position is apartment manager or building manager.

✔ **Real estate asset manager:** These managers act as the owner's real estate advisor for the property or properties. They advise owners on topics such as investment strategies and whether to buy, hold, or refinance. They don't focus on day-to-day operations, but on the owner's long-term financial strategies. They manage the assets.

A real estate license may or may not be required in your state to conduct the business of property management. Check with your state's real estate department for laws and licensing requirements.

Choosing the type of property you want to manage

The beauty of being a property manager is that every building needs one. You can choose from four basic types of properties to go into, and those categories have subcategories you can specialize in.

Residential:

✔ **Multifamily:** This area probably has the most opportunity because it serves our entire population. Everyone needs a roof over his or her head, right? Multifamily real estate falls into the category of apartment complexes, townhome developments, condominium and cooperative developments, and planned unit developments.

✔ **Mixed use:** These are typically multistory buildings with apartments on top and retail centers, shopping, or offices below.

✔ **Mobile home parks:** Cities typically designate certain areas where the "parks" call home. Basically, the homeowner rents space, or *pads,* as the concrete slabs are called, from the owner. Some park owners own the homes as well and rent out them to tenants.

Retail:

- ✔ **Shopping centers:** Size determines what bracket these centers fit into. From smallest to largest, they're strip centers, neighborhood centers, community centers, regional shopping centers, and super-regional malls.

- ✔ **Specialized centers:** This type of property can be a single-tenant-type property, such as a chain shoe store or sporting goods store, or it can extend to a factory outlet mall.

Office: Skyscrapers, business parks, multitenant office buildings, single-tenant office buildings, and medical offices are included here.

Industrial: Manufacturing plants, warehousing, distribution, and ministorage are included here.

Starting out as a property manager

As a property manager, you'll take care of the property's financial operations, making sure that tenants pay their rents in a timely fashion and paying monthly bills associated with the property. The property owners may also expect you to prepare financial statements and monthly reports for them. In those reports, you'll have to keep the owners abreast of current occupancy, repairs and maintenance, rent rolls, and any daily operational issues.

As for daily operations, the property owners will rely heavily on you for this portion of the workload. You'll have to contract on the owner's behalf for items such as utilities, landscaping, and security. If work needs to go out for bid, you'll be responsible for attaining those bids and selecting a bid winner. Monitoring the contractor's work is also your responsibility.

Keeping abreast of and adhering to the latest local, state, and federal laws and provisions are important parts of your role. Just as a normal business must obey all the laws of business owners, this falls on you as well. You must keep up with business permits and building codes. So, managing a property is much like a managing a business.

If you're required to be on-site, you'll be expected to monitor the property's grounds, any facilities, and/or equipment. Overseeing employees, such as maintenance staff and office personnel, falls to you. On the public side of the operation, be prepared to meet with and talk to tenants to handle their issues, which may include repair requests and/or complaints. An important task that most on-site managers have are *leasing duties* — coming up with a sales and marketing plan to draw in potential tenants, to negotiate leases, and to close the deal and get tenants moved in. Just as important is ensuring a healthy level of *tenant retention* — seeing to it that tenants are satisfied enough to stick around and remain paying clients of the property.

As you can see, to be a property manager requires you to like working with others, have a pretty tolerant disposition, be well organized, be a good time manager, and have sales and negotiation skills, in addition to being a solid communicator. Good computer skills will only help you too!

Finding a job as a property manager

You can get hired as a property manager in two ways. One way is to work your way up through the ranks. Working as an assistant manager under the wings of an experienced property manager is a good way to start. We don't know about you, but starting from the ground up, is the most fulfilling way to the top of the ladder in our opinion. The second way is to get your college degree and apply for a position. Most hired property managers typically have degrees in real estate, business administration, accounting, and finance. Great property management companies love new graduates whom they can train and groom from scratch.

When you're ready to look for that job, start at the very top of the food chain. Simply call local property management companies and ask whether they're hiring. Job turnover in this industry is no different than any other, so positions are always opening up. Send your résumé or general qualifications to as many property management companies as possible, and then follow up with a phone call. These actions will put you in the best position to get hired, or at least interviewed.

The property management industry in your town or city is a small world. Believe it or not, everyone knows everyone. Secrets are hard to keep and maintain in this industry. Contracts that management firms win, firms that lose customers, firms that don't pay their vendors, and firms that can do no wrong — this information is out there on the street for everyone to know and discuss. We don't know how it gets out there, but it does. When you think about it, you can't really control your reputation, but you can control your integrity and conduct. Therefore, no matter where you are, make sure that you mind your business.

Cashing In on a Commercial Mortgage Business Career

Our experiences with mortgage people have been interesting. Having worked for years with both sides, residential and commercial, we have found a common thread between them. They're very team oriented and seem to enjoy themselves and their work. So, if you like to work on teams, want to have fun, and make a good living, check out the mortgage business as a career.

Although the general responsibilities of residential and commercial lenders seem similar, the nitty-gritty details are starkly different. Checking borrower credit, underwriting the loan, and obtaining an appraisal for the property is the same for residential as it is for commercial. The processes run parallel, but the guidelines are different.

The commercial lender is required to have a more diverse skill set than a residential lender. As explained in Chapter 8, commercial loans are mainly made based on the property's quantity of income, quality of income and property condition, and last, on the merits of the borrower. Notice the order of priority — income, property, and then borrower. Borrower comes last in the ranking. In residential lending, it's the opposite more or less. The borrower is at the top of the list. With that said, commercial lenders are more focused on the property's financials. That's the skill set you must develop.

Choosing a role to play

You can explore many different career opportunities in the commercial mortgage business. And in some companies, it's likely that you may wear more than one of the following hats:

- ✔ **Mortgage broker:** This profession arranges loans between borrowers and banks. They shop other banks to match you with the best mortgage deal. They don't lend money directly.

- ✔ **Mortgage banker:** These folks are the bank. They lend money directly to the borrower.

- ✔ **Loan officer:** These are your frontline folks. They're salespeople who go out and get clients. They deal with the borrowers upfront and are the borrower's primary contact and source of information.

- ✔ **Loan originator:** This hat may be shared with the loan officer. Originators make the loan applications.

- ✔ **Loan processor:** They collect, review, and verify all borrower documentation that's used to decide whether to approve the loan. Their info is passed on to the loan underwriter.

- ✔ **Loan underwriter:** These folks are the "loan committee," so to speak. They make the final decision to grant the loan to the borrower or not. They put the property and the borrower under a microscope to evaluate and analyze the deal's risks. If the risks fit within their lending guidelines, the loan is approved. If not, it's denied or returned for resubmittal.

Jumping in

After thinking about a career in the commercial mortgage business, you may want to talk to some people who do this for a living. We recommend buying lunch for a couple of lending professionals and picking their brains. Ask them these types of questions:

- ✔ Why did you go into this business?
- ✔ How did you get into it?
- ✔ What is your favorite part of the business?
- ✔ What opportunities for growth do you see?

If you don't know any lenders personally, ask a reliable friend if she knows of anyone.

If you want to start off as a loan officer working for a loan brokerage company, you're required by law in nearly all states to have a real estate license. However, you're exempt in some states from the licensing requirement if you work for a bank. In this instance, the bank will provide you with all the training you need to get started as well as supervise you. A mortgage broker, believe it or not, may or may not have a broker's license because the requirement varies from state to state. Mortgage bankers are licensed and audited by the several state and federal agencies. Loan originators, processors, and underwriters may or may not be required by law to be licensed. Check into your state laws and regulations for your licensing and business requirements.

As far as college education, none is required to be a loan officer. What you'll find is that loan professionals in commercial lending tend to have more years of academic and college education than residential lender professionals have. That's just the nature of the business. But, by all means, it's not a requirement.

Consider these points to give you a little more clarity and maybe some confirmation:

- ✔ **Do you like crunching numbers and working with spread sheets?** Because getting a commercial loan approved relies heavily on current and projected net income, you're going to have to spend a decent amount of time proving that your borrower's property is a good risk to the bank. The bank's loan approval committee speaks a language called "analysis."

- ✔ **Do you mind holding hands?** What we mean by this is that the more relaxed, upfront, and honest you are with your clients, the smoother the transactions will go. Getting a loan to the closing table is a scary and daunting thing for some people, so a bit of hand-holding is required.

- ✔ **Are you a self-starter?** If your desire is to start off as a loan officer, then it calls for the same effort and focus as a successful real estate agent. You're going to have to do whatever it takes to bring in new customers, keep the current ones happy, and get loans to the closing table. This may mean thinking out of the box or going above and beyond what's typically done in handling situations.

Becoming a lending machine

In every one of the commercial professions that we mention in this chapter, there are always the chosen few who are considered super-duper, high-income producers in their fields. They're the ones we marvel at, watch, and envy because they generate a huge amount of business. What's their secret? Is it luck? Good looks?

Because we aren't super-duper, high-income-producing commercial loan officers, we went out and interviewed Terry and Eric, good friends of ours, who are. We wanted to find out what made these guys tick and so wildly successful. It's certainly not their good looks!

Terry, who owns his brokerage and takes on the title of chief lending officer, shared the following:

- ✔ **Have strong sales and marketing.** Market to a variety of sources — banks, real estate agents, and so on — using a variety of sources — direct mail, dynamic Web sites, and so on.

- ✔ **Don't wait for the phone to ring.** Put all leads and contacts into A, B, and C categories. Your A list contains clients who provide you with referrals on a consistent basis; call them at least twice a week. The people on your B list are clients who would refer you if asked and shown how. Call these contacts at least every other week. Your C list clients are folks who might refer you in the near future; stay in touch with them at least once a month.

- ✔ **Be a reliable advisor to your clients.** Be their source of commercial real estate information. When they have any question on commercial real estate financing, you want them to automatically think of you.

Our personal experiences in closing commercial loans around the country with Terry have been great throughout the years. The following list explains why we keep coming back, why he's our advisor, and why we refer him to other investors. You may want to keep these traits in mind when reflecting on how to become a super producer.

- ✔ He's accessible and full of the latest information, such as interest rate trends and the latest and greatest loan products out there.

- ✔ He delivers bad news quickly. He's upfront and doesn't try to hide unfavorable news from clients while trying to fix the problem. We appreciate this greatly because it allows us to see upcoming challenges and gives us the chance to be proactive rather than reactive.

✔ He's a teacher at heart. He explains how the commercial lending process works just like your fifth-grade teacher taught you social studies. This makes him approachable, which is important in the seemingly complex field of commercial financing.

Eric is one of the few lenders we know who rarely sees a slowdown in his lending business. There are good reasons why. Here's what he told us:

✔ **Stay focused and have a good work ethic.** Make goals and go after them.

✔ **Do loans for clients that you would personally do for yourself if you were in their position.** This says a lot to clients when you recommend a certain loan product.

✔ **"Explain stuff well," as Eric puts it.** Take your time and make sure that your clients have a good understanding of their loan options and that it fits in well with their investment goals.

Our personal experiences with Eric are the reasons why we think he's such a phenomenal producer. Consider these:

✔ Eric is absolutely the greatest at returning phone calls promptly. We honestly have no idea how he does it — all the time.

✔ Eric is a phenomenal real estate investor himself. How many lenders do you know who invest in real estate? Therefore, he understands our language of cash flows, exit strategies, and how the loan can impact the returns on investment. What a way to gain credibility, huh?

✔ Eric understands he can't do every loan. But even when he knows he can't do our loan, he still gives us advice on that particular deal.

To get more information on Terry, Eric, and a whole bunch of other professionals that we admire, go to www.commercialquickstart.com to register your copy of this book. Use code CFD101.

Arriving As a Commercial Appraiser

If you're in the process of loan approval for purchase or refinance for your strip center, office building, apartment complex, or land, the *appraiser* holds the key to your real estate value. Appraisers systematically analyze and compare properties to estimate the value of yours. Their findings are used for tax assessment, insurable value, "paper" value for your accountant, divorce, partnership dissolutions, expert witness testimony, condemnation, and of course, investment value for we investors.

Finding appraisal work

As an appraiser, you have several choices in whom to work for. Most appraisers turn their eye to residential property and are either self-employed or work for small appraisal companies. But it doesn't stop there. Every type of commercial property needs an appraiser to give the property a value. Commercial appraisers usually specialize in certain commercial properties because of the unique challenges in valuing a certain piece of property. For example, an appraiser may be asked to value an office building for purchase, or she may be asked to value a long-term lease on the same building. And each appraisal approach to reach the value is different.

Here's another use of an appraiser that we think is interesting. An appraiser can recommend, based on her findings, what will give you the "biggest bang for your buck." Let's say you have just inherited 20 acres of raw land sitting adjacent to the downtown district of your city. What in the world do you do with it? What do you build on it that will make you the most money? The appraiser will research the area, collect data on surrounding real estate, and come up with the "highest and best use" of your property. The highest and best use concept is defined as "the reasonably probable use that produces the highest property value."

Working as an appraiser

Some of the daily tasks that an appraiser may undertake in valuing a piece of real estate are gathering data on comparable sales, doing a physical inspection of the property, determining the income potential, measuring the property to prepare land diagrams, and figuring out the costs if the building were to be reproduced.

Appraisers may work for themselves, for small private firms, or for the government. The appraisal business can fluctuate as the market goes. For example, if interest rates are low, the purchase and refinance markets cause a lot of demand for appraisals. As the market slows, less demand is expected. Appraisers can either be paid per appraisal or can be salaried while working for an appraisal firm.

The main qualifications to become an appraiser vary from state to state. First and foremost, you must be licensed in your state or certified and have met certain educational and work experience requirements. Most times, the educational requirements can be met at local community colleges or through private, accredited courses. And the work experience can be met by working under a senior-level appraiser.

To advance in this career, years of experience and exposure play a large part. Earning accreditations and belonging to a professional appraisal organization are musts as well. The best-known organization is the Appraisal Institute (www.appraisalinstitute.org). It awards two professional designations — one is the Senior Residential Appraiser (SRA), which is for residential appraising, and the other is Member, Appraisal Institute (MAI) for commercial real estate. Both are looked on as setting the industry standards of excellence in the appraisal arena. A second organization to note is the American Society of Appraisers, or ASA (www.appraisers.org).

Part VI
The Part of Tens

The 5th Wave   By Rich Tennant

"What if we put the solid granite Jacuzzi on the first floor?"

In this part . . .

In this traditional *For Dummies* part, you quickly discover some really important stuff. For example, we provide the top ten ways to increase the value of your commercial properties. We also include ten great organizations that you should network with.

Chapter 18

Ten Ways to Increase Your Property Value

. . . .

In This Chapter

▶ Tried-and-true ways to increase commercial property values

▶ Increasing your net worth with a few simple steps

. . . .

After you close on your first piece of commercial real estate, we suggest investing in your own investment. You can take simple actions to increase the value of your property. Because commercial real estate is primarily valued on the amount of net operating income it generates, it's smart to think of ways to increase your net income and to increase the overall value, equity, and profit of the property.

Commercial real estate overall is very dynamic and not as immovable or inflexible as most people think. You can implement simple strategies, such as raising the rent or reducing your expenses, or you can do complex things, such as changing the use of the property or hiring a new management team. The choices are yours for the picking.

In this chapter, we offer ten ways to put more money into your pockets.

Raise the Rents

If your rents are below the market average, you're losing out on so.me precious earnings. Lucky for you, the easiest way to increase the value of your commercial property is to raise the rents. To find out if it's time to raise your rents, get on the phone and do a quick survey, call your broker and ask her to do a rent comparables report for you, or call a local leasing agent and pick his brain. One easy way to tell if your rents are below market is to find out whether you're the only apartment complex that rarely has vacancies. This is an indication that you have the best deal (cheapest rent) in town for tenants.

Rent increases are a very sensitive topic, and usually tenants expect noticeable improvements or a reason for the increase. So, if there's a large gap between their rent and the market rent, try increasing the rent only a bit at a time rather than in one lump sum. Huge one-time increases will upset and scare away tenants, so that's the last thing you want to do. However, if you're filling a vacant space, it's okay to charge the new tenant the highest rent possible.

Budget Your Way to Wealth

Reducing operating expenses increases your net operating income in the same way that raising the rent does. And as the net operating income goes up, so does the value of your property. The first thing to do is to review all the expenses with a fine-toothed comb and look for expenses that are out of the norm. You may need a similar property's expenses statements to compare, or consider combining heads with an experienced property manager. That person can go over your expenses with you.

An easy item to check out is property insurance. You humble coauthor Peter Harris once saved over 25 percent on his annual insurance because his property manager had the brilliant idea of getting a blanket policy under which she put all of her owner's properties. She got a bulk rate deal that way, and passed the savings on to him.

 Sometimes low-income apartments experience high turnover rates. And in those buildings, *turnover costs* (costs to fix up the property and make it rentable) tend to be the highest of all operating expenses. To cut costs, consider removing the contractors that are responsible for doing your turnover work. Hire staff to do this work instead. Simply give the staff a list of everything that needs to be done to each unit and the time allotted for each item. Doing this can save you hundreds of dollars per unit. But the added benefit that you can't overlook is that turnover-turnaround time for each unit will likely be reduced to days rather than weeks.

Give the Property a Makeover

Making improvements to your property can add value in more ways than one. First of all, giving your shopping center a new façade and repaving the parking lot gives your tenants a boost of new customers who are looking for the "new" shopping experience. This boost in turn enables you to raise your rents on new tenants and sets you up for higher rents when lease renewals come up. Plus, a well-done makeover and image enhancement always bodes well to add what investors call "prestige value."

For an apartment building, upgrading the interior of the units with new appliances, paint, and accents and giving the landscaping a face-lift allows you to raise rents, and it may also move your apartment into a new class entirely. Being upgraded to a higher class, say going from a "C" to a "B" class property, may also place you into a lower cap rate. After the property gets stamped with a lower cap rate, its value automatically increases. (Turn to Chapter 3 to find more on cap rates and classifications of properties.)

Change the Property's Use

Changing a property's use can significantly change the value of the property. In some instances, a property can be obsolete for what it was originally built for. We know of a hospital that was listed and vacant with no buyers in sight. Along comes a property asset manager for the nearby university. The university acquired the hospital property dirt-cheap and proceeded to convert it to apartments, primarily for students, but open to the public as well. The university spent $3.5 million for the renovations and turned the property into a 200-unit apartment complex now worth over $10 million based on the income it brings in.

Add Goodies to the Property

Most large apartments have swimming pools. So, adding a swimming pool is no big deal to tenants (and honestly, in some cases, adding one can be more of a hassle than it's worth). But other amenities are all the rage. Over the years, we have been networking with other property owners. All of us share our best practices with each other to determine the latest "in" things that we can do to wow our clients and our tenants. Here are some of the amenities that can have a huge positive impact on your property values, your client's property values, and the neighborhood values:

- A business center with computers (bolted down, of course!), fax machine, and copier
- A conference room to hold meetings
- A fitness center with trainers available for hire
- Free wireless Internet (especially near colleges and universities)
- A coffee bar (we copied the Starbucks theme)
- Concierge services

Obviously not every property has these amenities, so don't feel out of the loop if you can't add every one (or even more than one!). Because these items take money and time to plan out and construct, be sure to constantly look at the costs and benefits of each as they're used (or not used in some cases).

The goal here of course is to provide your tenants with a unique experience and well-thought-out service that they can't get elsewhere (or at least in your neighborhood). Tenant retention — keeping paying tenants happy and staying put — is the key to keeping a property stable.

As for a direct cash-generating amenity, consider putting coin-operated washing machines on the property. If your laundry facilities are accessible and well marketed, they can be a cash-flow factory (especially if your complex is near a college or university).

Stand Up to the Tax Man

Did you know that you can argue with the tax man that your property taxes are too high and get them reduced? We didn't know that either until one day we received a tax bill two years after purchasing the property — it had increased by 200 percent! After fainting and taking medicine for heart palpitations, we called the tax assessor's office and asked for an explanation. We were told that in our state, taxes are reassessed every three years. And the reassessment is based on market value, which happens to be the purchase price. The owner prior to us bought the property 17 years ago, so his tax bill was based on the price he paid. So, to make a long story short, we presented our case to the tax assessor board of appeals with the aid of an attorney who specializes in tax appeals. In the end, we were able to prove what we thought our property should have assessed for. The taxes still increased, but the percentage was much more manageable than 200 percent.

The best advice we can give you is to get an appraisal to determine the market value of your property. And second, get a real estate attorney who specializes in property tax grievances to fight on your behalf.

Pass Utility Expenses to Tenants

Utilities are one of the fastest growing expense categories for commercial property owners. Landlords are pretty much at the mercy of the utility companies, especially if they pay for any of the property's utility bills. On some properties, particularly those built in the 1970s and prior, landlords may pay for electric, gas, and water usage because back then, the spaces or units didn't have individual utility meters. So, the landlord is stuck with paying for every tenant's utility bills. This situation creates a sure opportunity for the tenants to abuse utilities, such as water usage, because they aren't paying for it.

You can implement some solutions that positively affect your bottom line and add value immediately. For example, if you have a gas-heated property that's warmed with boilers, but the electric is individually metered, consider removing the boiler and installing baseboard heaters that run off of the unit's electricity. That way, the tenant can control the heating of his own unit and pay for it. Your gas bill will go from thousands of dollars per month during the winter to nearly zero.

Unfortunately, the cost of water has increased dramatically over the last few years and most properties have one water meter that the landlord pays for. But we're finding that more and more landlords are passing most of the water costs to the tenants via a method called *sub-metering*. When you sub-meter the water bill, you install a meter outside of each unit and measure the usage per month. Then you, as the landlord, can charge the tenants for their usage. This accomplishes two things: Your water bill reduces dramatically, and the tenants start to conserve water now that they're paying for it. And the results go to boost your bottom line.

Renegotiate the Leases

Strong leases equal strong value. In other words, when you have solid leases with plenty of time left on them, you're more likely to receive a higher appraised value from an appraiser.

Leases are the lifeblood of commercial real estate. A ten-year lease with rent increases every three years is worth more to investors (and lenders) than a one-year lease with no intention of the tenant to renew. It is a good idea to sign new tenants to long-term leases and to renegotiate or extend current tenant leases to maximize the value of your property.

Here's an example: Timothy, a friend of ours, was in the middle of refinancing his mixed-use property on the outskirts of downtown. It was a total of 19 units; it had a mix of quality apartments upstairs and high-end retail stores on the bottom floor. He had spent hundreds of thousands of dollars rehab-bing the property. So, when his appraisal came in, he was shocked to find out that his property appraised for about 10 percent lower than what he conservatively expected. The reason for this decrease was because various tenant leases had expired and had turned to month-to-month agreements and others had less than a year left until they expired. Tim was instructed to go back to the tenants and do two things: have the expired lease tenants sign new long-term leases and renegotiate the others that were expiring to long-term leases. Even though only a few of the new leases were for higher rents, just by showing the appraiser that he had solid leases with a decent amount of time left on them, he was able to achieve his higher appraised value for his refinance to go through.

Bring in a New Management Team

You've seen it before. Big entertainment companies and sports franchises do it all the time. New management teams with new ideas, new philosophies, and totally different energies, come in and save the company or team from their demise or jolt them to brand-new levels of performance. The same can apply to your property. Bringing in a new management team to your property can add tremendous worth to your property. New management can bring in fresh ideas on increasing income, reducing expenses without harming the operations, enhance the tenant experience and satisfaction, and give the property appearance that "fresh" feeling. All of this does nothing but increase the value of the property.

Split Up Your Land

If you're a landlord of raw land, there are many ways to increase your property value. You can develop it and cash in when the properties are sold. But before you develop it, why not just add utilities and build roads? By doing this alone, you add value because now it has great development potential. You can sell it at this point because you've just fast tracked the land for development for an investor or developer.

Make it even simpler to add value by splitting the lot of land up into separate, smaller lots that are large enough to put a stand-alone property onto. After it's divided up and sold separately, the total will be far greater than selling it off as one lot.

Getting land that's *entitled* is a sequence of events leading up to having the land approved for more productive use. If the land is currently approved for industrial use, but it's found to be a poor location for such use, and the land was then approved and entitled for multifamily residential use, that's where the big dollars are made. Either splitting land into smaller pieces, or getting it approved for a higher use, makes land ownership very lucrative.

Chapter 19

Ten or So Easy Ways to Network

In This Chapter

▶ Making the most of your real estate relationships

▶ Discovering the essentials of networking

▶ Joining real estate organizations to meet the best of the best

*T*hroughout this book, we place an extremely high value on the "R" word — relationship. Why? Being successful in commercial real estate depends on your desire and ability to strike new relationships with people and professionals who hold something you want or need. No matter what you may have heard there's no such thing as a "self-made" person in the commercial real estate business. Anyone who has attained any level of success had help from an established relationship along the way.

In this chapter, we jump-start your relationship hunting by providing you with essential tips for networking in the commercial real estate world. These are just the tip of the iceberg when finding great relationships, great investments, and integrity-filled businesspeople to partner and network with, grow with, and realize your dreams with.

Get Your CCIM Designation

Ever want to attend medical school just to earn the prestigious "MD" stamp after your name? How about having the highly respected "CPA" added to your last name? Having earned either of these titles brings you automatic credibility in the respective industry. In commercial real estate, we have such a prestigious tag: CCIM, which stands for Certified Commercial Investment Member. This title designates you as a recognized expert in the disciplines of commercial and investment real estate. Once earned, you'll be among only 9,000 or so elite professionals worldwide who hold the CCIM title. Titleholders include brokers, asset managers, commercial lenders, leasing agents, developers, property managers, and investors, just to name a few.

To earn the CCIM designation, you must pass commercial core educational courses, submit a résumé of completed commercial investment transactions or consultations, and pass a comprehensive examination. These rigorous requirements ensure you and the public that you not only have a command of commercial real estate investment theory but that you also have relevant practical experience.

Put Power in Your Search Engines

It's easy to look for a house online in any city. You just go to the city's multiple listing service (MLS) and see what's out there. With this service, you see prices, pictures, property features — you name it. But for commercial real estate, no such service exists in each city. The next best things are independent online listing services for commercial real estate. Two companies have filled this niche, and they did it in a big way. One company is LoopNet and the other is CoStar Group.

LoopNet, Inc., (www.loopnet.com) refers to itself as the largest commercial real estate online listing service in the world. It's an easy-to-use Web site that lists properties that are for sale and for lease worldwide. LoopNet reports to have more than 500,000 commercial properties for sale and for lease on its Web site. You can also search for brokers nationwide who specialize in a field that you're interested in. LoopNet even provides reports on recent sales and closings nationwide in hundreds of cities. LoopNet is a powerful way to get immediate access to deals and commercial professionals of a broad nature. It's a great starting point for investors to contact brokers to get their investment ball rolling.

CoStar Group, Inc., (www.costar.com) calls itself the number one commercial real estate information company in the United States and United Kingdom. And judging from its extensive Web site and the wide range of services offered it would be difficult to disagree with its status as number one. CoStar offers a commercial property listing service that's similar to LoopNet.

CoStar has the most comprehensive database of property information we've ever seen in one Web site. If you're looking for an investment property for yourself or client, or if you want to expose your property (or your client's) to millions of people, CoStar can get the job done. When you need detailed, accurate, and up-to-date information on comparable sales, this company sets the bar; it tracks more than 1.9 million properties in its database. CoStar is invaluable for finding commercial deals of all types and for advertising your business. It's also a powerful networking tool for any commercial professional or would-be professional.

Go Directly to the Investment Firms

You can find firms to work with several ways, but the best way to find one is by referral from a fellow investor. After you find some firms you like, you need to make the call to see whether they fit your investment criteria. But most important, you must develop a relationship with a person within the firm. The best way to find an agent or advisor to begin work with is through referrals; referrals from another satisfied investor are best.

Begin by calling on a few of the following "big dogs" in the commercial real estate investment industry:

- ✔ Sperry Van Ness Commercial Real Estate (www.svn.com)
- ✔ CB Richard Ellis Group (www.cbre.com)
- ✔ Marcus & Millichap (www.marcusmillichap.com)
- ✔ Colliers International (www.colliers.com)
- ✔ Coldwell Banker Commercial (www.coldwellbankercommercial.com)
- ✔ Grubb & Ellis (www.grubb-ellis.com)
- ✔ Staubach (www.staubach.com)
- ✔ Cushman & Wakefield (www.cushwake.com)

There are hundreds of smaller local firms out there that can do the same level of work you require. We have great small firms that we continue to work with today and they were found in various ways — referrals, LoopNet, CoStar, and by going to commercial broker networking events.

Read the Trades

To stay ahead of the game, we suggest that you subscribe to (and read!) online commercial real estate newsletters and magazines. Here are a few online newsletters that we recommend:

- ✔ GlobeSt.com (www.globest.com)
- ✔ RealEstateJournal.com (www.realestatejournal.com/commercial), which is a property guide from the Wall Street Journal
- ✔ Commercial Property News Online (www.cpnonline.com)

- Multi-Housing News (www.multi-housingnews.com)
- MortgageDaily.com (www.mortgagedaily.com)

Here are some real estate magazines that can be helpful:

- *National Real Estate Investor* (www.nreionline.com)
- *Commercial Investment Real Estate Magazine,* which is the magazine of the CCIM Institute (www.ciremagazine.com)
- *Multifamily Executive* (www.multifamilyexecutive.com)
- *Shopping Center Business* (www.shoppingcenterbusiness.com)
- *Development Magazine* (www.naiop.org)

For Apartment Owners: Join the NAA

The National Association of Apartment Owners (NAA) was started in 1939 to serve as a legislative advocate (a government watchdog) and to serve the interests of apartment owners, property managers, leasing agents, developers, maintenance personnel, and apartment industry suppliers. The NAA has nearly 200 state and local chapters, and it supports over 50,000 multifamily housing companies and corporations that control over 6 million apartment units or homes in the United States.

The NAA is well known for its educational programs and training aimed at apartment or multifamily housing professionals. It focuses particularly on the management of properties. It awards six nationally recognized designations to members who complete its courses and requirements. As we see it, the NAA certainly sets the standards of excellence and professionalism in providing for the public's housing needs.

Joining one of the local chapters is the best way to get the most out of your NAA membership. The NAA also offers a useful tool to investors who are looking to set up an operating budget or who just want to see what income or expenses they could expect for a new property. This tool is the "Survey of Income and Expense Data" report. This report is taken from thousands of apartment owners nationwide as to where their properties are operating in terms of income and expenses. Other invaluable benefits of membership include admittance to its annual multifamily housing trade show and conference (which is by far the largest in the industry) and access to the career center connecting qualified professionals with great multifamily companies. Visit www.naahq.org for more information on the NAA.

For Office Building Owners: Get Involved with BOMA

The Building Owners and Managers Association (BOMA), which is more than a century old, is a huge network of professionals who take part in owning, managing, leasing, and developing office buildings, medical office buildings, and corporate facilities. BOMA states that current members collectively own or manage more than 9 billion square feet of office space, which represents more than 80 percent of the prime office space in North America. In addition, it reports 80 percent of its members have annual budgets over $1 million. With those figures, BOMA seems to be the place to go to get important information concerning office buildings as well as to network with the insiders. For more info, check out www.boma.org.

BOMA is the nation's largest and most influential lobbyist for office building legislation. It sets the industry standard for operations and reporting by producing research documents. Every year, it hosts the North American Real Estate Congress and Trade Show, which is the nation's largest gathering of office building professionals. Membership is available through any 1 of 92 local BOMA associations nationwide. You'll get access to its real estate advocacy group, live networking events, and access to vital information such as its publications and seminars.

For Shopping Center Owners: Enlist with the ICSC

The International Council of Shopping Centers (ICSC) originated in 1957 and is 70,000 members strong today in the United States, Canada, and many other countries worldwide. It supports shopping center investors, owners, property managers, developers, marketing specialists, commercial lenders, retailers, and other commercial professionals. The ICSC takes on the role of middleman between the government, consumers, and retailers in establishing fair business ethics, practices, and codes of conduct. It studies and reports on indicators in economics, operations (such as improving management and maintenance methods), and marketing affecting the shopping center industry.

The elite in the shopping center industry can be found among its 40,000-attendee annual convention held each spring. If you want to be seen and heard in this industry, this is the place to do it. The ICSC maintains a global-reaching research database of economic trends that includes tenant sales, entire shopping center sales, and operational expenses. It also offers world-class educational programs and certifications for all levels of marketing, management, and leasing.

The ICSC is a networking giant in the industry. It holds national and frequent regional conferences and trade shows, allowing shopping owner professionals of all levels to come together, do deals, brainstorm, and exchange best practices. For more info, go to www.icsc.org.

For Property Management Professionals: Become Affiliated with the IREM

For more than 70 years, the Institute of Real Estate Management (IREM) has been home for real estate professionals who are involved in property management of commercial and multifamily properties. IREM reports that its members manage more than 6.5 million square feet of commercial space and more than 11 million residential units, totaling over $848 billion in real estate assets.

Oftentimes, when commercial professionals look for experienced professionals and managers or need up-to-date and reliable property management information, they begin their search on the IREM Web site (www.irem.org).

IREM is an affiliate of the National Association of Realtors (NAR), which makes it, just by association, a reputable force in property-owner legislation. IREM is also well known for its award-winning magazine *Journal of Property Management*. Its credentialed membership educational program is world class and well respected in the industry of management. Nearly every manager that we have hired to manage or consult has an IREM designation. We begin all of our research for property management professionals, services, and education starting with IREM.

Stay Current and Connected

We love commercial real estate because it is constantly changing. Unfortunately, we promised you in the Introduction that this book is your "complete how-to guide" for investing in commercial real estate. To help you keep up with new places to network and other developments as they happen, make sure to get your free Commercial Training Package at www.commercialquickstart.com. By signing up, you will also have access to updated articles, online training, and other goodies for commercial investors.

Index

• *M* •

• *N* •

BUSINESS, CAREERS & PERSONAL FINANCE

0-7645-9847-3   0-7645-2431-3

Also available:
- Business Plans Kit For Dummies
  0-7645-9794-9
- Economics For Dummies
  0-7645-5726-2
- Grant Writing For Dummies
  0-7645-8416-2
- Home Buying For Dummies
  0-7645-5331-3
- Managing For Dummies
  0-7645-1771-6
- Marketing For Dummies
  0-7645-5600-2

- Personal Finance For Dummies
  0-7645-2590-5*
- Resumes For Dummies
  0-7645-5471-9
- Selling For Dummies
  0-7645-5363-1
- Six Sigma For Dummies
  0-7645-6798-5
- Small Business Kit For Dummies
  0-7645-5984-2
- Starting an eBay Business For Dummies
  0-7645-6924-4
- Your Dream Career For Dummies
  0-7645-9795-7

HOME & BUSINESS COMPUTER BASICS

0-470-05432-8   0-471-75421-8

Also available:
- Cleaning Windows Vista For Dummies
  0-471-78293-9
- Excel 2007 For Dummies
  0-470-03737-7
- Mac OS X Tiger For Dummies
  0-7645-7675-5
- MacBook For Dummies
  0-470-04859-X
- Macs For Dummies
  0-470-04849-2
- Office 2007 For Dummies
  0-470-00923-3

- Outlook 2007 For Dummies
  0-470-03830-6
- PCs For Dummies
  0-7645-8958-X
- Salesforce.com For Dummies
  0-470-04893-X
- Upgrading & Fixing Laptops For Dummies
  0-7645-8959-8
- Word 2007 For Dummies
  0-470-03658-3
- Quicken 2007 For Dummies
  0-470-04600-7

FOOD, HOME, GARDEN, HOBBIES, MUSIC & PETS

0-7645-8404-9   0-7645-9904-6

Also available:
- Candy Making For Dummies
  0-7645-9734-5
- Card Games For Dummies
  0-7645-9910-0
- Crocheting For Dummies
  0-7645-4151-X
- Dog Training For Dummies
  0-7645-8418-9
- Healthy Carb Cookbook For Dummies
  0-7645-8476-6
- Home Maintenance For Dummies
  0-7645-5215-5

- Horses For Dummies
  0-7645-9797-3
- Jewelry Making & Beading For Dummies
  0-7645-2571-9
- Orchids For Dummies
  0-7645-6759-4
- Puppies For Dummies
  0-7645-5255-4
- Rock Guitar For Dummies
  0-7645-5356-9
- Sewing For Dummies
  0-7645-6847-7
- Singing For Dummies
  0-7645-2475-5

INTERNET & DIGITAL MEDIA

0-470-04529-9   0-470-04894-8

Also available:
- Blogging For Dummies
  0-471-77084-1
- Digital Photography For Dummies
  0-7645-9802-3
- Digital Photography All-in-One Desk Reference For Dummies
  0-470-03743-1
- Digital SLR Cameras and Photography For Dummies
  0-7645-9803-1
- eBay Business All-in-One Desk Reference For Dummies
  0-7645-8438-3
- HDTV For Dummies
  0-470-09673-X

- Home Entertainment PCs For Dummies
  0-470-05523-5
- MySpace For Dummies
  0-470-09529-6
- Search Engine Optimization For Dummies
  0-471-97998-8
- Skype For Dummies
  0-470-04891-3
- The Internet For Dummies
  0-7645-8996-2
- Wiring Your Digital Home For Dummies
  0-471-91830-X

* Separate Canadian edition also available
† Separate U.K. edition also available

SPORTS, FITNESS, PARENTING, RELIGION & SPIRITUALITY

0-471-76871-5   0-7645-7841-3

Also available:
- Catholicism For Dummies
  0-7645-5391-7
- Exercise Balls For Dummies
  0-7645-5623-1
- Fitness For Dummies
  0-7645-7851-0
- Football For Dummies
  0-7645-3936-1
- Judaism For Dummies
  0-7645-5299-6
- Potty Training For Dummies
  0-7645-5417-4
- Buddhism For Dummies
  0-7645-5359-3

- Pregnancy For Dummies
  0-7645-4483-7 †
- Ten Minute Tone-Ups For Dummies
  0-7645-7207-5
- NASCAR For Dummies
  0-7645-7681-X
- Religion For Dummies
  0-7645-5264-3
- Soccer For Dummies
  0-7645-5229-5
- Women in the Bible For Dummies
  0-7645-8475-8

TRAVEL

0-7645-7749-2   0-7645-6945-7

Also available:
- Alaska For Dummies
  0-7645-7746-8
- Cruise Vacations For Dummies
  0-7645-6941-4
- England For Dummies
  0-7645-4276-1
- Europe For Dummies
  0-7645-7529-5
- Germany For Dummies
  0-7645-7823-5
- Hawaii For Dummies
  0-7645-7402-7

- Italy For Dummies
  0-7645-7386-1
- Las Vegas For Dummies
  0-7645-7382-9
- London For Dummies
  0-7645-4277-X
- Paris For Dummies
  0-7645-7630-5
- RV Vacations For Dummies
  0-7645-4442-X
- Walt Disney World & Orlando
  For Dummies
  0-7645-9660-8

GRAPHICS, DESIGN & WEB DEVELOPMENT

0-7645-8815-X   0-7645-9571-7

Also available:
- 3D Game Animation For Dummies
  0-7645-8789-7
- AutoCAD 2006 For Dummies
  0-7645-8925-3
- Building a Web Site For Dummies
  0-7645-7144-3
- Creating Web Pages For Dummies
  0-470-08030-2
- Creating Web Pages All-in-One Desk
  Reference For Dummies
  0-7645-4345-8
- Dreamweaver 8 For Dummies
  0-7645-9649-7

- InDesign CS2 For Dummies
  0-7645-9572-5
- Macromedia Flash 8 For Dummies
  0-7645-9691-8
- Photoshop CS2 and Digital
  Photography For Dummies
  0-7645-9580-6
- Photoshop Elements 4 For Dummies
  0-471-77483-9
- Syndicating Web Sites with RSS Feeds
  For Dummies
  0-7645-8848-6
- Yahoo! SiteBuilder For Dummies
  0-7645-9800-7

NETWORKING, SECURITY, PROGRAMMING & DATABASES

0-7645-7728-X   0-471-74940-0

Also available:
- Access 2007 For Dummies
  0-470-04612-0
- ASP.NET 2 For Dummies
  0-7645-7907-X
- C# 2005 For Dummies
  0-7645-9704-3
- Hacking For Dummies
  0-470-05235-X
- Hacking Wireless Networks
  For Dummies
  0-7645-9730-2
- Java For Dummies
  0-470-08716-1

- Microsoft SQL Server 2005 For Dummies
  0-7645-7755-7
- Networking All-in-One Desk Reference
  For Dummies
  0-7645-9939-9
- Preventing Identity Theft For Dummies
  0-7645-7336-5
- Telecom For Dummies
  0-471-77085-X
- Visual Studio 2005 All-in-One Desk
  Reference For Dummies
  0-7645-9775-2
- XML For Dummies
  0-7645-8845-1

HEALTH & SELF-HELP

0-7645-8450-2   0-7645-4149-8

Also available:

- ✔Bipolar Disorder For Dummies
  0-7645-8451-0
- ✔Chemotherapy and Radiation
  For Dummies
  0-7645-7832-4
- ✔Controlling Cholesterol For Dummies
  0-7645-5440-9
- ✔Diabetes For Dummies
  0-7645-6820-5* †
- ✔Divorce For Dummies
  0-7645-8417-0 †

- ✔Fibromyalgia For Dummies
  0-7645-5441-7
- ✔Low-Calorie Dieting For Dummies
  0-7645-9905-4
- ✔Meditation For Dummies
  0-471-77774-9
- ✔Osteoporosis For Dummies
  0-7645-7621-6
- ✔Overcoming Anxiety For Dummies
  0-7645-5447-6
- ✔Reiki For Dummies
  0-7645-9907-0
- ✔Stress Management For Dummies
  0-7645-5144-2

EDUCATION, HISTORY, REFERENCE & TEST PREPARATION

0-7645-8381-6   0-7645-9554-7

Also available:

- ✔The ACT For Dummies
  0-7645-9652-7
- ✔Algebra For Dummies
  0-7645-5325-9
- ✔Algebra Workbook For Dummies
  0-7645-8467-7
- ✔Astronomy For Dummies
  0-7645-8465-0
- ✔Calculus For Dummies
  0-7645-2498-4
- ✔Chemistry For Dummies
  0-7645-5430-1
- ✔Forensics For Dummies
  0-7645-5580-4

- ✔Freemasons For Dummies
  0-7645-9796-5
- ✔French For Dummies
  0-7645-5193-0
- ✔Geometry For Dummies
  0-7645-5324-0
- ✔Organic Chemistry I For Dummies
  0-7645-6902-3
- ✔The SAT I For Dummies
  0-7645-7193-1
- ✔Spanish For Dummies
  0-7645-5194-9
- ✔Statistics For Dummies
  0-7645-5423-9

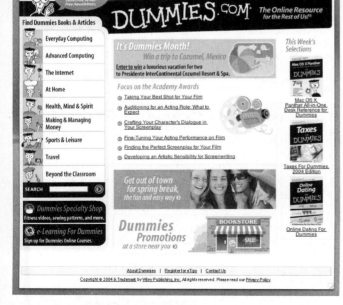

Get smart @ dummies.com®

- **Find a full list of Dummies titles**
- **Look into loads of FREE on-site articles**
- **Sign up for FREE eTips e-mailed to you weekly**
- **See what other products carry the Dummies name**
- **Shop directly from the Dummies bookstore**
- **Enter to win new prizes every month!**

* Separate Canadian edition also available
† Separate U.K. edition also available

Available wherever books are sold. For more information or to order direct: U.S. customers visit www.dummies.com or call 1-877-762-2974.
U.K. customers visit www.wileyeurope.com or call 0800 243407. Canadian customers visit www.wiley.ca or call 1-800-567-4797.